SELECTED LETTERS,
ORATIONS, AND
RHETORICAL DIALOGUES

THE
OTHER VOICE
IN
EARLY MODERN
EUROPE

A Series Edited by Margaret L. King and Albert Rabil Jr.

RECENT BOOKS IN THE SERIES

GABRIELLE DE COIGNARD
Spiritual Sonnets: A Bilingual Edition
Edited and Translated by Melanie E. Gregg

MARIE LE JARS DE GOURNAY
"Apology for the Woman Writing"
and Other Works
Edited and Translated by Richard Hillman
and Colette Quesnel

ANNIBAL GUASCO
Discourse to Lady Lavinia His Daughter
Edited, Translated, and with an Introduction
by Peggy Osborn

ANNE-MARIE-LOUISE D'ORLÉANS,
DUCHESSE DE MONTPENSIER
Against Marriage: The Correspondence
of La Grande Mademoiselle
Edited and Translated by Joan DeJean

OLYMPIA MORATA
The Complete Writings of an
Italian Heretic
Edited and Translated by Holt N. Parker

ISOTTA NOGAROLA
Complete Writings: Letterbook,
Dialogue on Adam and Eve, Orations
Edited and Translated by Margaret L. King
and Diana Robin

JACQUELINE PASCAL
"A Rule for Children" and
Other Writings
Edited and Translated by John J. Conley, S.J.

FRANÇOIS POULLAIN DE LA BARRE
Three Cartesian Feminist Treatises
Introductions and Annotations by
Marcelle Maistre Welch
Translation by Vivien Bosley

MARÍA DE SAN JOSÉ SALAZAR
Book for the Hour of Recreation
Introduction and Notes by Alison Weber
Translation by Amanda Powell

MADELEINE DE SCUDÉRY
The Story of Sapho
Translated and with an Introduction by
Karen Newman

ARCANGELA TARABOTTI
Paternal Tyranny
Edited and Translated by Letizia Panizza

ELISABETTA CAMINER TURRA
Selected Writings of an Eighteenth-
Century Venetian Woman of Letters
Edited and Translated by Catherine M. Sama

Madeleine de Scudéry

SELECTED LETTERS, ORATIONS, AND RHETORICAL DIALOGUES

☙

Edited and Translated by
Jane Donawerth and
Julie Strongson

THE UNIVERSITY OF CHICAGO PRESS
Chicago & London

Madeleine de Scudéry, 1607–1701

Jane Donawerth is professor of English and affiliate faculty in women's studies at the University of Maryland. She is author of *Shakespeare and the Sixteenth Century Study of Language*, editor of *Rhetorical Theory by Women before 1900: An Anthology*, and has published other books and essays on early modern women's writings, history of rhetoric, and science fiction by women.

Julie Strongson is a Ph.D. candidate in Comparative Literature at the University of Maryland. Her studies focus on issues of race and gender in nineteenth- and twentieth-century women's literature from France and Francophone countries, England, and the United States.

The University of Chicago Press, Chicago 60637
The University of Chicago Press, Ltd., London
© 2004 by The University of Chicago
All rights reserved. Published 2004
Printed in the United States of America
13 12 11 10 09 08 07 06 05 04   1 2 3 4 5

ISBN: 0-226-14403-8 (cloth)
ISBN: 0-226-14404-6 (paper)

Library of Congress Cataloging-in Publicaltion Data

Scudéry, Madeleine de, 1607–1701.
[Selections. English. 2004]
Selected letters, orations, and rhetorical dialogues / Madeleine de
Scudéry ; edited and translated by Jane Donawerth and Julie Strongson.
p. cm. — (Other voice in early modern Europe)
Includes bibliographical references and index.
ISBN 0-226-14403-8 (cloth : alk. paper) — ISBN 0-226-14404-6 (pbk. : alk. paper)
I. Donawerth, Jane, 1947–   II. Strongson, Julie.   III. Title.   IV. Series.
PQ1922.A1 2004
843'.7—dc22   2003023250

For our sisters, especially Lois Donawerth Bovard and
in memory of Lisa T. Strongson

CONTENTS

Acknowledgments ix

Series Editors' Introduction xi

Volume Editors' Introduction 1

Volume Editors' Bibliography 39

Model Letters from "Amorous Letters" (1641) 44

Fictional Orations from "Famous Women" (1665) 56

Rhetorical Dialogues 96

Series Editors' Bibliography 153

Index 167

ACKNOWLEDGMENTS

We found collaborative translation rewarding, supportive, and enlightening. We talked over the wording of most of the individual sentences, sometimes twice, and they improved through this process.

For her contribution, we express thanks to Lillian Doherty, who translated "Sappho to Erinna" and began "On Wit" with Jane Donawerth before she had to drop out of the project for other scholarly pursuits nearer to her classicist specialty; although we have retranslated these works, Lillian's mark is nevertheless still present. We also thank Stephanie Lenkey, an undergraduate French major in Professor Donawerth's history of rhetoric class, who helped solve some crucial problems in "On Conversation" and "On Speaking Too Much or Too Little." For answering questions, giving advice, or talking over definitions of words, we thank Harriett Andreadis, Virginia Walcott Beauchamp, Robert Coogan, Katie Field, Beth Goldsmith, Judy Hallett, Sue Lanser, Stephane Pillet, and Molly Wertheimer.

For their courteous and unfailing help, we would like to thank the staffs of McKeldin Library of the University of Maryland, the Folger Shakespeare Library in Washington, D.C., and the Library of Congress. For that wonderful librarian in the History Section of the Bibliothèque Nationale who miraculously found the *Mercure de France*, eternal gratitude. We are also grateful for the editorial suggestions of Albert Rabil and Margaret King and the anonymous reviewer for the University of Chicago Press.

Jane would like to remember Doris Lusk, for teaching her French in the morning during high school, and to thank her family, Woody, Kate, and Donnie, for putting up with yet another book, as well as her office mate, Shirley Logan, and other good friends at the university for offering support.

Julie would like to thank her big sister Lisa, whom she misses dearly, whose footsteps she followed into the world of studying French; Naomi

Berman, her ninth-grade French teacher, who introduced her to Paris and sparked her Francophilia; her mother, who bred her to be the feminist she is today and has always supported her along her life's path; her father and stepmother Susan, for their constant encouragement and enthusiasm for her work; and her Aunt Ruth, Uncle Jeff, and Uncle Aaron, for helping her to pursue her passions.

Figure 1, which appears on p. xxxii, is an engraving from Madeleine de Scudéry's *Conversations nouvelles* (1685). Reproduced by permission of the Folger Shakespeare Library (Acc. 171523). The medallions, figures 2–5, which appear on pp. 57, 68, 76, and 87, are from Scudéry's *Les femmes illustres; ou, Les harangues héroiques* (1667). Copyright The New York Public Library/Art Resource, New York.

THE OTHER VOICE IN EARLY MODERN EUROPE: INTRODUCTION TO THE SERIES

Margaret L. King and Albert Rabil Jr.

THE OLD VOICE AND THE OTHER VOICE

In western Europe and the United States, women are nearing equality in the professions, in business, and in politics. Most enjoy access to education, reproductive rights, and autonomy in financial affairs. Issues vital to women are on the public agenda: equal pay, child care, domestic abuse, breast cancer research, and curricular revision with an eye to the inclusion of women.

These recent achievements have their origins in things women (and some male supporters) said for the first time about six hundred years ago. Theirs is the "other voice," in contradistinction to the "first voice," the voice of the educated men who created Western culture. Coincident with a general reshaping of European culture in the period 1300–1700 (called the Renaissance or early modern period), questions of female equality and opportunity were raised that still resound and are still unresolved.

The other voice emerged against the backdrop of a three-thousand-year history of the derogation of women rooted in the civilizations related to Western culture: Hebrew, Greek, Roman, and Christian. Negative attitudes toward women inherited from these traditions pervaded the intellectual, medical, legal, religious, and social systems that developed during the European Middle Ages.

The following pages describe the traditional, overwhelmingly male views of women's nature inherited by early modern Europeans and the new tradition that the "other voice" called into being to begin to challenge reigning assumptions. This review should serve as a framework for understanding the texts published in the series the Other Voice in Early Modern Europe. Introductions specific to each text and author follow this essay in all the volumes of the series.

TRADITIONAL VIEWS OF WOMEN, 500 B.C.E.–1500 C.E.

Embedded in the philosophical and medical theories of the ancient Greeks were perceptions of the female as inferior to the male in both mind and body. Similarly, the structure of civil legislation inherited from the ancient Romans was biased against women, and the views on women developed by Christian thinkers out of the Hebrew Bible and the Christian New Testament were negative and disabling. Literary works composed in the vernacular of ordinary people, and widely recited or read, conveyed these negative assumptions. The social networks within which most women lived—those of the family and the institutions of the Roman Catholic Church—were shaped by this negative tradition and sharply limited the areas in which women might act in and upon the world.

GREEK PHILOSOPHY AND FEMALE NATURE. Greek biology assumed that women were inferior to men and defined them as merely child bearers and housekeepers. This view was authoritatively expressed in the works of the philosopher Aristotle.

Aristotle thought in dualities. He considered action superior to inaction, form (the inner design or structure of any object) superior to matter, completion to incompletion, possession to deprivation. In each of these dualities, he associated the male principle with the superior quality and the female with the inferior. "The male principle in nature," he argued, "is associated with active, formative and perfected characteristics, while the female is passive, material and deprived, desiring the male in order to become complete."[1] Men are always identified with virile qualities, such as judgment, courage, and stamina, and women with their opposites—irrationality, cowardice, and weakness.

The masculine principle was considered superior even in the womb. The man's semen, Aristotle believed, created the form of a new human creature, while the female body contributed only matter. (The existence of the ovum, and with it the other facts of human embryology, was not established until the seventeenth century.) Although the later Greek physician Galen believed there was a female component in generation, contributed by "female semen," the followers of both Aristotle and Galen saw the male role in human generation as more active and more important.

1. Aristotle, *Physics* 1.9.192a20–24, in *The Complete Works of Aristotle*, ed. Jonathan Barnes, rev. Oxford trans., 2 vols. (Princeton, 1984), 1:328.

In the Aristotelian view, the male principle sought always to reproduce itself. The creation of a female was always a mistake, therefore, resulting from an imperfect act of generation. Every female born was considered a "defective" or "mutilated" male (as Aristotle's terminology has variously been translated), a "monstrosity" of nature.[2]

For Greek theorists, the biology of males and females was the key to their psychology. The female was softer and more docile, more apt to be despondent, querulous, and deceitful. Being incomplete, moreover, she craved sexual fulfillment in intercourse with a male. The male was intellectual, active, and in control of his passions.

These psychological polarities derived from the theory that the universe consisted of four elements (earth, fire, air, and water), expressed in human bodies as four "humors" (black bile, yellow bile, blood, and phlegm) considered, respectively, dry, hot, damp, and cold and corresponding to mental states ("melancholic," "choleric," "sanguine," "phlegmatic"). In this scheme the male, sharing the principles of earth and fire, was dry and hot; the female, sharing the principles of air and water, was cold and damp.

Female psychology was further affected by her dominant organ, the uterus (womb), *hystera* in Greek. The passions generated by the womb made women lustful, deceitful, talkative, irrational, indeed—when these affects were in excess—"hysterical."

Aristotle's biology also had social and political consequences. If the male principle was superior and the female inferior, then in the household, as in the state, men should rule and women must be subordinate. That hierarchy did not rule out the companionship of husband and wife, whose cooperation was necessary for the welfare of children and the preservation of property. Such mutuality supported male preeminence.

Aristotle's teacher Plato suggested a different possibility: that men and women might possess the same virtues. The setting for this proposal is the imaginary and ideal Republic that Plato sketches in a dialogue of that name. Here, for a privileged elite capable of leading wisely, all distinctions of class and wealth dissolve, as, consequently, do those of gender. Without households or property, as Plato constructs his ideal society, there is no need for the subordination of women. Women may therefore be educated to the same level as men to assume leadership. Plato's Republic remained imaginary, however. In real societies, the subordination of women remained the norm and the prescription.

---

2. Aristotle, *Generation of Animals* 2.3.737a27–28, in *The Complete Works*, 1:1144.

The views of women inherited from the Greek philosophical tradition became the basis for medieval thought. In the thirteenth century, the supreme Scholastic philosopher Thomas Aquinas, among others, still echoed Aristotle's views of human reproduction, of male and female personalities, and of the preeminent male role in the social hierarchy.

ROMAN LAW AND THE FEMALE CONDITION. Roman law, like Greek philosophy, underlay medieval thought and shaped medieval society. The ancient belief that adult property-owning men should administer households and make decisions affecting the community at large is the very fulcrum of Roman law.

About 450 B.C.E., during Rome's republican era, the community's customary law was recorded (legendarily) on twelve tablets erected in the city's central forum. It was later elaborated by professional jurists whose activity increased in the imperial era, when much new legislation was passed, especially on issues affecting family and inheritance. This growing, changing body of laws was eventually codified in the *Corpus of Civil Law* under the direction of the emperor Justinian, generations after the empire ceased to be ruled from Rome. That *Corpus*, read and commented on by medieval scholars from the eleventh century on, inspired the legal systems of most of the cities and kingdoms of Europe.

Laws regarding dowries, divorce, and inheritance pertain primarily to women. Since those laws aimed to maintain and preserve property, the women concerned were those from the property-owning minority. Their subordination to male family members points to the even greater subordination of lower-class and slave women, about whom the laws speak little.

In the early republic, the *paterfamilias*, or "father of the family," possessed *patria potestas*, "paternal power." The term *pater*, "father," in both these cases does not necessarily mean biological father but denotes the head of a household. The father was the person who owned the household's property and, indeed, its human members. The *paterfamilias* had absolute power—including the power, rarely exercised, of life or death—over his wife, his children, and his slaves, as much as his cattle.

Male children could be "emancipated," an act that granted legal autonomy and the right to own property. Those over fourteen could be emancipated by a special grant from the father or automatically by their father's death. But females could never be emancipated; instead, they passed from the authority of their father to that of a husband or, if widowed or orphaned while still unmarried, to a guardian or tutor.

Marriage in its traditional form placed the woman under her husband's authority, or *manus*. He could divorce her on grounds of adultery, drinking wine, or stealing from the household, but she could not divorce him. She could neither possess property in her own right nor bequeath any to her children upon her death. When her husband died, the household property passed not to her but to his male heirs. And when her father died, she had no claim to any family inheritance, which was directed to her brothers or more remote male relatives. The effect of these laws was to exclude women from civil society, itself based on property ownership.

In the later republican and imperial periods, these rules were significantly modified. Women rarely married according to the traditional form. The practice of "free" marriage allowed a woman to remain under her father's authority, to possess property given her by her father (most frequently the "dowry," recoverable from the husband's household on his death), and to inherit from her father. She could also bequeath property to her own children and divorce her husband, just as he could divorce her.

Despite this greater freedom, women still suffered enormous disability under Roman law. Heirs could belong only to the father's side, never the mother's. Moreover, although she could bequeath her property to her children, she could not establish a line of succession in doing so. A woman was "the beginning and end of her own family," said the jurist Ulpian. Moreover, women could play no public role. They could not hold public office, represent anyone in a legal case, or even witness a will. Women had only a private existence and no public personality.

The dowry system, the guardian, women's limited ability to transmit wealth, and total political disability are all features of Roman law adopted by the medieval communities of western Europe, although modified according to local customary laws.

CHRISTIAN DOCTRINE AND WOMEN'S PLACE. The Hebrew Bible and the Christian New Testament authorized later writers to limit women to the realm of the family and to burden them with the guilt of original sin. The passages most fruitful for this purpose were the creation narratives in Genesis and sentences from the Epistles defining women's role within the Christian family and community.

Each of the first two chapters of Genesis contains a creation narrative. In the first "God created man in his own image, in the image of God he created him; male and female he created them" (Gn 1:27). In the second, God created Eve from Adam's rib (2:21–23). Christian theologians relied principally on Genesis 2 for their understanding of the relation between man and woman, interpreting the creation of Eve from Adam as proof of her subordination to him.

The creation story in Genesis 2 leads to that of the temptations in Genesis 3: of Eve by the wily serpent and of Adam by Eve. As read by Christian theologians from Tertullian to Thomas Aquinas, the narrative made Eve responsible for the Fall and its consequences. She instigated the act; she deceived her husband; she suffered the greater punishment. Her disobedience made it necessary for Jesus to be incarnated and to die on the cross. From the pulpit, moralists and preachers for centuries conveyed to women the guilt that they bore for original sin.

The Epistles offered advice to early Christians on building communities of the faithful. Among the matters to be regulated was the place of women. Paul offered views favorable to women in Galatians 3:28: "There is neither Jew nor Greek, there is neither slave nor free, there is neither male nor female; for you are all one in Christ Jesus." Paul also referred to women as his coworkers and placed them on a par with himself and his male coworkers (Phlm 4:2–3; Rom 16:1–3; 1 Cor 16:19). Elsewhere, Paul limited women's possibilities: "But I want you to understand that the head of every man is Christ, the head of a woman is her husband, and the head of Christ is God" (1 Cor 11:3).

Biblical passages by later writers (although attributed to Paul) enjoined women to forgo jewels, expensive clothes, and elaborate coiffures; and they forbade women to "teach or have authority over men," telling them to "learn in silence with all submissiveness" as is proper for one responsible for sin, consoling them, however, with the thought that they will be saved through childbearing (1 Tm 2:9–15). Other texts among the later Epistles defined women as the weaker sex and emphasized their subordination to their husbands (1 Pt 3:7; Col 3:18; Eph 5:22–23).

These passages from the New Testament became the arsenal employed by theologians of the early church to transmit negative attitudes toward women to medieval Christian culture—above all, Tertullian (*On the Apparel of Women*), Jerome (*Against Jovinian*), and Augustine (*The Literal Meaning of Genesis*).

THE IMAGE OF WOMEN IN MEDIEVAL LITERATURE. The philosophical, legal, and religious traditions born in antiquity formed the basis of the medieval intellectual synthesis wrought by trained thinkers, mostly clerics, writing in Latin and based largely in universities. The vernacular literary tradition that developed alongside the learned tradition also spoke about female nature and women's roles. Medieval stories, poems, and epics also portrayed women negatively—as lustful and deceitful—while praising good housekeepers and loyal wives as replicas of the Virgin Mary or the female saints and martyrs.

There is an exception in the movement of "courtly love" that evolved in southern France from the twelfth century. Courtly love was the erotic love between a nobleman and noblewoman, the latter usually superior in social rank. It was always adulterous. From the conventions of courtly love derive modern Western notions of romantic love. The tradition has had an impact disproportionate to its size, for it affected only a tiny elite, and very few women. The exaltation of the female lover probably does not reflect a higher evaluation of women or a step toward their sexual liberation. More likely it gives expression to the social and sexual tensions besetting the knightly class at a specific historical juncture.

The literary fashion of courtly love was on the wane by the thirteenth century, when the widely read *Romance of the Rose* was composed in French by two authors of significantly different dispositions. Guillaume de Lorris composed the initial four thousand verses about 1235, and Jean de Meun added about seventeen thousand verses—more than four times the original—about 1265.

The fragment composed by Guillaume de Lorris stands squarely in the tradition of courtly love. Here the poet, in a dream, is admitted into a walled garden where he finds a magic fountain in which a rosebush is reflected. He longs to pick one rose, but the thorns prevent his doing so, even as he is wounded by arrows from the god of love, whose commands he agrees to obey. The rest of this part of the poem recounts the poet's unsuccessful efforts to pluck the rose.

The longer part of the *Romance* by Jean de Meun also describes a dream. But here allegorical characters give long didactic speeches, providing a social satire on a variety of themes, some pertaining to women. Love is an anxious and tormented state, the poem explains: women are greedy and manipulative, marriage is miserable, beautiful women are lustful, ugly ones cease to please, and a chaste woman is as rare as a black swan.

Shortly after Jean de Meun completed *The Romance of the Rose*, Mathéolus penned his *Lamentations*, a long Latin diatribe against marriage translated into French about a century later. The *Lamentations* sum up medieval attitudes toward women and provoked the important response by Christine de Pizan in her *Book of the City of Ladies*.

In 1355, Giovanni Boccaccio wrote *Il Corbaccio*, another antifeminist manifesto, although ironically by an author whose other works pioneered new directions in Renaissance thought. The former husband of his lover appears to Boccaccio, condemning his unmoderated lust and detailing the defects of women. Boccaccio concedes at the end "how much men naturally surpass women in nobility" and is cured of his desires.[3]

WOMEN'S ROLES: THE FAMILY. The negative perceptions of women expressed in the intellectual tradition are also implicit in the actual roles that women played in European society. Assigned to subordinate positions in the household and the church, they were barred from significant participation in public life.

Medieval European households, like those in antiquity and in non-Western civilizations, were headed by males. It was the male serf (or peasant), feudal lord, town merchant, or citizen who was polled or taxed or succeeded to an inheritance or had any acknowledged public role, although his wife or widow could stand as a temporary surrogate. From about 1100, the position of property-holding males was further enhanced: inheritance was confined to the male, or agnate, line—with depressing consequences for women.

A wife never fully belonged to her husband's family, nor was she a daughter to her father's family. She left her father's house young to marry whomever her parents chose. Her dowry was managed by her husband, and at her death it normally passed to her children by him.

A married woman's life was occupied nearly constantly with cycles of pregnancy, childbearing, and lactation. Women bore children through all the years of their fertility, and many died in childbirth. They were also responsible for raising young children up to six or seven. In the propertied classes that responsibility was shared, since it was common for a wet nurse to take over breast-feeding and for servants to perform other chores.

Women trained their daughters in the household duties appropriate to their status, nearly always tasks associated with textiles: spinning, weaving, sewing, embroidering. Their sons were sent out of the house as apprentices or students, or their training was assumed by fathers in later childhood and adolescence. On the death of her husband, a woman's children became the responsibility of his family. She generally did not take "his" children with her to a new marriage or back to her father's house, except sometimes in the artisan classes.

Women also worked. Rural peasants performed farm chores, merchant wives often practiced their husbands' trades, the unmarried daughters of the urban poor worked as servants or prostitutes. All wives produced or embellished textiles and did the housekeeping, while wealthy ones managed

---

3. Giovanni Boccaccio, *The Corbaccio, or The Labyrinth of Love,* trans. and ed. Anthony K. Cassell, rev. ed. (Binghamton, N.Y., 1993), 71.

servants. These labors were unpaid or poorly paid but often contributed substantially to family wealth.

WOMEN'S ROLES: THE CHURCH. Membership in a household, whether a father's or a husband's, meant for women a lifelong subordination to others. In western Europe, the Roman Catholic Church offered an alternative to the career of wife and mother. A woman could enter a convent, parallel in function to the monasteries for men that evolved in the early Christian centuries.

In the convent, a woman pledged herself to a celibate life, lived according to strict community rules, and worshiped daily. Often the convent offered training in Latin, allowing some women to become considerable scholars and authors as well as scribes, artists, and musicians. For women who chose the conventual life, the benefits could be enormous, but for numerous others placed in convents by paternal choice, the life could be restrictive and burdensome.

The conventual life declined as an alternative for women as the modern age approached. Reformed monastic institutions resisted responsibility for related female orders. The church increasingly restricted female institutional life by insisting on closer male supervision.

Women often sought other options. Some joined the communities of laywomen that sprang up spontaneously in the thirteenth century in the urban zones of western Europe, especially in Flanders and Italy. Some joined the heretical movements that flourished in late medieval Christendom, whose anticlerical and often antifamily positions particularly appealed to women. In these communities, some women were acclaimed as "holy women" or "saints," whereas others often were condemned as frauds or heretics.

In all, although the options offered to women by the church were sometimes less than satisfactory, they were sometimes richly rewarding. After 1520, the convent remained an option only in Roman Catholic territories. Protestantism engendered an ideal of marriage as a heroic endeavor and appeared to place husband and wife on a more equal footing. Sermons and treatises, however, still called for female subordination and obedience.

THE OTHER VOICE, 1300–1700

When the modern era opened, European culture was so firmly structured by a framework of negative attitudes toward women that to dismantle it was a monumental labor. The process began as part of a larger cultural movement that entailed the critical reexamination of ideas inherited from the ancient and medieval past. The humanists launched that critical reexamination.

THE HUMANIST FOUNDATION. Originating in Italy in the fourteenth century, humanism quickly became the dominant intellectual movement in Europe. Spreading in the sixteenth century from Italy to the rest of Europe, it fueled the literary, scientific, and philosophical movements of the era and laid the basis for the eighteenth-century Enlightenment.

Humanists regarded the Scholastic philosophy of medieval universities as out of touch with the realities of urban life. They found in the rhetorical discourse of classical Rome a language adapted to civic life and public speech. They learned to read, speak, and write classical Latin and, eventually, classical Greek. They founded schools to teach others to do so, establishing the pattern for elementary and secondary education for the next three hundred years.

In the service of complex government bureaucracies, humanists employed their skills to write eloquent letters, deliver public orations, and formulate public policy. They developed new scripts for copying manuscripts and used the new printing press to disseminate texts, for which they created methods of critical editing.

Humanism was a movement led by males who accepted the evaluation of women in ancient texts and generally shared the misogynist perceptions of their culture. (Female humanists, as we will see, did not.) Yet humanism also opened the door to a reevaluation of the nature and capacity of women. By calling authors, texts, and ideas into question, it made possible the fundamental rereading of the whole intellectual tradition that was required in order to free women from cultural prejudice and social subordination.

A DIFFERENT CITY. The other voice first appeared when, after so many centuries, the accumulation of misogynist concepts evoked a response from a capable female defender: Christine de Pizan (1365–1431). Introducing her *Book of the City of Ladies* (1405), she described how she was affected by reading Mathéolus's *Lamentations*: "Just the sight of this book . . . made me wonder how it happened that so many different men . . . are so inclined to express both in speaking and in their treatises and writings so many wicked insults about women and their behavior."[4] These statements impelled her to

---

4. Christine de Pizan, *The Book of the City of Ladies*, trans. Earl Jeffrey Richards, foreword by Marina Warner (New York, 1982), 1.1.1, pp. 3–4.

detest herself "and the entire feminine sex, as though we were monstrosities in nature."[5]

The rest of *The Book of the City of Ladies* presents a justification of the female sex and a vision of an ideal community of women. A pioneer, she has received the message of female inferiority and rejected it. From the fourteenth to the seventeenth century, a huge body of literature accumulated that responded to the dominant tradition.

The result was a literary explosion consisting of works by both men and women, in Latin and in the vernaculars: works enumerating the achievements of notable women; works rebutting the main accusations made against women; works arguing for the equal education of men and women; works defining and redefining women's proper role in the family, at court, in public; works describing women's lives and experiences. Recent monographs and articles have begun to hint at the great range of this movement, involving probably several thousand titles. The protofeminism of these "other voices" constitutes a significant fraction of the literary product of the early modern era.

THE CATALOGS. About 1365, the same Boccaccio whose *Corbaccio* rehearses the usual charges against female nature wrote another work, *Concerning Famous Women*. A humanist treatise drawing on classical texts, it praised 106 notable women: ninety-eight of them from pagan Greek and Roman antiquity, one (Eve) from the Bible, and seven from the medieval religious and cultural tradition; his book helped make all readers aware of a sex normally condemned or forgotten. Boccaccio's outlook nevertheless was unfriendly to women, for it singled out for praise those women who possessed the traditional virtues of chastity, silence, and obedience. Women who were active in the public realm—for example, rulers and warriors—were depicted as usually being lascivious and as suffering terrible punishments for entering the masculine sphere. Women were his subject, but Boccaccio's standard remained male.

Christine de Pizan's *Book of the City of Ladies* contains a second catalog, one responding specifically to Boccaccio's. Whereas Boccaccio portrays female virtue as exceptional, she depicts it as universal. Many women in history were leaders, or remained chaste despite the lascivious approaches of men, or were visionaries and brave martyrs.

The work of Boccaccio inspired a series of catalogs of illustrious women of the biblical, classical, Christian, and local pasts, among them Filippo da

5. Ibid., 1.1.1–2, p. 5.

Bergamo's *Of Illustrious Women*, Pierre de Brantôme's *Lives of Illustrious Women*, Pierre Le Moyne's *Gallerie of Heroic Women*, and Pietro Paolo de Ribera's *Immortal Triumphs and Heroic Enterprises of 845 Women*. Whatever their embedded prejudices, these works drove home to the public the possibility of female excellence.

THE DEBATE. At the same time, many questions remained: Could a woman be virtuous? Could she perform noteworthy deeds? Was she even, strictly speaking, of the same human species as men? These questions were debated over four centuries, in French, German, Italian, Spanish, and English, by authors male and female, among Catholics, Protestants, and Jews, in ponderous volumes and breezy pamphlets. The whole literary genre has been called the *querelle des femmes*, the "woman question."

The opening volley of this battle occurred in the first years of the fifteenth century, in a literary debate sparked by Christine de Pizan. She exchanged letters critical of Jean de Meun's contribution to *The Romance of the Rose* with two French royal secretaries, Jean de Montreuil and Gontier Col. When the matter became public, Jean Gerson, one of Europe's leading theologians, supported de Pizan's arguments against de Meun, for the moment silencing the opposition.

The debate resurfaced repeatedly over the next two hundred years. *The Triumph of Women* (1438) by Juan Rodríguez de la Camara (or Juan Rodríguez del Padron) struck a new note by presenting arguments for the superiority of women to men. *The Champion of Women* (1440–42) by Martin Le Franc addresses once again the negative views of women presented in *The Romance of the Rose* and offers counterevidence of female virtue and achievement.

A cameo of the debate on women is included in *The Courtier*, one of the most widely read books of the era, published by the Italian Baldassare Castiglione in 1528 and immediately translated into other European vernaculars. *The Courtier* depicts a series of evenings at the court of the duke of Urbino in which many men and some women of the highest social stratum amuse themselves by discussing a range of literary and social issues. The "woman question" is a pervasive theme throughout, and the third of its four books is devoted entirely to that issue.

In a verbal duel, Gasparo Pallavicino and Giuliano de' Medici present the main claims of the two traditions. Gasparo argues the innate inferiority of women and their inclination to vice. Only in bearing children do they profit the world. Giuliano counters that women share the same spiritual and mental capacities as men and may excel in wisdom and action. Men and women are of the same essence: just as no stone can be more perfectly a stone than another, so no human being can be more perfectly human than others, whether male or female. It was an astonishing assertion, boldly made to an audience as large as all Europe.

THE TREATISES. Humanism provided the materials for a positive counterconcept to the misogyny embedded in Scholastic philosophy and law and inherited from the Greek, Roman, and Christian pasts. A series of humanist treatises on marriage and family, on education and deportment, and on the nature of women helped construct these new perspectives.

The works by Francesco Barbaro and Leon Battista Alberti—*On Marriage* (1415) and *On the Family* (1434–37)—far from defending female equality, reasserted women's responsibility for rearing children and managing the housekeeping while being obedient, chaste, and silent. Nevertheless, they served the cause of reexamining the issue of women's nature by placing domestic issues at the center of scholarly concern and reopening the pertinent classical texts. In addition, Barbaro emphasized the companionate nature of marriage and the importance of a wife's spiritual and mental qualities for the well-being of the family.

These themes reappear in later humanist works on marriage and the education of women by Juan Luis Vives and Erasmus. Both were moderately sympathetic to the condition of women without reaching beyond the usual masculine prescriptions for female behavior.

An outlook more favorable to women characterizes the nearly unknown work *In Praise of Women* (ca. 1487) by the Italian humanist Bartolommeo Goggio. In addition to providing a catalog of illustrious women, Goggio argued that male and female are the same in essence, but that women (reworking the Adam and Eve narrative from quite a new angle) are actually superior. In the same vein, the Italian humanist Maria Equicola asserted the spiritual equality of men and women in *On Women* (1501). In 1525, Galeazzo Flavio Capra (or Capella) published his work *On the Excellence and Dignity of Women*. This humanist tradition of treatises defending the worthiness of women culminates in the work of Henricus Cornelius Agrippa *On the Nobility and Preeminence of the Female Sex*. No work by a male humanist more succinctly or explicitly presents the case for female dignity.

THE WITCH BOOKS. While humanists grappled with the issues pertaining to women and family, other learned men turned their attention to what they perceived as a very great problem: witches. Witch-hunting manuals, explorations of the witch phenomenon, and even defenses of witches are not at first glance pertinent to the tradition of the other voice. But they do relate in this way: most accused witches were women. The hostility aroused by supposed witch activity is comparable to the hostility aroused by women. The evil deeds the victims of the hunt were charged with were exaggerations of the vices to which, many believed, all women were prone.

The connection between the witch accusation and the hatred of women is explicit in the notorious witch-hunting manual *The Hammer of Witches* (1486) by two Dominican inquisitors, Heinrich Krämer and Jacob Sprenger. Here the inconstancy, deceitfulness, and lustfulness traditionally associated with women are depicted in exaggerated form as the core features of witch behavior. These traits inclined women to make a bargain with the devil—sealed by sexual intercourse—by which they acquired unholy powers. Such bizarre claims, far from being rejected by rational men, were broadcast by intellectuals. The German Ulrich Molitur, the Frenchman Nicolas Rémy, and the Italian Stefano Guazzo all coolly informed the public of sinister orgies and midnight pacts with the devil. The celebrated French jurist, historian, and political philosopher Jean Bodin argued that because women were especially prone to diabolism, regular legal procedures could properly be suspended in order to try those accused of this "exceptional crime."

A few experts such as the physician Johann Weyer, a student of Agrippa's, raised their voices in protest. In 1563, he explained the witch phenomenon thus, without discarding belief in diabolism: the devil deluded foolish old women afflicted by melancholia, causing them to believe they had magical powers. Weyer's rational skepticism, which had good credibility in the community of the learned, worked to revise the conventional views of women and witchcraft.

WOMEN'S WORKS. To the many categories of works produced on the question of women's worth must be added nearly all works written by women. A woman writing was in herself a statement of women's claim to dignity.

Only a few women wrote anything before the dawn of the modern era, for three reasons. First, they rarely received the education that would enable them to write. Second, they were not admitted to the public roles—as administrator, bureaucrat, lawyer or notary, or university professor—in which they might gain knowledge of the kinds of things the literate public thought worth writing about. Third, the culture imposed silence on women, considering speaking out a form of unchastity. Given these conditions, it is remarkable that any women wrote. Those who did before the fourteenth century were almost always nuns or religious women whose isolation made their pronouncements more acceptable.

From the fourteenth century on, the volume of women's writings rose. Women continued to write devotional literature, although not always as cloistered nuns. They also wrote diaries, often intended as keepsakes for their children; books of advice to their sons and daughters; letters to family members and friends; and family memoirs, in a few cases elaborate enough to be considered histories.

A few women wrote works directly concerning the "woman question," and some of these, such as the humanists Isotta Nogarola, Cassandra Fedele, Laura Cereta, and Olympia Morata, were highly trained. A few were professional writers, living by the income of their pens; the very first among them was Christine de Pizan, noteworthy in this context as in so many others. In addition to *The Book of the City of Ladies* and her critiques of *The Romance of the Rose*, she wrote *The Treasure of the City of Ladies* (a guide to social decorum for women), an advice book for her son, much courtly verse, and a full-scale history of the reign of King Charles V of France.

WOMEN PATRONS. Women who did not themselves write but encouraged others to do so boosted the development of an alternative tradition. Highly placed women patrons supported authors, artists, musicians, poets, and learned men. Such patrons, drawn mostly from the Italian elites and the courts of northern Europe, figure disproportionately as the dedicatees of the important works of early feminism.

For a start, it might be noted that the catalogs of Boccaccio and Alvaro de Luna were dedicated to the Florentine noblewoman Andrea Acciaiuoli and to Doña María, first wife of King Juan II of Castile, while the French translation of Boccaccio's work was commissioned by Anne of Brittany, wife of King Charles VIII of France. The humanist treatises of Goggio, Equicola, Vives, and Agrippa were dedicated, respectively, to Eleanora of Aragon, wife of Ercole I d'Este, duke of Ferrara; to Margherita Cantelma of Mantua; to Catherine of Aragon, wife of King Henry VIII of England; and to Margaret, duchess of Austria and regent of the Netherlands. As late as 1696, Mary Astell's *Serious Proposal to the Ladies, for the Advancement of Their True and Greatest Interest* was dedicated to Princess Anne of Denmark.

These authors presumed that their efforts would be welcome to female patrons, or they may have written at the bidding of those patrons. Silent themselves, perhaps even unresponsive, these loftily placed women helped shape the tradition of the other voice.

THE ISSUES. The literary forms and patterns in which the tradition of the other voice presented itself have now been sketched. It remains to highlight the major issues around which this tradition crystallizes. In brief, there are four problems to which our authors return again and again, in plays and catalogs, in verse and letters, in treatises and dialogues, in every language: the problem of chastity, the problem of power, the problem of speech, and the problem of knowledge. Of these the greatest, preconditioning the others, is the problem of chastity.

THE PROBLEM OF CHASTITY. In traditional European culture, as in those of antiquity and others around the globe, chastity was perceived as woman's quintessential virtue—in contrast to courage, or generosity, or leadership, or rationality, seen as virtues characteristic of men. Opponents of women charged them with insatiable lust. Women themselves and their defenders— without disputing the validity of the standard—responded that women were capable of chastity.

The requirement of chastity kept women at home, silenced them, isolated them, left them in ignorance. It was the source of all other impediments. Why was it so important to the society of men, of whom chastity was not required, and who more often than not considered it their right to violate the chastity of any woman they encountered?

Female chastity ensured the continuity of the male-headed household. If a man's wife was not chaste, he could not be sure of the legitimacy of his offspring. If they were not his and they acquired his property, it was not his household, but some other man's, that had endured. If his daughter was not chaste, she could not be transferred to another man's household as his wife and he was dishonored.

The whole system of the integrity of the household and the transmission of property was bound up in female chastity. Such a requirement pertained only to property-owning classes, of course. Poor women could not expect to maintain their chastity, least of all if they were in contact with high-status men to whom all women but those of their own household were prey.

In Catholic Europe, the requirement of chastity was further buttressed by moral and religious imperatives. Original sin was inextricably linked with the sexual act. Virginity was seen as heroic virtue, far more impressive than, say, the avoidance of idleness or greed. Monasticism, the cultural institution that dominated medieval Europe for centuries, was grounded in the renunciation of the flesh. The Catholic reform of the eleventh century imposed a similar standard on all the clergy and a heightened awareness of sexual requirements on all the laity. Although men were asked to be chaste, female unchastity was much worse: it led to the devil, as Eve had led mankind to sin.

To such requirements, women and their defenders protested their innocence. Furthermore, following the example of holy women who had escaped the requirements of family and sought the religious life, some women began to conceive of female communities as alternatives both to family and to the cloister. Christine de Pizan's city of ladies was such a community. Moderata Fonte and Mary Astell envisioned others. The luxurious salons of the French *précieuses* of the seventeenth century, or the comfortable English drawing rooms of the next, may have been born of the same impulse. Here women not only might escape, if briefly, the subordinate position that life in the family entailed but might also make claims to power, exercise their capacity for speech, and display their knowledge.

THE PROBLEM OF POWER. Women were excluded from power: the whole cultural tradition insisted on it. Only men were citizens, only men bore arms, only men could be chiefs or lords or kings. There were exceptions that did not disprove the rule, when wives or widows or mothers took the place of men, awaiting their return or the maturation of a male heir. A woman who attempted to rule in her own right was perceived as an anomaly, a monster, at once a deformed woman and an insufficient male, sexually confused and consequently unsafe.

The association of such images with women who held or sought power explains some otherwise odd features of early modern culture. Queen Elizabeth I of England, one of the few women to hold full regal authority in European history, played with such male/female images—positive ones, of course—in representing herself to her subjects. She was a prince, and manly, even though she was female. She was also (she claimed) virginal, a condition absolutely essential if she was to avoid the attacks of her opponents. Catherine de' Medici, who ruled France as widow and regent for her sons, also adopted such imagery in defining her position. She chose as one symbol the figure of Artemisia, an androgynous ancient warrior-heroine who combined a female persona with masculine powers.

Power in a woman, without such sexual imagery, seems to have been indigestible by the culture. A rare note was struck by the Englishman Sir Thomas Elyot in his *Defence of Good Women* (1540), justifying both women's participation in civic life and their prowess in arms. The old tune was sung by the Scots reformer John Knox in his *First Blast of the Trumpet against the Monstrous Regiment of Women* (1558); for him rule by women, defects in nature, was a hideous contradiction in terms.

The confused sexuality of the imagery of female potency was not reserved for rulers. Any woman who excelled was likely to be called an Amazon, recalling the self-mutilated warrior women of antiquity who repudiated all men, gave up their sons, and raised only their daughters. She was often said to have "exceeded her sex" or to have possessed "masculine virtue"—as the very fact of conspicuous excellence conferred masculinity even on the female subject. The catalogs of notable women often showed those female heroes dressed in armor, armed to the teeth, like men. Amazonian hero-ines romp through the epics of the age—Ariosto's *Orlando Furioso* (1532) and Spenser's *Faerie Queene* (1590–1609). Excellence in a woman was perceived as a claim for power, and power was reserved for the masculine realm. A woman who possessed either one was masculinized and lost title to her own female identity.

THE PROBLEM OF SPEECH. Just as power had a sexual dimension when it was claimed by women, so did speech. A good woman spoke little. Excessive speech was an indication of unchastity. By speech, women seduced men. Eve had lured Adam into sin by her speech. Accused witches were commonly accused of having spoken abusively, or irrationally, or simply too much. As enlightened a figure as Francesco Barbaro insisted on silence in a woman, which he linked to her perfect unanimity with her husband's will and her unblemished virtue (her chastity). Another Italian humanist, Leonardo Bruni, in advising a noblewoman on her studies, barred her not from speech but from public speaking. That was reserved for men.

Related to the problem of speech was that of costume—another, if silent, form of self-expression. Assigned the task of pleasing men as their primary occupation, elite women often tended toward elaborate costume, hairdressing, and the use of cosmetics. Clergy and secular moralists alike condemned these practices. The appropriate function of costume and adorn-ment was to announce the status of a woman's husband or father. Any further indulgence in adornment was akin to unchastity.

THE PROBLEM OF KNOWLEDGE. When the Italian noblewoman Isotta Nogarola had begun to attain a reputation as a humanist, she was accused of incest—a telling instance of the association of learning in women with unchastity. That chilling association inclined any woman who was educated to deny that she was or to make exaggerated claims of heroic chastity.

If educated women were pursued with suspicions of sexual misconduct, women seeking an education faced an even more daunting obstacle: the as-sumption that women were by nature incapable of learning, that reasoning was a particularly masculine ability. Just as they proclaimed their chastity, women and their defenders insisted on their capacity for learning. The major work by a male writer on female education—that by Juan Luis Vives, *On the Education of a Christian Woman* (1523)—granted female capacity for intellec-tion but still argued that a woman's whole education was to be shaped around the requirement of chastity and a future within the household. Female writers of the following generations—Marie de Gournay in France, Anna Maria van Schurman in Holland, and Mary Astell in England—began to envision other possibilities.

The pioneers of female education were the Italian women humanists who managed to attain a literacy in Latin and a knowledge of classical and Christian literature equivalent to that of prominent men. Their works implicitly and explicitly raise questions about women's social roles, defining problems that beset women attempting to break out of the cultural limits that had bound them. Like Christine de Pizan, who achieved an advanced education through her father's tutoring and her own devices, their bold questioning makes clear the importance of training. Only when women were educated to the same standard as male leaders would they be able to raise that other voice and insist on their dignity as human beings morally, intellectually, and legally equal to men.

THE OTHER VOICE. The other voice, a voice of protest, was mostly female, but it was also male. It spoke in the vernaculars and in Latin, in treatises and dialogues, in plays and poetry, in letters and diaries, and in pamphlets. It battered at the wall of prejudice that encircled women and raised a banner announcing its claims. The female was equal (or even superior) to the male in essential nature—moral, spiritual, and intellectual. Women were capable of higher education, of holding positions of power and influence in the public realm, and of speaking and writing persuasively. The last bastion of masculine supremacy, centered on the notions of a woman's primary domestic responsibility and the requirement of female chastity, was not as yet assaulted—although visions of productive female communities as alternatives to the family indicated an awareness of the problem.

During the period 1300–1700, the other voice remained only a voice, and one only dimly heard. It did not result—yet—in an alteration of social patterns. Indeed, to this day they have not entirely been altered. Yet the call for justice issued as long as six centuries ago by those writing in the tradition of the other voice must be recognized as the source and origin of the mature feminist tradition and of the realignment of social institutions accomplished in the modern age.

We thank the volume editors in this series, who responded with many suggestions to an earlier draft of this introduction, making it a collaborative enterprise. Many of their suggestions and criticisms have resulted in revisions of this introduction, although we remain responsible for the final product.

PROJECTED TITLES IN THE SERIES

Isabella Andreini, *Mirtilla*, edited and translated by Laura Stortoni

Tullia d'Aragona, *Complete Poems and Letters*, edited and translated by Julia Hairston

Tullia d'Aragona, *The Wretch, Otherwise Known as Guerrino*, edited and translated by Julia Hairston and John McLucas

Giuseppa Eleonora Barbapiccola and Diamante Medaglia Faini, *The Education of Women*, edited and translated by Rebecca Messbarger

Francesco Barbaro et al., *On Marriage and the Family*, edited and translated by Margaret L. King

Laura Battiferra, *Selected Poetry, Prose, and Letters*, edited and translated by Victoria Kirkham

Giulia Bigolina, *Urania and Giulia*, edited and translated by Valeria Finucci

Francesco Buoninsegni and Arcangela Tarabotti, *Menippean Satire: "Against Feminine Extravagance" and "Antisatire,"* edited and translated by Elissa Weaver

Rosalba Carriera, *Letters, Diaries, and Art*, edited and translated by Shearer West

Madame du Chatelet, *Selected Works*, edited by Judith Zinsser

Vittoria Colonna, *Sonnets for Michelangelo*, edited and translated by Abigail Brundin

Vittoria Colonna, Chiara Matraini, and Lucrezia Marinella, *Marian Writings*, edited and translated by Susan Haskins

Princess Elizabeth of Bohemia, *Correspondence with Descartes*, edited and translated by Lisa Shapiro

Isabella d'Este, *Selected Letters*, edited and translated by Deanna Shemek

Fairy-Tales by Seventeenth-Century French Women Writers, edited and translated by Lewis Seifert and Domna C. Stanton

Moderata Fonte, *Floridoro*, edited and translated by Valeria Finucci

Moderata Fonte and Lucrezia Marinella, *Religious Narratives*, edited and translated by Virginia Cox

Francisca de los Apostoles, *Visions on Trial: The Inquisitional Trial of Francisca de los Apostoles*, edited and translated by Gillian T. W. Ahlgren

Catharina Regina von Greiffenberg, *Meditations on the Life of Christ*, edited and translated by Lynne Tatlock

In Praise of Women: Italian Fifteenth-Century Defenses of Women, edited and translated by Daniel Bornstein

Louise Labé, *Complete Works*, edited and translated by Annie Finch and Deborah Baker

Madame de Maintenon, *Dialogues and Addresses*, edited and translated by John J. Conley, S.J.

Lucrezia Marinella, *L'Enrico, or Byzantium Conquered*, edited and translated by Virginia Cox

Lucrezia Marinella, *Happy Arcadia*, edited and translated by Susan Haskins and Letizia Panizza

Chiara Matraini, *Selected Poetry and Prose*, edited and translated by Elaine MacLachlan

Eleonora Petersen von Merlau, *Autobiography (1718)*, edited and translated by Barbara Becker-Cantarino

Alessandro Piccolomini, *Rethinking Marriage in Sixteenth-Century Italy*, edited and translated by Letizia Panizza

Christine de Pizan et al., *Debate over the "Romance of the Rose,"* edited and translated by Tom Conley with Elisabeth Hodges

Christine de Pizan, *Life of Charles V,* edited and translated by Charity Cannon Willard

Christine de Pizan, *The Long Road of Learning,* edited and translated by Andrea Tarnowski

Madeleine and Catherine des Roches, *Selected Letters, Dialogues, and Poems,* edited and translated by Anne Larsen

Oliva Sabuco, *The New Philosophy: True Medicine,* edited and translated by Gianna Pomata

Margherita Sarrocchi, *La Scanderbeide,* edited and translated by Rinaldina Russell

Justine Siegemund, *The Court Midwife of the Electorate of Brandenburg* (1690), edited and translated by Lynne Tatlock

Gabrielle Suchon, *"On Philosophy" and "On Morality,"* edited and translated by Domna Stanton with Rebecca Wilkin

Sara Copio Sullam, *Sara Copio Sullam: Jewish Poet and Intellectual in Early Seventeenth-Century Venice,* edited and translated by Don Harrán

Arcangela Tarabotti, *Convent Life as Inferno: A Report,* introduction and notes by Francesca Medioli, translated by Letizia Panizza.

Laura Terracina, *Works,* edited and translated by Michael Sherberg

Katharina Schütz Zell, *Selected Writings,* edited and translated by Elsie McKee

CONVERSATIONS.
Par Mademoiselle de Scudery.

Fig. 1. "The Salon"

VOLUME EDITORS'
INTRODUCTION

THE OTHER VOICE

M adeleine de Scudéry was arguably the most popular European novelist of the seventeenth century. Her works were read avidly and translated into many languages (Italian, English, German, Spanish, and Arabic). Her rhetorical writings, only slightly less well-known, influenced salon culture throughout Europe and were used in France for girls' education. Scudéry published *Amorous Letters from Various Contemporary Authors* in 1641, *Famous Women, or Heroic Speeches* in 1642, *Conversations on Diverse Subjects*, including the dialogues "On Conversation," "On Speaking Too Much or Too Little," and "On Wit," in 1680, and *New Conversations on Diverse Subjects*, including the dialogue "On the Manner of Writing Letters," in 1684.[1] While Scudéry published *Famous Women* under her brother's name and the others anonymously, she was well-known in France and in knowledgeable circles around Europe to be the author of most of these works. Her volume of speeches by women and her first volume of conversational dialogues were widely translated and popular throughout Europe.

Scudéry was one of the rare women in seventeenth-century Europe to make her living as a writer. In addition, she was an important voice in countering the misogyny of the period through her portraits of strong, intelligent, talkative women in her novels, speeches, and conversational dialogues and in

---

1. See Madeleine de Scudéry, *Lettres amoureuses de divers autheurs de ce temps* (Paris, 1641); *Les femmes illustres; ou, Les harangues héroiques, de Mr de Scudéry* (Paris, 1665); *Conversations sur divers sujets,* 2 tomes (Paris, 1680); *Conversations nouvelles sur divers sujets, dedie'es au Roy* (Paris, 1684); and the modern editions, *Choix de conversations de Mlle de Scudéry,* ed. Phillip J. Wolfe (Ravenna: Longo Editore, 1977); and *De l'air galant et autres conversations,* ed. Delphine Denis (Paris: Honoré Champion, 1998). On the use of Scudéry's *Conversations* to teach conversation to the girls at Mme de Maintenon's school from 1686 to 1691, see Elizabeth Goldsmith, *"Exclusive Conversations": The Art of Interaction in Seventeenth-Century France* (Philadelphia: University of Pennsylvania Press, 1988), 66.

her argument for women's education in one of the heroic speeches, "Sappho to Erinna." Moreover, in that speech and in her *Amorous Letters*, she helped to construct a socially acceptable discourse of eroticism for female-female relationships.

Scudéry was well-known as an important presence in French salons and a founder of the *précieuse* movement.[2] When these were attacked and fell out of fashion (for the quite misogynist reason that they encouraged uppity women, as well as for matters of changing taste), Scudéry was vilified, and in contemporary French studies she still has a reputation for stylistic excess. However, we have not found her style difficult, pretentious, or ridiculous. In her *Amorous Letters*, she helped to popularize the passionate figures and extravagant language of female friendship that became a staple of women's literature for the next two and a half centuries. In the *Heroic Speeches*, she adapted the heightened humanist oratorical style to the vernacular and to women. In her many volumes of *Conversations*, she creates an easy, modern, conversational style that is playful and still amusing and engaging.

LIFE AND WORKS   In his work on conversation in French literature, M Fumaroli called Madeleine de Scudéry one of the "best theorists of con-

---

2. For a definition of *"précieuses,"* see Ian Maclean, *Woman Triumphant: Feminism in French Literature 1610–1652* (Oxford: Clarendon Press, 1977), 152–53: *"Préciosité* offered women a system of existence conceived of as an antidote to their plight as wards and wives . . . the purification and enrichment of language, [and] the creation of a self-conscious intellectual élite . . . . The *précieuse* develops essentially feminine qualities, such as 'finesse,' elegance, sensibility; she is neither pedantic nor unlearned, but 'savante' . . . ; she exists in a universe in which love is deified, but only that love which has been purified from constraint, from considerations of convenience and financial gain, from the dangers of habit and monotony. It is, in fact, the love of the world of the novel, where the lover displays infinite patience, where adventures and dangers serve to keep passion alive, where marriage is always just out of sight." On *précieuses,* see also Myriam Maître, *Les précieuses: Naissance des femmes de lettres en France au XVII, siècle* (Paris: Honoré Champion, 1999), especially pp. 419–96, on the characteristics of preciosity; and pp. 397–414, on the role of the *précieuses* after the Fronde—Maître argues that they were part of the propaganda machine of Louis XIV to erase the damaging effects of the Fronde. For a dissenting voice, see Roger Duchêne, who suggests, in "A la recherche d'une espèce rare et mêlée: les Précieuses avant Molière," *Papers on French Seventeenth-Century Literature* 43 (1995): 331–57, that *"précieuse"* was a term of approbation for elegant society women and did not signify a special group until after so designated by Molière; see also his "Le Nouveau dictionnaire des Précieuses," *Papers on French Seventeenth-Century Literature* 50 (1999): 91–109, where he argues that we should *not* call Scudéry *"précieuse"* because it was a limiting term that was dismissive of women with pretensions to education; and *Les Précieuses, ou, Comment l'esprit vin aux femmes* (Paris: Fayard, 2001), which supports the opinion that the term was a vague one signifying a fashion, not a specific circle, and reprints many documents in the pro and anti-*précieuse* debate.

versation in the seventeenth century."[3] During her lifetime, her works were published either anonymously or under the name of her brother, Georges de Scudéry, also a well-known writer. Scudéry seems to have felt strongly the limitations imposed on women writers. In her biography of Scudéry, Nicole Aronson quotes from Scudéry's novel, *Le grand Cyrus*, in which the heroine, Sapho, exclaims, "There is nothing more unpleasant than to be a woman of letters and be treated as one when one is of noble birth."[4] "Sapho" being Scudéry's salon name and the character Sapho almost certainly a self-portrayal in her works, this sentiment probably reflects her own attitude toward her work.

Named for her mother, Madeleine de Scudéry, one of two children who survived infancy, was born, according to tradition, in Le Hâvre on 15 November 1607. Her baptism is recorded on 1 December 1608, and her brother Georges had been baptized on 12 August 1601. Their father, Georges de Scudéry, was captain of the port in Le Hâvre, where he married Madeleine de Martel de Goutimesnil in 1599. Both parents died in 1613, leaving Madeleine and Georges in the custody of an uncle in Rouen, where they spent their childhood. Her uncle gave her an abnormally well-rounded education for a girl at the time: she studied writing, spelling, drawing, dancing, painting, and needlework. In addition to these subjects, Scudéry studied others on her own, such as agriculture, medicine, cooking, Spanish, and Italian. Her works also demonstrate such a comprehensive knowledge of ancient history that we suspect she may also have received some instruction in Greek and Latin.[5]

In 1637, after the death of their uncle, Scudéry moved to Paris to live with her brother Georges, who had achieved great success with his play, *Le Prince Déguisé* (1635). The two lived in Rue Vieille-du-Temple in the Marais district and soon became integrated into the "best society,"[6] frequenting the famous salon at the Hôtel de Rambouillet. Although not noted for her beauty, Scudéry was reported to have a gift for wit and clever conversation

3. Quoted in Elisa Biancardi, "Madeleine de Scudéry et son cercle: spécificité socioculturelle et créativité littéraire," *Papers on French Literature* 22 (1995): 415, Strongson's translation.

4. Aronson, *Mademoiselle de Scudéry*, trans. Stuart R. Aronson (Boston: G. K. Hall and Co., 1978), 19.

5. On her education, see Charles Augustin Sainte-Beuve, "Mademoiselle de Scudéry," *Portraits of the Seventeenth Century: Historic and Literary*, trans. Katherine P. Wormeley (New York: Frederick Ungar Publishing Co., 1964), 2:58–59; Aronson, *Mademoiselle de Scudéry*, 22; and Nathalie Grande, *Stratégies de romancières de Clélie à La Princesse de Clèves (1645–1678)* (Paris: Honoré Champion, 1999), 211.

6. Sainte-Beuve, "Mademoiselle de Scudéry," 63.

that made her quite popular within this circle.[7] Scudéry remained unmarried her whole life.[8]

Scudéry's first literary success was her four-volume novel *Ibrahim; ou, L'illustre Bassa*, published in 1641 under her brother's name. In 1641 she also published *Lettres amoureuses* anonymously, a collection of model letters ranging from an intimate correspondence between women that emphasized impassioned sentiments to templates for various personal business and social obligations. In 1642, under her brother's name, she published *Les femmes illustres; ou, Les harangues héroiques*, a collection of fictional speeches attributed to historical women. We present selections in this collection from both *Lettres* and *Femmes illustres*.[9]

In 1642, with the help of Madame de Rambouillet, Georges was appointed governor of Nôtre-Dame-de-la-Garde in Marseille. Scudéry followed him there, where they remained from 1644 to 1647. Although it was expected for women to live with their father or brother until married, these were difficult years for Scudéry, who missed the active social life she had enjoyed in Paris. Nevertheless, she and her brother developed a collaborative, creative relationship through coauthorship. According to contemporary accounts, the siblings were almost arrested when they were overheard in a Lyon hotel discussing the assassination of a prince; the police let them go when they realized that these authors were discussing the plot of their latest novel.[10] In 1650, Georges was elected to the Académie Française.

In 1648 began the Fronde, an uprising of the Parlement led by aristo-

7. Aronson, *Mademoiselle de Scudéry*, 27

8. According to Aronson, this decision "probably lay in her well-known aversion to anything that could rob her of her freedom" (*Mademoiselle de Scudéry*, 45). Biancardi supposes that Paris society was satisfying enough that she chose not to take up the responsibilities of marriage ("Madeleine de Scudéry et son cercle," 419).

9. There is controversy over what Scudéry wrote and what her brother wrote, although generally scholars believe that Scudéry wrote the novels and the speeches of *Famous Women*, while her brother wrote the plays; Scudéry certainly wrote the *Conversations*, which appeared after her brother died, and these works contain many excerpts from the novels. Scudéry's authorship was an open secret during her lifetime. For Aronson's opinions on authorship, see *Mademoiselle de Scudéry*, 29 and 118. We follow Joan DeJean, "La lettre amoureuse revue et corrigée: Un texte oublié de Madeleine de Scudéry," *Revue d'Histoire Littéraire de la France* 1 (1988): 17–22; and *Fictions of Sappho, 1546–1937* (Chicago: University of Chicago Press, 1989); as well as Maître, *Les Précieuses*, in assigning *Lettres amoureuses*, published anonymously, to Madeleine de Scudéry. *Lettres amoureuses* is included under Scudéry's authorship in the *History of Women Microfilm Series*, reel 78, no. 502 (New Haven, Conn.: Research Publications).

10. Aronson, *Mademoiselle de Scudéry*, 34. Aronson claims that "this story proves . . . [that] the collaboration of brother and sister is clearly established, and . . . that the police knew the Scudéry name at once indicates just how celebrated it was" (*Mademoiselle de Scudéry*, 34).

crats against what they perceived to be excessive power of the king's ministers (Louis XIV was still in his minority). Scudéry's political position at this time is difficult to ascertain. Through her family she was friend to the brother and sister who led the resistance, Mme de Longueville and the great Condé. In the midst of this political turmoil, in 1649, Scudéry published the ten-volume novel, *Artamène; ou, Le grand Cyrus,* under her brother's name, dedicating it to Mme de Longueville and portraying Condé as the king. Nevertheless, when the Fronde failed, and later when her brother Georges went into voluntary exile under threat of punishment, Scudéry remained safely in Paris and dedicated many of her works to Louis XIV. Even her earlier works, dedicated to women and featuring women in central roles, might not have been entirely aimed at *Frondeuses,* since Anne of Austria, the regent, liked books about powerful queens.[11] In 1651, Scudéry wrote, "The King seems to hate those who want to lessen his authority, and, judging from appearances, he will remember tomorrow what they are doing today."[12] Most biographers take these clues as indications of her royalist position. Dorothy McDougall, however, claims that Scudéry, and those like her, "although staunch Royalists at heart . . . refused to support a cause in which they saw only the glorification of the hated Mazarin [chief minister and Cardinal, whose reign was full of cruelty by all accounts] identifying himself with the Crown."[13] We must remember that women were rarely punished for political crimes in the Renaissance, the general opinion being that men were responsible for the politics of the family and the women in it. In addition, since Georges's name was on the novel, there was no legal proof of Scudéry's loyalties. Nathalie Grande points out that Scudéry's clientalism never gained her, as a woman,

---

11. See Ian Maclean, *Woman Triumphant,* 79; and Faith E. Beasley, *Revising Memory: Women's Fiction and Memoirs in Seventeenth-Century France* (New Brunswick, N.J.: Rutgers University Press, 1990), 13. Her summary of the Fronde is especially concise and helpful: "There was no one overriding purpose, except perhaps a general hatred for the regent's (Anne D'Autriche's) foreign-born prime minister, Mazarin . . . . the parliament instigated the troubles in 1648 with a series of decrees designed to call royal authority, especially the role of the prime minister, into question . . . . A second wave of protest and rebellion, termed . . . the princely Fronde, added to the revolt and enlarged the sphere of participants. This group . . . incited the peasants in [their] various principalities to civil disobedience. The princes' primary objective was to profit from a relatively weak regency to increase their own power. They opposed Mazarin and sought to replace both the regent and the prime minister with a leader from among their ranks who could rule both the country and the young Louis XIV more to their satisfaction" (Beasley, *Revising Memory,* 43). On the women who played powerful political and military roles in the Fronde, see pp. 45–47.

12. Aronson, *Mademoiselle de Scudéry,* 36.

13. McDougall, *Madeleine de Scudéry: Her Romantic Life and Death* (London: Methuen and Co., 1938) 72.

the political posts that it did her brother and her friend Paul Pellisson, but also, consequently, it did not result in the same damage to her—she suffered neither exile nor imprisonment.[14]

In 1654, after Georges fled to Le Hâvre, he married a woman twenty-six years his junior, Marie-Madeleine de Montcal de Martinvast.[15] Around this time, Scudéry began her famous *Samedis*, named for the day, Saturday, on which she held social gatherings in her salon in her new residence in the Marais, on the Rue de Beauce. Politics had given her the opportunity to live alone: there had been rumors that there were many incidents of personal and political conflict with her brother and that she suffered from his lack of financial responsibility. At her new home, Scudéry and her guests at the salon took part in one of her favorite activities: conversation. It was at these *Samedis* that Scudéry became acquainted with Pellisson, a much younger man who became a close friend. Biographers usually interpret their relationship as a Platonic romance. In what is generally taken as a metaphorical description of their relationship, in her novel, *Le grand Cyrus*, she describes the relationship between Sapho and Phaon: "There were never two hearts so united, and never did love join together so much innocence and so much ardor . . . . They saw in each other's eyes what was in their hearts, and the tender feelings they saw caused them to love each other all the more."[16] As Scudéry herself explained, however, in her conversational dialogue on letter writing, there is a fine distinction between love and gallantry.[17] Scudéry's relationship with Pellisson has often been the focus of renditions of her life, and yet most of these studies exclude her many passionate friendships with women, which we believe were equally important. For example, there exists in manuscript a passionate epistolary verse exchange between Scudéry and a young poet, Catherine Descartes.[18]

14. Grande, *Stratégies de romancières*, 269.

15. Some sources cite her name as Marie-Françoise, not Madeleine, but this seems unlikely, for her correspondence is sometimes confused with that of Georges's sister (Aronson, *Mademoiselle de Scudéry*, 36). Georges's wife became his partner in writing, coauthoring *Almahide, ou, L'esclave-reine,* published in 1658, the only work by Georges without the participation of Scudéry.

16. Aronson, *Mademoiselle de Scudéry*, 44.

17. McDougall says that in a biography of Pellisson, the author speaks of *"leur amour* for want, as he confesses, of any other term to describe their affinity. And within the bounds that the old romantic gallantry prescribed, they certainly were 'in love'" (*Madeleine de Scudéry*, 143).

18. In the workshop on "Changing Stories: Attending to Early Modern Lesbianism," facilitated by Harriette Andreadis, Susan Lanser, and Valerie Traub, 9 November 2000, at the University of Maryland "Attending to Early Modern Women" conference, Elizabeth Wahl provided handouts with copies of the letters and verses by Madeleine de Scudéry and Catherine Descartes from

In 1654, Scudéry published her most important novel, *Clélie, histoire romaine*, in ten volumes, again under her brother's name. In 1661, she published *Célinte, nouvelle première* anonymously.[19] In November of that year, as a result of the fall of the royal financier Fouquet, to whom he was secretary, Pellisson was imprisoned by the king and not released until five years later, the same year that Scudéry lost her hearing entirely.[20] Scudéry's brother Georges died on 14 May 1667, but the two seem to have been estranged for several years before that. In 1667, Scudéry published *Mathilde d'Aguilar* and, in 1669, after a visit to Versailles, *La promenade de Versailles*, also anonymously.

For *Discours de la gloire*, a hyperbolic eulogy of Louis XIV published in 1671, Scudéry earned the first Académie Française Prize ever awarded. In 1680, she anonymously published *Conversations sur divers sujets* in two volumes; followed by *Conversations nouvelles sur divers sujets*, also in two volumes, in 1684; *Conversations morales* in two volumes in 1686; *Nouvelles conversations de morale* in two volumes in 1688; and *Entretiens de morale* in two volumes in 1692. After 1683, when she was granted a royal pension, Scudéry dedicated all of her books to Louis XIV (while previously most of her works had been dedicated to women).[21] In this volume, we include selections from the first two sets of these dialogues.

Pellisson's death, in February 1693, devastated Scudéry, who wrote of him in eulogy

> The king has lost the most zealous of his subjects, the century one of its great ornaments, literature one of its brightest lights, and religion one of its great defenders. But I have lost much more than all the others because I have lost a wonderful friend of forty years, with whom I have shared both good and bad times and for whom I have always felt the greatest of admiration.[22]

Mademoiselle de Scudéry: Sa vie et sa correspondance, ed. Routhery and Boutron (Paris, 1873), and "The 'Unpublished' Poems of Mlle. de Scudéry and Mlle. Descartes," *Modern Language Notes* 40 (March 1925): 155–57. See also Wahl, *Invisible Relations* (Stanford: Stanford University Press, 1999), 110–17.

19. In *From Dawn to Decadence: 500 Years of Western Cultural Life, 1500 to the Present* (New York: Harper-Collins, 2000), Jacques Barzun explains the popularity of Scudéry's novels: "What pleases most people in the art of their time is work that deals with the bits and pieces of knowledge and feeling that make up the common stock in everybody's mind . . . . It is popular as long as the mental mosaic of the time persists" (340).

20. For more information on politics, Pellisson, and political issues in the Scudéry circle, see Alain Niderst, *Madeleine de Scudéry, Paul Pellisson, et Leur Monde* (Paris: Presses Universitaires de France, 1976); for keys linking characters in the novels to specific persons, see pp. 525–32.

21. See Goldsmith, *Exclusive Conversations*, 60–64.

22. Aronson, *Mademoiselle de Scudéry*, 52.

Scudéry died at the age of ninety-three or ninety-four, on 2 June 1701, her mental faculties intact. She is buried at her parish church, Saint-Nicolas des Champs, in Paris. Her death was recorded in both *La gazette* and *Le mercure de France.*[23]

Biographers have debated Scudéry's gender politics. According to Aronson, Scudéry "always encouraged women to develop their intelligence, to learn to read, and to be able to take part in discussions with friends of their choice"; she further adds that Scudéry felt that achieving "intellectual independence" resulted in a woman's achieving true individuality.[24] Charles Augustin Sainte-Beuve points out, however, that in *Le grand Cyrus* Scudéry remarks, "I am often shocked to see many *women of rank* so grossly ignorant that, in my opinion, they dishonor our sex."[25] Elisa Biancardi claims that Scudéry was not a feminist per se, in that she "never actually proposed real collective solutions to make [relations between men and women in society] better"; however, she used her outgoing personality and independent lifestyle to serve as a model for other women who had the ability to follow suit, professing not to speak for all women but only for those who "were like her."[26] On the other hand, Constant Venesoen sees Scudéry as a feminist, pointing out that *Clélie* offers a model for progressive early modern women; and Linda Timmermans categorizes Scudéry as feminist because of her early dialogue, "Sappho to Erinna," and the progressive development of her ideas on women's education and independence as depicted in *"L'histoire de Sapho"* in *Le grand Cyrus.*[27] In the context of the seventeenth century, when the issue debated was whether women had the same intellectual capacity as men and therefore could profit from education, Scudéry was an important progressive voice who warrants attention from contemporary feminists. Adapting the public relations practices of earlier Italian and French regional courts, where humanists were used to publicize the civility and learning of

---

23. On Scudéry's life, see also Barbara Krajewska, "Du nouveau sur la Correspondence de Mlle de Scudéry," *Essays in French Literature* 25 (1988): 9–15. In the commentary on Scudéry's death in the newsletter, the *Mercure Galant*, she was eulogized as "The Sappho of France," and "a Christian Amazon" (88–89).

24. Aronson, *Mademoiselle de Scudéry,* 129.

25. Aronson, *Mademoiselle de Scudéry,* 66, emphasis added.

26. Biancardi, "Madeleine de Scudéry et son cercle," 420–21 (Strongson translation).

27. See Constant Venesoen, *Études sur la littérature féminine au XVII_e siècle: Mademoiselle de Gournay, Mademoiselle de Scudéry, Madame de Villedieu, Madame de Lafayette* (Birmingham, Ala.: SUMMA Publications, 1990), 44–45; and Linda Timmermans, *L'accès des femmes à la culture (1598–1715): Un débat d'idées de Saint François de Sales à la Marquise de Lambert* (Paris: Honoré Champion, 1993), 303 and 327.

the monarch and the society that he enabled, Louis XIV collected a stable of writers and painters praising his regime; at the same time, humanists and artists sought to raise their social status and benefit from this opportunity by exercising their rhetorical and artistic skills. Madeleine de Scudéry adapted this humanist relationship between patron and writer to the advancement of women. Her conversations showcase the elegance of the French vernacular and offer a rhetoric of conversation to allow others to take advantage of cultural opportunities to rise in society. Her praise of the monarch and of the courtly society he generated even beyond the court garnered her a position of influence and an annual allowance from the king.

Although Scudéry argued that women are as intelligent and as educable as men, she shared in other regards the prejudice of her age. Her works record no protest against contemporary hierarchies of social rank and prestige, although she herself had benefited from increased social mobility in France in the seventeenth century. Even her involvement in the Fronde shows no indication of desire for social reform, but merely a nostalgic desire for a government where the aristocracy once again would have the powers it had lost under the growth of absolutism and the nation-state in the seventeenth century. On political issues Scudéry always identified up the social ladder, not down.

WOMEN AND RHETORIC IN THE RENAISSANCE In the Renaissance, as Margaret King and Albert Rabil detail in the introduction to the series, women were viewed as inferior, and conduct books and social convention prepared women to be chaste, silent, obedient, and modest.[28] Consequently, women were also excluded from most forms of education, especially rhetoric, which was presumed to make them talkative and rebellious against authority.[29]

---

28. See also Suzanne W. Hull, *Chaste, Silent and Obedient* (San Marino, Calif.: Huntington Library Press, 1982 and 1988); Anthony Grafton and Lisa Jardine, *From Humanism to the Humanities: Education and the Liberal Arts in Fifteenth-and Sixteenth-Century Europe* (London: Duckworth, 1986), esp. 37–38, on Isotta Nogarola, a fifteenth-century Italian woman who apologizes in her letter to a male humanist for transgressing "those rules of silence especially imposed on women"; and the introduction to Juan Luis Vives, *The Instruction of a Christen Woman*, ed. Virginia Walcott Beauchamp, Elizabeth H. Hageman, and Margaret Mikesell (Urbana, Ill.: University of Illinois Press, 2002), esp. xxiii—xxvi and xxxix—lxxvi. On women's inferiority, see Maclean, *Woman Triumphant*, 1–24, and *The Renaissance Notion of Woman* (Cambridge: Cambridge University Press, 1980).

29. Renaissance educators warned that women should proceed no farther than grammar and devotional texts, even if they were of a class to be educated in classical matters: see Joan Gibson, "Educating for Silence: Renaissance Women and the Language Arts," *Hypatia* 4 (spring

Humanism in the Renaissance was characterized by a return to the classical model of education centering on language and rhetoric (as well as history, moral philosophy, and poetry). After boys and girls learned to read in schools, at home, or under tutors, the two groups were generally separated, and boys studied rhetoric, beginning with Aphthonius either with tutors or in grammar school and progressing to Cicero, Quintilian, Erasmus, and others in late grammar school and university. In Aphthonius's *Progymnasmata* (fourth to fifth century), Renaissance boys learned to write themes (such as commonplaces, refutations and confirmations, praise and blame, the *chreia* or relation of a deed or saying of a person, and the *ethopoeia* or imitation of an historical or fictional character speaking). They further learned to speak short orations in Latin and to argue on both sides of an issue in the tradition of sophistic rhetoric. In Cicero's *De inventione* (84 B.C.E.) and *De oratore* (55 B.C.E.) and the anonymous *Rhetorica ad Herennium* (ca. 84 B.C.E., believed in the Renaissance to be by Cicero), boys learned the fundamental Aristotelian appeals in all speeches to character (*ethos*), reason (*logos*), and emotion (*pathos*); the special techniques for forensic or legal, deliberative or political, and epideictic or celebratory praise-blame oratory; the organization of speeches or other compositions into a traditional pattern of introduction, narration of events, proposition, confirmation, refutation, and conclusion; and ways to deliver or perform speeches. In addition, they were drilled in the Ciceronian style that was a hallmark of humanists: the long, periodic sentences that suspended the sense until the end, parallel structure, heightened diction, and elaborate schemes (patterned language like alliteration) and tropes (metaphor, hyperbole, paradox, irony, and many more). From Cicero, boys might further learn to see the orator as an eclectic philosopher, interested in acquiring all sorts of knowledge. From Quintilian, boys might gain all these fundamentals, but also a view of the orator as the good man speaking well (in both performative and moral senses). Renaissance humanists more rarely studied Aristotle's *Rhetoric*, but they did read carefully his *On Sophistical Refutations*, which influenced styles of wit and wordplay, as well as logic, since it taught how to avoid (and so how to use) tricks with language. Boys also studied some of the numerous works by Desiderius Erasmus, the great Renaissance popularizer of classical rhetoric: they memorized proverbs or hunted ideas for their themes in his *Adagia* (1500), studied sentence and argument variation in his *De copia verborum et rerum* (c. 1512), or learned good Latin and ethics through his dialogues in *Colloquia* (1518). Scudéry seems to

---

1989): 9–27; and Margaret Hannay, introduction to *Silent but for the Word* (Kent, Ohio: Kent State University Press, 1985).

have been more influenced by this classical humanist form of rhetoric than
the revision of Aristotle by Peter Ramus, which was also frequently taught
in France, especially among Protestants.

But how might Scudéry have acquired such humanist rhetorical knowledge if girls were shunted off, after learning to read the vernacular, into quite
a different education for household responsibilities and religious piety? Exceptional women, those destined to be rulers (such as Queen Elizabeth I of
England) or brides of rulers (such as Mary Stuart, betrothed to the French
Dauphin) were given rhetorical educations.[30] But by the sixteenth and seventeenth centuries, women of the merchant and professional classes were also
being given classical educations and rhetorical training. For example, Beatrix Galindo, a professor of rhetoric at the University of Salamanca, taught
Catherine of Aragon.[31] Cassandra Fedele, a Venetian, was taught Latin and
Greek by her father, circulated her humanist letter book in manuscript, published an oration, and even delivered public Latin orations in several instances, once at the University of Padua.[32] Tullia d'Aragona, an Italian courtesan, in 1547 published a *Dialogue on the Infinity of Love*, demonstrating her
knowledge of this popular humanist genre and Platonic and Aristotelian philosophy and thus participating in the plan of Cosimo I, Duke of Florence,
to proclaim the cultural supremacy of Tuscany.[33] Catherine des Roches, who
published two volumes of poetry with her mother Madeleine, also wrote a
defense of women's education, *Dialogues de placide et sévère*, that circumscribed
women's learning within the bounds of feminine modesty set by the earlier humanists, Juan Luis Vives and Erasmus, in their discussions of women's
education.[34] Laura Cereta, from a professional Italian family, learned Latin
and read classical authors during convent schooling, participating with great

30. On Elizabeth I, see Leah Marcus, "Shakespeare's Comic Heroines, Elizabeth I, and the
Political Uses of Androgyny," in *Women in the Middle Ages and the Renaissance*, ed. Mary Beth Rose
(Syracuse, N.Y.: Syracuse University Press, 1986), 135–53; Mary Thomas Crane, " 'Video et
Taceo': Elizabeth I and the Rhetoric of Counsel,' " *Studies in English Literature* 28 (1988): 1–15; and
Kathi Vosevich, "Tutoring the Tudors," in *Women, Writing, and the Reproduction of Culture in Tudor and
Stuart Britain*, ed. Mary E. Burke et al. (Syracuse, N.Y.: Syracuse University Press, 2000), 61–76.
On Mary Stuart, see Wilbur Samuel Howell, *Logic and Rhetoric in England 1500–1700* (New York:
Russell & Russell, 1956, 1961), 166–67.

31. Susan Bassnett, *Elizabeth I: A Feminist Perspective* (Oxford: Berg, 1989), 21.

32. See Cassandra Fedele, *Letters and Orations*, ed. and trans. Diana Robin (Chicago: University
of Chicago Press, 2000).

33. See Tullia d'Aragona, *Dialogue on the Infinity of Love*, ed. and trans. Rinaldina Russell and Bruce
Merry (Chicago: University of Chicago Press, 1997).

34. On Catherine des Roches's dialogue, see Madeleine Lazard, *Les avenues de fémynie* (Paris: Fayard, 2001), 230–31.

distinction in humanist debates of her time in Brescia, where she lived after her marriage. There is even a report in early biographies of Cereta that she lectured in local salons and academies, and, although she was not published until Scudéry's lifetime in 1640, her letters and epistolary essays on humanist topics circulated in manuscript and made her famous in Italy.[35] In *The Nobility and Excellence of Women* (1601), Lucrezia Marinella defended women against misogynist attacks in pamphlets and poetry in the Italian *querelle des femmes*, basing her arguments on the rhetorical commonplaces: beginning with arguments from the name "woman" in several languages, she argues for women's worth through causes, nature and essence (definition), testimony from men to women's worth, women's actions and virtues, and refutation of men who cast blame on women.[36] Anna Maria van Schurman was known as the most learned woman in Europe, having studied Latin and Greek with her brothers under the tutelage of their father and having attended lectures at the institution that became the University of Utrecht, hidden behind the curtains of a special loge, learning Hebrew, Ethiopian, Chaldean, Arabic, and Syriac. In 1646, her Latin treatise defending women's right to learning was translated into French.[37] Bathsua Makin, who tutored the Stuart princesses during the English Civil War and who was known as the most learned woman in England, corresponded with van Schurman and wrote her own defense of women's education.[38]

The most likely explanation for the rhetorical training of all these women is that they were tutored with brothers or by uncles or fathers who had a special interest in humanist learning (as we know occurred in the case of van Schurman). Such family education in rhetoric over the course of these two centuries changed women's status and views on the nature of women remarkably, although it took many more centuries for other changes to result.[39] The women just cited for their rhetorical capabilities clearly had

---

35. See Laura Cereta, *Collected Letters of a Renaissance Feminist*, trans. and ed. Diana Robin (Chicago: University of Chicago Press, 1997).

36. See Lucrezia Marinella, *The Nobility and Excellence of Women and the Defects and Vices of Men*, ed. and trans. Anne Dunhill, intro. by Letizia Panizza (Chicago: University of Chicago Press, 1999).

37. See Anna Maria van Schurman, *Whether a Christian Woman Should be Educated and Other Writings from Her Intellectual Circle*, ed. and trans. Joyce L. Irwin (Chicago: University of Chicago Press, 1998).

38. See Bathsua Makin, *An Essay to Revive the Antient Education of Gentlewomen* (1673), introduction by Paula Barbour, publication 202 (Los Angeles: William Andrews Clark Memorial Library and University of California, 1980).

39. Historians debate the nature of the political influence of study of rhetoric on society in the Renaissance. Some think that rhetoric reinforced hierarchy; see, for example, Wayne Rebhorn,

humanist training in the languages as well. That is not so necessary from the mid-seventeenth century onward, since the main work of humanists for a century and a half had been translations into the vernacular. We do not know whether or not Scudéry studied Greek or Latin; at any rate, she does not display such knowledge by citing proverbs and by quotation in a classical language. But we do know that it was possible by Scudéry's lifetime to acquire a humanist rhetorical education through vernacular textbooks and translations, for her English contemporary, Margaret Cavendish, Duchess of Newcastle, demonstrates a wide knowledge gleaned from reading and from salon conversations, even though she states that she has no languages other than her native English (and despite many years spent in exile on the continent). In her encyclopedic *The Worlds Olio* (1655), in her *Orations of Divers Sorts* (1662), in her *Sociable Letters* (1664), and in her bookish plays, often more dialogue in form than theatrical drama—especially "The Female Academy" in *Plays* (1662)—Cavendish demonstrates just such erudition and rhetorical education as Scudéry's, although Cavendish's is decidedly more empiricist in flavor.[40]

Many recently recovered writings by early modern women and the Other Voice series in general, as well as Scudéry's writings in particular, suggest that humanism was a significant influence in the increased status of women. Through humanist education in rhetoric and composition and through adaptations of the most popular humanist forms—the letter, the

•

The Emperor of Men's Minds (Ithaca, N.Y.: Cornell University Press, 1995). Some think that rhetoric provided the Renaissance with models for participatory government and tools to begin a reformulation of society; see, for example, David Norbrook, "Rhetoric, Ideology and the Elizabethan World Picture," in *Renaissance Rhetoric*, ed. Peter Mack (Boston: St. Martin's Press, 1994), 140–64. Cheryl Glenn suggests that women's rhetoric in the English Renaissance ranged across these purposes, with some women in each camp, in *Rhetoric Retold: Regendering the Tradition from Antiquity through the Renaissance* (Carbondale, Ill.: Southern Illinois University Press, 1997). Other historical studies of women's rhetoric of this time period are offered in Carole Levin and Patricia A. Sullivan, eds., *Political Rhetoric, Power, and Renaissance Women* (Albany, N.Y.: State University of New York Press, 1995); Andrea A. Lunsford, ed., *Reclaiming Rhetorica: Women in the Rhetorical Tradition* (Pittsburgh: University of Pittsburgh Press, 1995); and Molly Meijer Wertheimer, ed., *Listening to Their Voices: The Rhetorical Activities of Historical Women* (Columbia, S.C.: University of South Carolina Press, 1997).

40. On Cavendish, see Jane Donawerth, "The Politics of Renaissance Rhetorical Theory by Women," in *Political Rhetoric, Power, and Renaissance Women*, ed. Levin and Sullivan, 260–61; Donawerth, "Conversation and the Boundaries of Public Discourse in Rhetorical Theory by Renaissance Women," *Rhetorica* 16 (Spring 1998): 188–92; Christine Mason Sutherland, "Aspiring to the Rhetorical Tradition: A Study of Margaret Cavendish," in *Listening to Their Voices*, 255–71; Ryan John Stark, "Margaret Cavendish and Composition Style," *Rhetoric Review* 17 (Spring 1999): 264–81; and Donawerth, ed., *Rhetorical Theory by Women before 1900* (Lanham, Md.: Rowman & Littlefield, 2002), 45–58.

oration, and the dialogue—women writers across Europe argued for the equality of women's intellect and the necessity of education for women. These forms, as humanists practiced them, were especially amenable to these purposes because of their position straddling the boundary of private and public and because of the frequently acknowledged goal of social mobility for the writers.

In addition, there was a crucial change in social institutions and so in rhetoric in the Renaissance: the development of the salon. Under the leadership of Catherine de' Médicis, the queen mother and regent of France, Queen Marguerite of Navarre in exile, and many French nobles in the sixteenth century, France adopted the institution of the salon, borrowing from its successful use in the Italian city-states. There, as idealized in Castiglione's *The Book of the Courtier,* rulers of city-states established salons to further art, culture, and civility in their states, to give the aristocracy goals other than internecine rivalry and warfare, and to promote the rulers' ideology and fame as benevolent philosopher-kings. According to the Italian model, established in France under Catherine, women were integral to the institution of the salon: they provided beauty, grace, and a civilizing influence, and they were educated to participate in the intellectual pastimes of the salon—at least as intelligent respondents and audience members. Especially influential on Scudéry's conception of the salon must have been the salon of Claude Catherine de Clermont-Dampierre, maréchale de Retz, and her husband Albert de Gondi, for the ladies of their salon took the names of the nine muses during their cultural games and festivities and the father of the Marquise de Rambouillet was a regular participant there.[41]

Most famous of the seventeenth-century salons was the Hôtel de Rambouillet or the *chambre bleue* of Catherine de Vivonne, Marquise de Rambouillet, where Georges and Madeleine de Scudéry were introduced to Paris society in 1637 and where they garnered enough influence and support to achieve a government post for Georges in Marseilles in 1642. The Marquise de Rambouillet retired from court life in 1608 and began to gather intellectuals in regular conversations at her home. The salon was not a sedentary activity (see fig. 1 [p. xxxii], which was a frontispiece from a volume of Scudéry's *Conversations*). Participants conversed in small groups and circulated around the room; the clever hostess offered paintings, exotic displays, and new books, as well as games and charades to further conversational interaction. Between 1620 and 1645, the salon of the Marquise de Rambouil-

---

41. On the development of the salon in sixteenth-century France and its relationship to powerful and intellectual women, see Madeleine Lazard, *Les avenues de fémynie*, esp. 258 and 291–308.

let was the center and model of Parisian culture: her salon was frequented by Mme de Sévigné, Mme de La Fayette, both Georges and Madeleine de Scudéry, the Duchesses de Longueville and de Montpensier, Guez de Balzac, Jean Chapelain, Richelieu, Pierre Corneille, François de Malherbe, Vincent Voiture, La Rochefoucauld, and many other political or artistic celebrities. This salon generally focused on literature, debated general aesthetics and the value of individual new works, and, as can be seen from the list of participants, welcomed women as well as men to equal participation, providing support for many of the women as authors.[42] As Carolyn Lougee has argued in her study of seventeenth-century salon culture, the salon provided social mobility, mixing old and new aristocracy with rising middle-class politicians and artists, and also revised notions of women's inferiority, transforming the old view of women as by nature irrational and weak into women as inherently intuitive, sweet, and delicate—values which then became hallmarks of the society of the *honnêtes gens*, the decent, discerning, well-educated people of high society.[43]

From 1653 on, Madeleine de Scudéry lived in a house in the Marais, the most fashionable section of Paris, and there began her *Samedis* (Saturdays), her own salon, which became as famous as that of Mme de Rambouillet. Her brother lived with her the first year, but after a threat of arrest for his activities during the Fronde, he went into voluntary exile at Granville, near Le Hâvre. Scudéry's salon and the salon as an institution in general centered on conversation. Salon culture included excursions, elegant dinners, surprise visits to friends in the country, scientific experiments, exchange of

---

42. On the salon, see Beasley, *Revising Memory*, 47–52; Maclean, *Woman Triumphant*, 141–54; Renate Baader, *Dames de lettres, autorinnen des preziösen, hocharistokratischen und "modernen" salons (1649–1698): Mlle de Scudéry—Mlle de Montpensier—Mme d'Aulnoy* (Stuttgart: J.B. Metzlersche Verlagsbuchhandlung, 1986), who discusses Cartesianism, educational reform, the church, and the salon as influencing the changing roles of women in seventeenth-century France and Scudéry's novels; and Dena Goodman, *The Republic of Letters: A Cultural History of the French Enlightenment* (Ithaca, N.Y.: Cornell University Press, 1994), esp. 2–9 and 90–135. While Dorothy Backer's *Precious Women* (New York: Basic Books, 1974) is an enthusiastic and engaging portrait of the salon and its practitioners, we cannot recommend it because of its many inaccuracies.

43. On the salon fostering social mobility, see Carolyn Lougee, *Le Paradis des Femmes: Women, Salons, and Social Stratification in Seventeenth-Century France* (Princeton: Princeton University Press, 1976), esp. chs. 2–3, 31–55. See also Erica Harth, "The Salon Woman Goes Public . . . or Does She?" in *Going Public: Women and Publishing in Early Modern France*, ed. Elizabeth Goldsmith and Dena Goodman (Ithaca, N.Y.: Cornell University Press, 1995), 179–93. On women's writing as "natural," as opposed to men's writing as "artful," see Katherine A. Jensen, "Male Models of Female Epistolarity; or How to Write Like a Woman in Seventeenth-Century France," in *Writing the Female Voice: Essays on Epistolary Literature*, ed. Elizabeth C. Goldsmith (Boston, Mass.: Northeastern University Press, 1989), 25–45.

poems, impromptu games of verse composition, dramatic improvisations, concerts, and impassioned literary debates that made and unmade writers' careers. Because of the mixing of classes and the importance of the people who frequented the salons, they were a "private" space that had enormous influence on public issues, especially because under an absolute monarch, influence is the only form of power for anyone other than the monarch. In any case, the salon certainly furthered the aspirations of women, for in this space men and women seemed equal.

SCUDÉRY AS A RHETORICAL THEORIST   Rhetoric comes in many guises in the Renaissance, not only in textbooks, but also in conversational dialogues (as in *The Courtier*), in conduct books, in manuals of style, and in formulary rhetorics, or collections of models for imitation. In her conversations, Scudéry not only theorizes a new sort of rhetoric for seventeenth-century salon culture, but also models elegant conversation.[44] In her orations, she experiments with a literary form of the public speech, which had been a standard rhetorical exercise since ancient Greece, but revolutionizes it by composing speeches for historical women, thus recovering great women of the past as models for current women's speaking. In her *Amorous Letters,* she both offers standard formulary models of business letters (the letter asking a patron or friend for a favor, for example) and also adapts the form to a novel-like construction of a relationship between two loving women. In addition, Scudéry adapts humanist rhetorical forms, the letter, the oration, and the dialogue, to women.

Précieuse style has been much criticized, but Scudéry's style is conversational and easy except in her highly ornamented speeches for fictional women, which are meant to be rhetorical exercises. Thus, we would term her style rhetorical but not ornate. Like all Renaissance writers trained in a humanist rhetorical tradition, Scudéry uses a great deal of parallel construction in her sentences, especially balance (where two or more clauses of related meaning are composed in similar grammatical constructions with the same rhythm), antithesis (where two clauses or phrases are set up as opposed in meaning but similar in grammatical constructions), and climax

44. For a history of conversation as an art in Europe, see Peter Burke, *The Art of Conversation* (Ithaca, N.Y.: Cornell University Press, 1993), 89–122; for an extremely useful survey of men's writings on conversation in the Renaissance and eighteenth century, see Ann Cline Kelly, "Swift's *Polite Conversation*: An Eschatological Vision," in *Studies in Philology* 73 (April 1976): 204–24. On the rhetoric of conversation—compliments, graciousness, elegant self-presentation—for the courtier, see Frank Whigham, *Ambition and Privilege: The Social Tropes of Elizabethan Courtesy Theory* (Berkeley: University of California Press, 1984).

(where parallel phrases or clauses are constructed in a sequence so that each section is longer and the most meaningful section occupies the privileged longest final position to give it more weight). Unlike earlier humanists, Scudéry uses metaphor and related figurative imagery lightly—this is perhaps a consequence of the changing taste in style in the seventeenth century, where growing empiricism had made writers more and more suspicious of metaphor, more and more desirous of having a language that is clear and transparent, rather than rich and ambiguous. Especially in the heroic speeches, Scudéry occasionally uses periodic sentences, the type of sentence that was Cicero's hallmark, where the sense is suspended until the end, usually by postponing the verb or other key part of speech through several long clauses. But Scudéry prefers the loose style, which had replaced Ciceronian patterns in seventeenth-century Europe. Following the characteristics of that style, which favors coordinate over subordinate grammatical structures and more natural rhythms, Scudéry often uses pleonasm, superfluous words that give weight and more elegant rhythm to the sentence.

In *Amorous Letters*, Scudéry's style is not the informal, conversational style of Cicero's letters to friends, but instead, the more heightened polite style of seventeenth-century society and romantic fiction. Especially in the letters between the two loving women, Scudéry heightens the emotional impact of the letters through exclamation, antithesis, climax, analogy, and metaphor when speaking of the love between the two (metaphor was thought to be more appropriate for expressing emotions in the Renaissance) and through complaints and lengthy descriptions of the suffering resulting from "neglect" by the other correspondent. As Scudéry says in her own later conversation on letter writing, "happy letters get you nowhere in love," and "when you do not have a reason for complaint, you should do it anyway."

In *Famous Women*, Scudéry pulls out all the stops and produces resounding oratorical style. In most cases she imagines the historical woman she has chosen in a significant crisis where she must plead for her life, although usually not in public, since rarely in Scudéry's culture would a woman speak in public. Scudéry's style in these orations is fully oratorical: long, often periodic sentences; frequent exclamation, interjection, and heroic epithets (adjectives or titles preceding names, a characteristic of epic style); metaphor, personification, irony, vivid description, catalogues, hyperbole, and all the other resources of figurative language; and clever, well-formulated arguments, drawing on all the commonplaces of rhetorical training (arguments from cause, effect, definition, comparison, opposites, names or etymology, associations or adjuncts, etc.).

In contrast, in the *Conversations*, Scudéry helps to formulate an elegant, but easy and natural-sounding French literary style for conversational dialogue. In these dialogue essays, her loose rhythms follow the patterns of conversation; there is almost no metaphor, although comparisons abound; she uses vivid description, catalogue, hyperbole, irony, and occasional exclamation. But most of all, she threads through her conversations all the forms of *ésprit* or wit: broad knowledge of the world, intelligent and insightful commentary, witty descriptions of absent fools and playful thrusts at present companions, and occasional wordplay (although almost never puns). Especially characteristic of Scudéry's formulation of *ésprit* is the patrolling of its boundaries: each dialogue formulates the "rules" for being a skilled participant in conversation, and these rules at the same time mark the boundaries of class (while dismantling the walls between lower gentry and upper aristocrats and between educated middle-class professionals and the classes above them).

In all of Scudéry's works, but especially theoretically developed in the conversations, certain central terms and concepts recur. Besides *ésprit* or wit, which we have just defined in the discussion of style, two others are most important: *l'agréable*, or the agreeable, and *honnêtes gens*, or the concept of decent, well-educated gentlefolk. The agreeable is the central principle for salon conversation, for polite society, and for aesthetic pleasure. A person is agreeable if she is sympathetic, if she allows others a share in the conversation, if she is pleasing in appearance and manner, if she is well educated and interesting, and if she has concern for her friends and those around her. Being agreeable is not mere politeness but, instead, the cornerstone of harmonious social interaction. *Honnêtes gens* are discriminating, honest, decent, polite middle- and upper-class people, who understand virtue and elegance as a standard of taste for polite society and know a great deal about a great many subjects, but not too much about any one—they are wits not scholars.[45] As Domna Stanton has pointed out, the *honnête homme* is a reworking of the classical model of the ideal rhetor as found in Cicero and Quintilian.[46]

Now let us turn to the content and nature of each of Scudéry's rhetorical works from which we have translated selections. *Amorous Letters from Various Contemporary Authors* (1641) participates in two rhetorical traditions: from the Middle Ages onward, many handbooks on how to write letters were pub-

---

45. Maclean, *Woman Triumphant*, 126–35.

46. Stanton, *The Aristocrat as Art: A Study of the* Honnête Homme *and the Dandy in Seventeenth- and Nineteenth-Century French Literature* (New York: Columbia University Press, 1980), 16; see also 7 and 14–130.

lished, a corpus of works often called the *ars dictaminis*, or art of letter writing. In the Renaissance, these advice books on how to write proper Latin requests for business or patronage in formats appropriate to class differences were revolutionized by the rediscovery of Cicero's informal personal letters.[47] By the seventeenth century, handbooks on letter writing often served two purposes, still instructing people on how to write business letters or requests for favors, but also guiding the increasing number of literate people in how to write interesting personal letters. From the Renaissance on, humanists often demonstrated their education and erudition, as well as their international and cross-class contacts, by publishing collections of their letters, and friends often published such collections at the death of a humanist.

Scudéry's *Amorous Letters* seems to be a combination of these two genres of letter books. The first thirty-four letters and thirty-one responses are a correspondence between two women of middling or upper classes, although one seems to be slightly more apologetic and so perhaps of slightly lesser social rank. These letters demonstrate what kinds of topics and concerns are appropriate in letters between two women who share a passionate friendship. They sound very much like love letters, although the headings make clear that they are two women addressing each other. We will treat them at length in the section on "Sappho." Following these initial letters are thirty-seven more, with no responses, which offer models for the general polite social business that an ordinary well-off person would need to transact: included are letters of sympathy at the death of a family member (nos. 29, 56, 63), a letter requesting a favor (no. 35), a letter of introduction (no. 39), a letter of recommendation (for a young girl who wants to enter religious orders!) (no. 41), letters of praise (nos. 49, 53, 65), and letters of complaint at the silence of a friend (nos. 50, 61). In addition, there are three letters (nos. 53–55) that praise the responder's style of writing letters and in the process offer advice on writing witty, personal, informal but elegant letters. An argument could be made that most of these letters are part of a series, and that after letter 34 the responder stops responding, becoming unfaithful to the friendship, but that would make the inclusion of the letters of recommendation to the Abbess and the formal letter requesting a favor inconsistent and confusing.

We think, instead, that this volume constitutes a formulary rhetoric of letter writing, one like many other Renaissance handbooks, which offers models for those who have difficulty with composition to simply copy, with

47. On the development of the personal vernacular letter and publication of "letter books," see Janet Gurkin Altman, "The Letter Book as a Literary Institution 1539–1789: Toward a Cultural History of Published Correspondences in France," *Yale French Studies* 71 (1995): 17–62.

small changes to personalize them. What is remarkable, then, is that this formulary rhetoric addresses women as an audience who will need to write letters constantly and so will need models appropriate to female recipients. In addition, we think that Scudéry is putting forward her first humanist credentials in print, by offering a humanist-style letter collection, albeit fictional rather than actual letters. This purpose is especially noticeable in the letters on style, which would be the kind of topic of concern to the fashionable and well-educated classes, for letter writing would be one of the ways, in an increasingly socially mobile society, that one could tell the upper and well-educated from the lower and less literate classes.

Should we take the title, *Amorous Letters from Various Contemporary Authors,* at face value? Did Scudéry's friends contribute model letters to the second half of this volume?[48] We think that the style is too consistent and uniform for that, but we would not rule out the idea of collaboration and advice on some of the letters. As in the Heian Period in Japan, where a lady who received a letter would call in her friends and waiting-women to help her respond, the salon culture was extremely collaborative, with its members often composing poetry and stories together for their own entertainment.

Joan DeJean has argued that Scudéry's *Famous Women, or Heroic Speeches* is original in adapting the catalogue of women worthies, a popular form of the defense of women in the *querelle de femmes* (the pamphlet controversy about women), to the new form of speech or oration.[49] These speeches also suggest that Scudéry had acquired some specific rhetorical and Latin education, perhaps from her uncle when he tutored her brother Georges, because the fictional speech or *ethopoeia* is a standard figure in classical rhetoric, assuming great importance in Renaissance rhetorical education because of its appearance in the list of themes required of boys studying elementary Latin in the most popular beginning Renaissance composition text, Aphthonius's *Progymnasmata* (ca. 300–400 C.E.). In this Latin composition exercise, the eleventh in Aphthonius's graduated series of exercises, the student composes a speech to fit a specific occasion in the life of a famous historical person, a speech one imagines that the person actually spoke. This rhetorical set piece was an extremely popular one in classical and Renaissance histories and so contributes to both their vivid narrative qualities and also our modern sense that

---

48. On collaborative authorship among the *précieuses* in the prefatory letter to one of Scudéry's novels, see Leonard Hinds, "Literary and Political Collaboration: The Prefatory Letter of Madeleine de Scudéry's *Artamène, ou le grand Cyrus,*" *Papers on French Seventeenth-Century Literature* 45 (1996): 491–500.

49. See DeJean, *Fictions of Sappho, 1546–1937,* esp. 101–2.

they are not accurate or reliable. But Scudéry coyly plays with our double expectations of historical veracity and imaginative creativity in her prefatory "Argument" to each piece.

Furthermore, as Erica Harth has pointed out, the portrait, especially of mythological or historical characters, was a favorite short form of the *précieuses,* and verbally drawing portraits of each other was a parlor game popular in the salons.[50] On the title page to *Famous Women,* de Scudéry promises *"les veritable Portraicts de ces Heroïnes,"* faithful or accurate portraits of these heroines. Since reading aloud was a popular entertainment at the salons, perhaps Scudéry imagines her heroic speeches as rhetorical exercises similar to late Roman collections of speeches, which were written for performance before a small audience, to be judged for their artistic qualities. Since women in Scudéry's time were forbidden to speak in public, such a venue for her speeches would be a means of evading such constraints. Moreover, Scudéry is also adapting another favorite rhetorical exercise, one that reaches back to the Sophists, the debate on both sides of an issue, a rhetorical exercise that was by the Renaissance composed as often for print as for oral performance. Finally, humanists of the Renaissance were often called upon to display the results of patronage by giving orations at public occasions. Since women were not allowed to give public speeches in seventeenth-century France (although there are instances of Italian and French women recorded earlier in the sixteenth century), publishing a volume of fictional speeches, and ones addressed mainly to family members rather than public audiences, allows Scudéry to demonstrate her humanist oratorical credentials without violating the gendered norms of her society.

In her collection of fictional orations for historical women, Scudéry offers a wonderful range of women from ancient Greece and Rome, in each case specifying the audience, almost always a private, family audience. Besides the speeches that we have translated here, "Mariam to Herod," "Sophonisba to Masinissa," "Zenobia to her Daughters," and "Sappho to Erinna," Scudéry includes "Cleopatra to Mark Antony," "Lucretia to Colatine," "Pulcheria to the Patriarch of Constantinople," and, in the rare public speech, "Agrippina to the Roman People," as well as many others.[51] This genre was

---

50. See Erica Harth, *Ideology and Culture in Seventeenth-Century France* (Ithaca, N.Y.: Cornell University Press, 1983), esp. 68: "The 'precious' polite society of the time . . . loved nothing more than to exercise its wit on portraits in the highly polished, often esoteric, metaphorical languages that it employed to perfection."

51. On *Famous Women or Heroic Speeches,* see also Nicole Aronson, *Mademoiselle de Scudéry, ou Le voyage au Pays de Tendre* (Paris: Fayard, 1986), 125–37.

popular enough that Margaret Cavendish, Duchess of Newcastle, also published fictional speeches, although she emphasized not historical characters
but issues that could be debated on both sides, sophistic fashion, and included mainly speeches by men, with only a small section of speeches by
women.[52]

We include "Mariam to Herod" because a major recovered text in English Renaissance studies is Elizabeth Cary's *The Tragedy of Mariam*, and it is
interesting to see what a different writer makes of this story. In Cary's play,
Mariam regrets her marriage to the tyrannous Herod, who has murdered her
grandfather and her brother, and resolves to separate herself from him and
deny him her bed; insanely jealous, Herod kills her.[53] In the speech from
Famous Women, Scudéry imagines Mariam on trial for her life before a jealous
Herod who is both accuser and judge.

Of all Scudéry's speeches, "Mariam to Herod" is the most elegantly Ciceronian in style and classical form of argument. Since Cicero's orations defined rhetorical style for the Renaissance, although in Scudéry's time it is on
the verge of being replaced by newer empiricist-influenced styles, we think
that to some degree Scudéry is demonstrating her intellectual credentials in
this speech—her right to be a writer. This speech is full of periodic sentences
(like the first one in the speech), theatrical rhetorical questions, exclama-
tions, and climactic parallel structures, such as "He was young, he was virtuous, he was a model [young man] in all ways, and his greatest fault, no doubt,
was to resemble me." Scudéry marshals effective, well-organized arguments,
giving Mariam arguments that she could not have plotted Herod's death because of her birth, her obedience (first to her father in marrying Herod, then
to her husband), and drawing from the who-what-where-when-how list of
forensic rhetoric to refute allegations that she had flirted with Mark Antony
and sent him her picture. Scudéry constructs a fascinating argument based
on class bias for Mariam: Mariam could not have had an affair with Joseph,
whom Herod had killed out of jealousy, because Joseph was beneath her in
social status and kings contested for Mariam's queenly hand. Scudéry allots
Mariam many effective appeals to pathos, including "I was the mother of
your children."

We offer the speeches by Sophonisba and Zenobia because they form
a paired set in the tradition of the sophistic and humanist rhetorical exercise

52. See Margaret Cavendish, Duchess of Newcastle, *Orations of Divers Sorts, Accommodated to Divers Places* (London, 1662), esp. "Female Orations," 225–32.
53. See Elizabeth Cary, the Lady Falkland, *The Tragedy of Mariam, The Fair Queen of Jewry*, ed. Barry Weller and Margaret W. Ferguson (Berkeley: University of California Press, 1994).

of arguing on both sides of a question. Here the question is whether a queen who has been conquered and will be led in a Roman Triumph in the face of public shame should commit suicide or would be more courageous to live and endure. In "Sophonisba to Masinissa" Sophonisba persuades her husband that suicide is preferable to being led in Triumph by the Roman Emperor, for it preserves her honor, while in "Zenobia to her Daughters," Zenobia tries to convince her daughters that suicide is cowardly and dishonorable and she has only demonstrated her fortitude by enduring the ordeal of the Triumph. Scudéry uses the "Argument" introducing "Zenobia to her Daughters" to reinforce the contrast in the two positions.

In "Sophonisba to Masinissa," Scudéry portrays a Sophonisba who is fierce and courageous: she begins her speech reminding her husband that she had refused to marry him until he promised that she would never fall under the power of the Romans, and she roundly criticizes Roman imperialism and vanity, barbarically expressed in the custom of the Triumph. Sophonisba appeals to her husband's emotions of love and fear of shame on behalf of his wife. But she centers her speech on reasoned arguments from definition: Sophonisba, a queen, is too great of soul to follow a chariot; wife and husband are one, and so Scipio, the Roman general, cannot triumph over an ally (Masinissa); and only foolish philosophers thinks that "true generosity consists in suffering fatal accidents with constancy" (the Stoic definition of virtue), while kings know that it consists in "heroic examples of courage." The sophistic exercise was a common "test" for schoolboys in Latin education, so again Scudéry seems to be demonstrating her knowledge of classical forms and her rhetorical competence in them.

In "Zenobia to her Daughters," Scudéry portrays a queen who is also a philosopher, placing this speech in the final position of the debate to give it more authority, but in her commentary also delighting in the intellectual play of good arguments on opposite sides of a question. Zenobia appeals to the pride of her daughters, arguing that the sorrow and shame that they feel at having been displayed in a Roman Triumph creates anew their bondage; that their mother is an example of fortitude and endurance for them, having suffered the loss of husband and son, and the sacrifices of many battles (in most of which she was victorious); that their very enemy, Aurelian, testifies to the virtue of Zenobia; that enduring a Triumph displays strength, not weakness, as the applause of the crowds along the way demonstrated; and that virtue consists of constancy and equanimity (a Stoic, philosophical definition), while suicide demonstrates only dishonorable despair.

We include "Sappho to Erinna" because it seems to be Scudéry's manifesto, since she herself took the name of "Sapho" in salon culture. Almost every woman of letters in the sixteenth and seventeenth centuries has such a defense of education for women. Indeed, in the sixteenth and seventeenth centuries, the right to an education might be said to define the feminist position, just as in the eighteenth century marriage reform did and in the nineteenth century women's property rights and suffrage. Scudéry's defense of women's education may be considered rhetorical theory because she defends a particular form of education, the humanist focus on rhetoric, style, and *belles lettres*.

In "Sappho to Erinna," Scudéry represents herself, under the name of Sappho, as an educated older woman mentoring an aspiring poet—the dialogue thus embodies its message, that women will best achieve fame by becoming educated and by publishing their writings. In this speech, Sappho enters the *querelle des femmes* and defends women's worth by arguing that women are not inferior in intellect to men and that they consequently deserve a liberal arts education. This speech is on the playful end of the Renaissance controversy about women; it is the kind of contribution to the debate that Linda Woodbridge argues most pamphlets in the debate about women were—a rhetorical exercise.[54] Since rhetoric is the foundation of Renaissance humanism, this does not mean that a rhetorical exercise could not also be a meaningful political intervention, as Scudéry's "Sappho to Erinna" certainly is.

In playful guise, Sappho begins her argument by explaining that we must not view women as possessing only beauty and men only intellect, because there exist ugly women and stupid men. She continues in this virtuoso manner, inventing new and playful reasons for granting women intelligence and education equal to men: when Nature gives the gift of beauty as the purpose of a creation, it lasts, but women's beauty fades; beauty is to women as valor is to men, but both share intelligence that can be improved by the study of *belles lettres*; if we women have imagination, mental vivacity, and good memories, then we must also have reasonable judgment, because these talents constitute this capacity; if we do have these gifts, it is terrible to waste them, learning no more than how to curl your hair. Scudéry also argues that men have no leisure for study, since they are too busy managing families, property, and the state, so women must fill the gap, since they have the leisure to study; that the gods do not make useless creations, and so women, too, are useful; and that it is not shameful for women to publish verses, but rather shameful for either sex to publish bad verses. She points out

---

54. See Linda Woodbridge, *Women and the English Renaissance: Literature and the Nature of Womankind, 1540–1620* (Urbana, Ill.: University of Illinois Press, 1986).

that study does not destroy women's beauty through hard work and anxiety, for through study women acquire a lasting beauty that Time cannot destroy, and urges women not to settle for immortality through men's poetic portrayal of them, for people admire the maker more than the portrait. Drawing one's own portrait, not through self-praise but through elegant language, one achieves true fame; women should not, then, be deterred by false modesty. This playful, elegant contribution to the controversy about women, Scudéry supposes, is extremely effective—Erinna, after all, is convinced by Sappho to become a great poet. Thus Scudéry has created not only a successful argument for women's education, but also a vision of utopian mentoring of women by women.

Unlike many women writers of the seventeenth century, Scudéry does not depend on classical or biblical authorities in her arguments. In this respect she demonstrates a certain modernism, influenced perhaps by the empiricist rebellion against authority that characterizes science and letters after Francis Bacon's championing of experience as the basis of truth. Scudéry, however, grounds her orations in dialectical reasoning based on the commonplaces—the standard form of rhetorical argumentation taught in the seventeenth century. She gives reasons for her opinions, rather than citing authorities.

In the *Conversations*, Scudéry reworks the Renaissance humanist tradition of the dialogue in light of the institution of the salon. She had begun this process in her novels, and many of the conversations are lifted, but with significant revisions, from the novels. The models Scudéry seems to have in mind for her dialogues include not only Castiglione's *The Book of the Courtier*, which set the standard for two centuries of salon conversation but, more broadly, rhetorical dialogues in general, including those of the classical rhetorical theorists—Plato, Cicero, and Augustine.[55] While Scudéry's conversations encompass many topics (see the collections by Phillip J. Wolfe and Delphine Denis), we have chosen those on conversation, wit, and letter writing, where Scudéry develops a theory of rhetoric appropriate to women and the institution of the salon: "On Conversation," "On Speaking Too Much or Too Little," "On Wit," and "On the Manner of Writing Letters." Scudéry's conversations were very popular during her lifetime and were used as textbooks in Mme de Maintenon's school for girls from 1686 to 1691.[56]

---

55. Many major statements in classical rhetoric take the form of the dialogue—Plato's *Gorgias, Menexenus*, and *Phaedrus*, Cicero's *De oratore*, and Augustine's *De magistro*.

56. See note 1.

"On Conversation" is a dialogue comprised of eight speakers. Unlike classical dialogues, where specific philosophers are featured and promote their ideas, or even *The Courtier,* where speakers are assigned topics of discourse, the group as a whole agrees on a topic—in this case, conversation—and the rhythms of interaction are very like conversation, albeit idealized. Still, all the speakers contribute to the final conclusion, which is reached not by one speaker's arguments overpowering another's, but by consensus. In addition, unlike any of these classical or Renaissance models, women in Scudéry's dialogues contribute as much as men, and the person who comes in at the end to distill the results—in the role of facilitator rather than leader—is often a woman.

"On Conversation" opens with Cilénie introducing the topic by reiterating the sophistic principle popularized by Cicero, that speech is the bond of human society.[57] But here Scudéry begins her adaptation of rhetorical theory to the salon by restating the principle: "conversation is the bond of society for all humanity, the greatest pleasure of discriminating people [*honnêtes gens*]." Amilcar takes up this idea and adds that conversation is *not* for business purposes and conversation is not what judges, merchants, generals, even the king in his Council speak. Conversation is, rather, for that special, leisured, well-educated elite who participate in salon culture. Here Scudéry demonstrates her recognition that classical rhetorical theory and dialogues had done the ideological work of setting class boundaries, and she energetically adapts their techniques to a new social configuration, the limited seventeenth-century social mobility of upper middle-class and lower gentry mixing with new and old nobility in the new institution of the salon. Scudéry excludes from conversation and the salon the lower classes, including the mercantile middle class, but also is careful to claim some special power for the remaining classes that even the king does not necessarily possess.

Indeed, "On Conversation" polices the boundaries further, for most of the dialogue is a list of topics to avoid in conversation, as the speakers, each in turn, jump in with their pet peeves. One should not talk about domestic cares, children, and servants; clothes and what they cost; intrigues and affairs; genealogies and family histories; business affairs and lawsuits; resi-

---

57. On the sophistic idea that language preceded and caused the civilization of humanity, that language is the main social bond, see Isocrates, *Isocrates,* trans. George Norlin (Cambridge, Mass.: Harvard University Press, 1928), "Nicocles," vol. 1, 77–81 and "Antidosis," vol. 2, 327–29. On Cicero's adaptation of this principle, see *De inventione,* trans. H. M. Hubbell (Cambridge, Mass.: Harvard University Press, 1960), I.ii.2–3; *De re publica,* trans. Clinton Walker Keyes (London: William Heinemann, 1928), 3.2.3; and esp. *De oratore,* trans. E. W. Sutton and H. Rackham (London: William Heinemann, 1948), 1.8.23.

dences and furniture; tragic adventures and life's misfortunes; gossip about the neighborhood; current events; or academic subjects and especially science. One should not be too serious or too silly or too long-winded or too secretive. In this dialogue, which is perhaps Scudéry's most conservative statement on gender roles, two speakers argue the role of women in conversation and conclude—with dissent—that men are better conversationalists and that women are interesting speakers only when men are present. With reassuring lack of consistency, at the end of the dialogue, the group pushes Valeria to the center to sum up for them, asking what, then, can one talk about that is "rational and pleasing." Here Scudéry adopts the principle from Horace's *Ars Poetica* that had long been part of rhetorical theory as well as poetics: art, spoken or written, must be *utile et dulce,* useful and sweet[58] —here recast as reasonable and amusing or agreeable.

Gathering the strands of the preceding conversation, Valeria pronounces that, nevertheless, all of the topics put forth are actually appropriate for conversation if the speaker employs judgment and wit. She sets standards, which the group agrees on, for conversation: conversation must be natural and varied, appropriate to the occasion and the people gathered together; conversation must never be hurried, and speakers must keep the tone at a high level even when speaking of trivial things. Most important is the spirit of the group: people must be civil, polite, and joyful in conversation, and they must work together as a group to provide enjoyment for all to avoid boring each other. Then, both trivial and important matters may be discussed, as long as they are discussed well—with wit, judgment, concern for those participating, and enthusiasm.

In "On Speaking Too Much or Too Little," the central characters are Plotine and Amilcar, her suitor or gallant, as well as five other friends who gather for a salon-style conversation. Plotine begins the conversation by complaining about two of her suitors, one who talks too much and will not let her get in a word, and another who speaks scarcely at all and makes her do all the work of conversation. In an animated discussion, the group agrees that one should talk neither too much nor too little and that one should not interrupt. They agree that there should be "no tyranny in conversation," that "each person has a role and a right to speak in turn," and that listening is an obligation and a skill. Characteristically, Scudéry signals that this conversation will be one where alternative opinions will be entertained, even welcomed, by having Emile point out how much disagreement exists on what topics and styles of conversation are acceptable. Shifting the discussion and

58. See Horace, *Ars poetica,* 1.343.

the method of argumentation to opinion is also a shift from the strictures of demonstrative logic, or aesthetic rules, into the field of argumentation based on probability, the field of rhetorical dialectic. Modeling this flexible method, Amilcar gives an amusing satiric portrait of the man who speaks too much and will not let others into the conversation, and then is skewered by Plotine, who points out that his portrait, while quite amusing, is too long.

The speakers then set out a delightful inventory of conversational sophistics, modeled on the kind of catalogue Aristotle gives in *On Sophistical Refutations* for public speaking. They agree, despite the variety of opinions on good conversation, that everyone wants to avoid obscurity and pompous nonsense. Borrowing Aristotle's division into mistakes of words and matter, Scudéry's *salonnières* cleverly divide conversational obscurity into problems with finding what to say and problems stemming from confusing word choice. They add that confusion in conversation also results from speaking before hearing the whole question, from answering mechanically while distracted, from the desire to be elegant, from misuse of fashionable words, and from speaking without enough knowledge.

Having dispatched the subject of faults in conversation, in the second half of the dialogue the speakers discuss how to speak well. They agree that good conversation requires wit, memory, and judgment, as well as language in the style of well-bred people. They agree that Plotine is the model for such conversational expertise: she "speaks as a rational woman should speak—agreeably." They analyze Plotine's talent in terms that would be recognizable to this audience as the canons of classical rhetoric: Plotine does not hunt around for something to say (invention); she does not hesitate (good memory); her speech is clear and easy (arrangement); her expressions are noble and natural (style); and her movement, voice, and facial expressions avoid affectation and match her words (delivery). This whole section seems very much an adaptation of Quintilian's advice on public speaking to the different circumstances of conversational speech.

The group reinforces again the class boundary that dialect enforces: well educated people do not use vulgar accents, but standard French. Finally, after a brief, open-ended debate on the differences between men's and women's speech (that nevertheless precludes women from using oaths or making pronouncements and recommends modesty for them), the conversation ends with the group agreeing that the best way to learn to converse well is to frequent the company of well-bred people, listening to and participating in their conversations—the classical rhetorical trio of practice, experience, and imitation. In this dialogue, the ideal speaker is thus a woman, a member of the well-educated leisure class, and a member of a salon.

The conversation titled "On Wit" has more narrative framework than most of the other dialogues, as well as an unnamed "I" narrator. The narrator, along with several friends, journeys to visit a gentleman, Antigene, in the country at his estate near the sea in order to have a view of the ocean for the first time. They are joined by Antigene's long-lost son and an old friend who has rescued him, as well as several other local ladies on this particular day. The dialogue encompasses two debates, the first a friendly, brief skirmish between Clarice, who loves travel stories, and Melinta, who hates them—and here Melinta wins, for Clearchus and Dom Alvarez never do relate their travel adventures. The second, more important debate, concerns wit. Here the group generally divides between Euridamia, who takes a fairly conservative view of wit appropriate to elegant conversation, and Melinta, who prefers to tease with her gloves off. The group in general agrees that wit exists everywhere but is flavored by the customs of the local people, that wit is a natural talent and that those who do not have it should not attempt it, that wit depends on place (university, law court, military, court, etc.), and that wit depends not just on what you say, but how you say it and your facial expression and body movements. With Melinta dissenting, they agree that you should never make fun of a lover, your friends or acquaintances, your enemies, people of no merit or people with merit, of crimes, misfortunes, disabilities, old age, or foreigners, and that ladies should not tease gentlemen and gentlemen should not tease ladies. Indeed, they share the consensus that teasing is a great danger to friendship. The group further agrees that saying insulting things or using rude or vulgar language is not amusing. In this discussion, we can see that the mid-seventeenth century begins a century-long debate about the nature of social conversation and social relationships, and eventually the more combative mode of wit is replaced by the more sociable mode of sympathetic sentiment.

Here the group asks Euridamia to sum up and elaborate, and she explains that teasing is a natural talent, that good wit is surprising, that it stings but does not hurt, and that it requires lively imagination and brilliance. She cautions that joking should not be too frequent because it destroys the sense of surprise, that it should not be announced ahead of time that something is funny, that funny stories should never be repeated by the teller, that proverbs should be avoided, that the ending of a story must be funnier than the beginning, and that you should stick to your talent—whether naïveté or wordplay—and not imitate others. Good wit, according to Euridamia, requires a fiery spirit, a lively imagination, a sensitive judgment, and a well-stocked memory, and must be gallant and bold but not audacious. The Golden Rule is never to hurt your friends. Melinta, all agree, is the exception to all these rules, for she breaks the rules—especially making fun of her friends and being too sharp—but she is still funny, amusing, and good.

At the end of the dialogue, the group returns to the debate about travel stories and reaches a compromise with Antigene's promise to relate a portrait or character of a great prince. Under the guise of telling about a historical, foreign prince, Antigene praises his own king—thus allowing Scudéry to praise her own king, Louis XIV. According to the portrait, this king is handsome, with easy manners (civil and heroic at once), a reformer of government and laws, an excellent military commander but moderate as a conqueror, and possessor of a formidable range of intellectual interests, promoting building projects and creating scientific and exotic collections that attract visitors from all over the world. Scudéry adds that when "he himself began to steer the ship [of state] . . . contrary to the inveterate practice of rulers during his time . . . he made all his ministers his instruments"—instead of falling under their influence. Here Scudéry comments on her own political position, since she had praised and supported the rebellious aristocratic *Frondeuses* when Anne of Austria, Louis's mother, had allowed her chief councilor, Mazarin, too much influence, and reasserted her loyalty to the government when Louis XIV came of age and took control. Indeed, Stanton has argued that hyperbole was a political strategy of the *honnêtes gens* after the Fronde and that underlying the praise, "the hyperbolic register of [the] compliments tell us that [they are], in fact, playing a conscious, obvious game that does not reflect or affect . . . inner being."[59]

"On Wit" as a whole also provides a model for elegant entertainment. The dialogue begins with visits, progresses through a banquet of many courses in rooms perfumed by indoor orange trees, moves to a long conversation and debate about travel stories and wit, includes a praise of the current king, and finishes with a walk through the gardens and a short opera written by the host and performed for the guests outdoors in a bower.

"On the Manner of Writing Letters" is a dialogue set at the country estate of Aminte, a few hours from the city, where four of her friends have joined her to urge her to write them letters while she is away. Aminte has often said that writing poems is easier than writing letters (making her the ideal, creative *honnête femme*), and her cousin Cléante has sent her a whole library of famous letters—classical as well as recent—to convince her that writing letters is necessary. When they arrive and tell her the purpose of her visit, Aminte dismisses all these letters (by men) as elegant, public letters that are no good as models of familiar letters (for women).

---

59. Stanton, *The Aristocrat as Art*, 72.

The visitors then join to convince Aminte that everyone writes letters and so should she. Aminte gives an example of a contemporary who left no published letters, but Cléante assures her that he did write, according to a good friend, but just did not keep copies. Aminte suggests that women just do not write as much as men do, but another guest replies that they are generally just too modest to publish their letters.

All the friends then join in giving advice to Aminte and each other on how to write good letters. They each contribute, but reach a consensus that the best writers write as they speak, do not put much wit in a letter, eschew grand or vulgar words, write decorously according to the purpose (business, news, love, etc.), and avoid elegance but display gallantry, politeness, passion, wit, and judgment.

The four friends then set out a catalogue of different kinds of letters. Business letters must be precise, concise, and well organized and must demonstrate civility. Letters of sympathy should be short, without long eulogies for the deceased or expressions of great grief—just a brief note to express sympathy. Cléante adds that some people, after all, do not need consoling, since they are not sad that they lost a husband or gained a fortune. They agree that letters of congratulation are easy to compose. They puzzle over the various purposes of letters of recommendation and agree that for a person you are obligated to recommend but do not really know you must write a short, dry letter without specifics, while for a recommendation that you want to succeed you must detail the good qualities of the person, put yourself in the place of her protector, think of the specific audience and engage their pride, and write a second note to reinforce your first. They describe letters of compliment, the letters responding to a business or social obligation, and recommend short, bland, general, and civil writing that will not encourage a lengthy correspondence. The letter of news must describe only news that is fresh and must fit the audience, giving news of battles, floods, fires, and uprisings to those who like that sort of news, and the local rumors and gossip about famous people to those who like that sort, and so for each audience. The serious letter, formal, literate, employing all your knowledge, is given short shrift; this is Scudéry's dismissal not of the letter of business or public affairs, but of the humanist letter that discusses philosophical or current affairs as a self-advertisement, the sort of letter that made humanists of the previous century famous, but is out-of-date by the seventeenth century. The letter of gallantry should contain wit and flattery; mock everything; cover a broad range of subjects; be expressed in easy, natural, noble, and urbane style; and avoid grand eloquence but include the charm that comes from "speaking well about trifles." Finally, in this pretelephone society, notes keep people in touch: to connect employer and employee, to get up-to-date news from friends, to let them know things you might forget before you see them.

Good love letters, all agree, are rare, but also rarely seen, because they are not made public, even to friends. They require infinite, passionate love combined with delicacy, so that the passion becomes "agreeable." In love letters, the fire of passion takes the place of wit, and such letters must be gallant, spiritual and yet playful, full of both passion and respect. They also must include complaints and a little anxiety, for "happy letters get you nowhere in love." They must display more sentiment than wit and must be expressed in deferential but impassioned style. Women write better love letters than men do, the group agrees, because men may express their love directly, while women may not, and the essence of art is indirection. Women's responses to men's love letters—if they respond at all—must be characterized by virtue, modesty, and fear mingled with tenderness. While most letters are short, lovers are allowed long letters because of the extravagance of the passion— they cannot help themselves, cannot be selective because their judgment is obscured by passion. Women must *never* admit to having written or received love letters, for men are by nature indiscreet.

Faced with these arguments and advice, Aminte admits defeat and agrees to write. Her friends go back to the city, Aminte writes for a while, then goes back to her old ways.

As Elizabeth Goldsmith observes, the group dynamic in Scudéry's conversations moves from a negative survey of what other speakers do wrong to positive praise of one of themselves as a model for speakers. The speakers participate in the new consumer culture by creating "a kind of feast of words that is displayed and consumed in the act of conversation"—no more so than in Scudéry's *Conversations,* where these conversations are then memorialized in print.[60] But as Aronson points out, Scudéry's dialogues rarely offer a solution to the problem posed and, instead, show various sides of the argument, allowing the reader to decide for herself.[61]

SCUDÉRY AND SAPPHO   In salon circles, Scudéry took the name "Sapho" (the French spelling of Sappho). Scudéry's *Amorous Letters* includes

60. See Goldsmith, *Exclusive Conversations,* esp. pp. 41–75 on Scudéry's *Conversations.* On Scudéry's *conversations,* see also Erica Harth, *Cartesian Women: Versions and Subversion of Rational Discourse in the Old Regime* (Ithaca, N.Y.: Cornell University Press, 1992), 33–37 and 44–54; Harth argues that Scudéry's anonymous publication and salon conversations recorded in print exemplify seventeenth-century discomfort with the idea of women writers and learned women.

61. Aronson, *Mademoiselle de Scudéry,* 121.

a long, passionate exchange of letters between two women. In one of the speeches in *Famous Women or Heroic Speeches*, Sappho persuades Erinna to educate herself and take up a career as a poet and so to make herself famous for her intellect. In her novel *Clélie*, in the section called "Histoire de Sapho," Scudéry again brings this historical figure to life. In manuscript there exists a passionate epistolary verse exchange between Scudéry and Catherine Descartes, and Scudéry was an intimate friend with many of the famous women of Paris. What does this mean?

Let us first look at the namesake Scudéry chose. By all accounts, Sappho was a real historical person, the earliest writer of love poetry in Western literature whose works, at least in fragments, have survived. She was born ca. 610 B.C.E., just at the close of the seventh century B.C.E., at a time of rapid colonial expansion on the part of Greek city-states. Her name is properly transliterated as "Psappho." Her parents were Skamandronymos and Kleis of Mytilene on Lesbos, the third largest island in the Aegean Sea near what was then Lydia and what is now Turkey. She had three brothers whose connections to Egypt and service on the state council suggest that the family was aristocratic. She married Kerkylas of Andros and perhaps had a daughter named "Kleis" for her mother (depending on whether you translate a reference in her poems as "daughter" or "girl"—both possibilities in Ancient Greek).[62] While the Greek poets who preceded Sappho, such as Homer and Hesiod, celebrated war, farming, drinking, and masculine camaraderie, Sappho wrote about love. Enough fragments of her poetry survive to testify that her poetry consisted of both marriage songs and celebrations of women's erotic attraction to other women.[63]

The ancient Latin poets rewrote Sappho while imitating her verse forms and use of female speakers and pathos. As DeJean has shown, the most widespread view of Sappho in the French Renaissance was based in the sixteenth century on Catullus's allusions to Sappho and in the seventeenth century on Ovid's *Heroides*, that great and influential compendium of letters by women to men who have seduced and abandoned them; the result is a view of "Sappho as sexually pitiable woman."[64] In Ovid's poem, Sappho has

62. See Jane Snyder, *The Woman and the Lyre: Women Writers in Classical Greece and Rome* (Carbondale, Ill.: Southern Illinois University Press, 1989), ch. 1 on Sappho, pp. 1–37.

63. See *Sappho's Lyre: Archaic Lyric and Women Poets of Ancient Greece*, ed. and trans. Diane Rayor (Berkeley: University of California Press, 1991), 1–5 and 51–81. See also Marilyn B. Skinner, "Woman and Language in Archaic Greece, or Why Is Sappho a Woman?" in *Feminist Theory and the Classics*, ed. Nancy Sorkin Rabinowitz and Amy Richlin (New York: Routledge, 1993), 125–44; as well as Judith P. Hallett, "Sappho and Her Social Context: Sense and Sensuality," *Signs* 4 (1979): 447–71.

64. See DeJean, *Fictions of Sappho*, 1–48, quotation 44. See also Snyder 4–13.

fallen in love with Phaon, a much younger man who rejects and mocks her. Overcome with grief, she leaves her female companions and leaps to her death into the sea from the White Rock of Leucas.[65] Modern biographers have remade Scudéry, using the friendship with Pellisson, in the same way that the ancient Latin poets remade Sappho: into a foolish older woman in love with a younger man.[66]

Recently, there has been a critical rethinking of Sappho's place in the Renaissance, prompted by the growth of gay and lesbian studies. This newer view differs markedly from Lillian Faderman's view that same-sex erotic poetry by women indicated "female friendship" in a different culture's rhetorical codes,[67] for example, or even DeJean's view in *Fictions of Sappho* that, while the Roman revisions of a heterosexual and abandoned Sappho dominated in the French Renaissance, nevertheless, the homoerotic Sappho was available in newly recovered and translated fragments, but mainly invoked to be discounted in a male poet's move to assert poetic superiority. Recent scholars have begun to suggest that women writers' allusions to Sappho often signaled transgressive literary achievements and same-sex eroticism. Harriette Andreadis has analyzed the friendship poetry of many midcentury Englishwomen and concluded that they created a discourse for female same-sex erotics that could be disassociated from an increasingly negative view of tribadism.[68] Valerie Traub has called for a complicated understanding of female same-sex eroticism that will replace the double problem of lesbian invisibility and over-idealized views of women's community. She argues that there was a renaissance of representation of female homoeroticism in sixteenth- and seventeenth-century England, fashioned of two very different discourses: the medical anxiety about the clitoris expressed as satiric denunciation of the tribade (a seventeenth-century deprecatory term for "lesbian") and a philosophical and literary idealization of female friendship.[69] Susan

65. On Ovid's Sappho in the Renaissance, see also Harriette Andreadis, *Sappho in Early Modern England: Female Same-Sex Literary Erotics 1550–1714* (Chicago: University of Chicago Press, 2001), 28–37.

66. See, for example, Aronson, who, in the biography, *Mademoiselle de Scudéry*, makes much of the Platonic amour between Scudéry and Pellisson, but fails to mention *Lettres amoureuses* in her study of Scudéry's writings, *Mademoiselle de Scudéry ou le voyage au Pays de Tendre*.

67. See Lillian Faderman, *Surpassing the Love of Men: Romantic Friendship and Love between Women from the Renaissance to the Present* (New York: William Morrow and Company, 1981).

68. See Andreadis, *Sappho in Early Modern England: Female Same-Sex Literary Erotics 1550–1714.*

69. See Valerie Traub, "The Rewards of Lesbian History," *Feminist Studies* 25 (1999): 363–94; "The Perversion of 'Lesbian' Desire," *History Workshop Journal* no. 41 (1996): 23–49; and *The Renaissance of Lesbianism in Early Modern England* (New York: Cambridge University Press, 2002).

Lanser has suggested that the cultural tradition of female friendship might be used to cover unconventional behavior and female intimacy, as well as lesbian erotics in women's writings.[70]

Following this new scholarship, we think that, at the very least, Scudéry is revising history to rework the conception of the irrational, hysterical woman into the passionate, embattled, struggling, but courageous *savante*, taking "Sapho" as her name in the salon and revising the story of Sappho as a foolish old woman into a story of Sappho as a wise old woman, mentoring young women, in "Sappho to Erinna." In both ancient and Renaissance times, Sappho's poetry was admired and imitated by both men and women, so Scudéry's self-identification with her is a savvy claim to the authority of a poet laureate, a bold move for a seventeenth-century woman. If we look more closely at *Amorous Letters*, however, we think that Scudéry had a further role in the reworking of literary sapphics that occurred in the seventeenth century.

In *Amorous Letters*, Scudéry offers a remaking of the letter-writing manual, as well as a revision of possibilities for the range of women's discourse. In remaking the formulary rhetoric for letters, during the first thirty-four letters and responses, Scudéry models a "conversation between absent friends," intimacy between two women expressed through letters. The friendship is portrayed as highly idealized, extremely passionate, and reflecting social ambition, for the letter writer seems to be of a slightly lower station than the respondent and so often apologizes for boring her or imposing on her. The sequence of letters and responses begins with the kinds of topics that were the subject of poetic and literary exercises: which is better—country or city? should one be happy and ignorant or wise and sad? are women more constant than men? But these familiar topics are personalized. The writer prays that the respondent return to the city because the country is disgusting, and the two consider whether stupidity causes happiness in decidedly feminine terms, immediately making a turn into the question of whether thoughtless people are happier in marriage. The two debate whether or not to retire from ordinary life into a nunnery. The middle sequence of the letters is filled

70. See Susan S. Lanser, "Befriending the Body: Female Intimacies as Class Acts," *Eighteenth-Century Studies* 32 (1998–99): 179–98, esp. 180: "I will suggest that female friendship emerged through women's agency as a powerful resource in the struggle for autonomy and authority; that it also implicated women in the consolidation of gentry-class interests; that it operated through a discourse of passionate love and physical longing that carried at least the theoretical possibility of seeming 'lesbian'; that social hierarchies worked to separate the monstrous sapphist from the tender friend; and that the very prominence of passionate female friendship enabled cover stories for less conventional behaviors and relationships."

with anxiety and reassurance: the writer fears that the respondent thinks she writes too often, or is not grateful enough for their correspondence, and the respondent reassures her; the writer rejoices that the respondent has finally reconciled with her, and the respondent reassures her that her disaffection was only a false rumor; the writer threatens to retire to a convent, and the respondent reacts with dismay; the writer paints her misery in her friend's absence and fears she does not care enough since her letters are few, and the respondent reassures her, calling her her life, her goddess; the writer worries that her letters are not well written enough, and the respondent reassures her of her joy at receiving them. While the letters have content, they do not form a narrative plot, as in the epistolary novel. Rather, they depict the range of emotions and intellectual pleasures attendant on an intimate friendship, much like many sonnet sequences.

In *Amorous Letters*, Scudéry also offers a revision of the range of possibilities for women's discourse, especially a discourse of same-sex erotics. The men's tradition, in Platonism, had always had this kind of discourse, for Platonism meant at once homoeroticism and also passionate but bodiless idealism. In her depiction of expressions of passionate friendship between women, Scudéry reworks the conventions of the love letter to express love between women. The letters reveal the anxiety that characterizes courtship: does the respondent care for the writer or not? Letter number 20 even explicitly expresses this anxiety as courtship: "you will say to me that this is a language of courtship and that my friendship sounds like love." Scudéry defends and disguises this love when the writer answers herself, "But why would [love] not have the same vocabulary, since it has the same intensity?" Finally, Scudéry adapts the intense emotionality of love discourse to these letters between women: the writer is the servant of the respondent, as well as her goddess; to prove her loyalty, the writer writes even when she is extremely ill from fever and is chastised by the respondent.

Scudéry is important because she creates a female-to-female discourse in the vernacular similar to what male humanists in Renaissance Italy crafted in their Latin letters—a way for nonreligious, well-educated, high-status people who like each other to relate in words. Moreover, she extends beyond earlier models the ways in which women can participate in mixed-gender conversations in the salon, completing a process that the Italian Renaissance began. These models are necessary in order to redesign the rules of society of upper-class and well-educated people so that women are included. In her formulary letter manual, which is also an experiment with the form of the fictional epistle, Scudéry also contributes significantly to the construction of a socially acceptable erotic discourse for female-female relationships.[71]

TEXTS   No manuscripts of Madeleine de Scudéry's works have come to light, except for personal correspondence housed in the Bibliothèque Nationale. Fortunately, her works were all published during her lifetime since she supported herself, and often her brother, through writing. The lack of problems in her texts suggests that the printer followed clear manuscripts or else Scudéry herself saw her works through press.

Our translations of the conversations are based on recent critical editions: "On Conversation," "On Wit," and "On the Manner of Writing Letters" on the edition of selected conversations by Delphine Denis in *De l'air galant et autres conversations* (Paris: Honoré Champion, 1998), and "On Speaking Too Much or Too Little," on the edition of selected conversations by Phillip J. Wolfe, *Choix de conversations de Mlle de Scudéry* (Ravenna: Longo Editore, 1977). Because Denis inexplicably used the dialogues from the novels of the 1640s and 1650s as the copy text for her edition of the conversations (even though there were substantial changes to turn these dialogues into the conversations) and edited the actual conversations only in her notes, we have also carefully followed the original texts in the Paris editions of "On Conversation" and "On Wit" in *Conversations sur divers sujets* (1680) and of "On the Manner of Writing Letters" in *Conversations nouvelles sur divers sujets, dedie'es au Roy* (1684) in order to make sure that we were not confused by Denis's arrangement. Both Wolfe and Denis agree that the Paris editions of each collection are the only reliable copy text. Because Scudéry's brother was exiled from Paris and perhaps continuously in straitened circumstances, there is a theoretical possibility that the Le Haye and Amsterdam editions might also be authorial, brokered by the brother or his widow. However, textual evidence shows otherwise: the only changes were the sort of deletions or single-word changes that a printer might make as errors setting type from the Paris edition; there are no additions to suggest authorial revision in these editions outside Paris.

Our translation for the speeches by Mariam, Sophonisba, Zenobia, and Sappho are based on the second Paris edition, *Les femmes illustres; ou, les harangues*

---

71. We do not agree with DeJean's reading of *Lettres amoureuses* (in both "La lettre amoureuse revue et corrigée," 17–22, and in *Fictions of Sappho*, 98–101) as a collection of letters from one man to a series of mistresses—the letters are, after all, marked letter and response, and both are addressed to Madame.

héroiques, de Mr de Scudéry (Paris, 1665). There is a recent French edition (in 1991) of the 1644 Paris edition of *Les femmes illustres,* but it does not seem to be a reliable edition, for there are many passages missing that seem to be errors in transcription on the part of the editor rather than the original printer. In any case, we follow here the Anglo-British editing tradition of using the last reliable text published during the author's lifetime.

There is only one edition of *Lettres amoureuses de divers autheurs de ce temps* (Paris, 1641), and so that is our copy text for all the letters.

VOLUME EDITORS'
BIBLIOGRAPHY

PRIMARY SOURCES

d'Aragona, Tullia. *Dialogue on the Infinity of Love*. Edited and translated by Rinaldina Russell and Bruce Merry. Chicago: University of Chicago Press, 1997.

Cary, Elizabeth, the Lady Falkland. *The Tragedy of Mariam, The Fair Queen of Jewry*. Edited by Barry Weller and Margaret W. Ferguson. Berkeley: University of California Press, 1994.

Cavendish, Margaret, Duchess of Newcastle. *Orations of Divers Sorts, Accommodated to Divers Places*. London, 1662.

Cereta, Laura. *Collected Letters of a Renaissance Feminist*. Translated and edited by Diana Robin. Chicago: University of Chicago Press, 1997.

Cicero. *De Inventione*. Translated by H. M. Hubbell. Cambridge, Mass.: Harvard University Press, 1960.

———. *De re publica*. Translated by Clinton Walker Keyes. London: William Heinemann, 1928.

———. *De oratore*. Translated by E. W. Sutton and H. Rackham. London: William Heinemann, 1948.

Fedele, Cassandra. *Letters and Orations*. Edited and translated by Diana Robin. Chicago: University of Chicago Press, 2000.

Isocrates. "Nicocles" and "Antidosis." In *Isocrates*. Translated by George Norlin, 1:77–81 and 2:327–29. Cambridge, Mass.: Harvard University Press, 1928. .

Makin, Bathsua. *An Essay to Revive the Antient Education of Gentlewomen* (1673). Introduction by Paula Barbour. Los Angeles: William Andrews Clark Memorial Library and University of California, 1980.

Marinella, Lucrezia. *The Nobility and Excellence of Women and the Defects and Vices of Men*. Edited and translated by Anne Dunhill, with an introduction by Letizia Panizza. Chicago: University of Chicago Press, 1999.

Sappho. *Sappho's Lyre: Archaic Lyric and Women Poets of Ancient Greece*. Edited and translated by Diane Rayor. Berkeley: University of California Press, 1991.

Schurman, Anna Maria van. *Whether a Christian Woman Should Be Educated and Other Writings from Her Intellectual Circle*. Translated by Joyce L. Irwin. Chicago: University of Chicago Press, 1998.

Scudéry, Madeleine de. *Artamène ou Le Grand Cyrus*. 10 vols. Paris, 1653.

—————. *Choix de Conversations de Mlle de Scudéry*. Edited by Phillip J. Wolfe. Ravenna: Longo Editore, 1977.

—————. *Clélie*. 10 vols. Paris, 1655.

—————. *Conversations sur divers sujets*. 2 vols.. Paris, 1680.

—————. *Conversations nouvelles sur divers sujets, dedie'es au Roy*. Paris, 1684.

—————. *Conversations upon Several Subjects Written in French by Mademoiselle de Scudéry*. Translated by Ferrand Spence. 2 vols. London, 1683.

—————. *De l'air galant et autres conversations*. Edited by Delphine Denis. Paris: Honoré Champion, 1998.

—————. *Les Illustres or the Heroick Harangues of the Illustrious Women*. Translated by James Innes. 2 vols. Edinburgh, 1681.

—————. *Les illustres; ou, les harangues héroiques, de Mr de Scudéry*. Paris, 1665.

—————. *Lettres amoureuses de divers autheurs de ce temps*. Paris, 1641.

—————. *Mademoiselle de Scudéry: sa vie et sa correspondence*. Edited by Routhery and Boutron. Paris, 1873.

Vives, Juan Luis. *The Instruction of a Christen Woman*. Edited by Virginia Walcott Beauchamp, Elizabeth H. Hageman, and Margaret Mikesell. Urbana, Ill.: University of Illinois Press, 2001.

SECONDARY SOURCES

Altman, Janet Gurkin. "The Letter Book as a Literary Institution 1539–1789: Toward a Cultural History of Published Correspondences in France." *Yale French Studies* 71 (1995): 17–62.

Andreadis, Harriette. *Sappho in Early Modern England: Female Same-Sex Literary Erotics 1550–1714*. Chicago: University of Chicago Press, 2001.

Andreadis, Harriette, Susan Lanser, Valerie Traub, and Elizabeth Wahl. Workshop on "Changing Stories: Attending to Early Modern Lesbianism." Attending to Early Modern Women Conference at the University of Maryland, 9 November 2000.

Aronson, Nicole. *Mademoiselle de Scudéry*. Translated by Stuart R. Aronson. Boston: Twayne Publishers, 1978.

—————. *Mademoiselle de Scudéry ou le voyage au Pays de Tendre*. Paris: Fayard, 1986.

Baader, Renate. *Dames de lettres, autorinnen des preziösen, hocharistokratischen und "modernen" Salons (1649–1698): Mlle de Scudéry—Mlle de Montpensier—Mme d'Aulnoy*. Stuttgart: J. B. Metzlersche Verlagsbuchhandlung, 1986.

Backer, Dorothy. *Precious Women*. New York: Basic Books, 1974.

Barzun, Jacques. *From Dawn to Decadence: 500 Years of Western Cultural Life: 1500 to the Present*. New York: HarperCollins, 2000.

Bassnett, Susan. *Elizabeth I: A Feminist Perspective*. Oxford: Berg, 1989.

Beasley, Faith E. *Revising Memory: Women's Fiction and Memoirs in Seventeenth-Century France*. New Brunswick, N.J.: Rutgers University Press, 1990.

Biancardi, Elisa. "Madeleine de Scudéry et son cercle: spécificité socioculturelle et créativité littéraire," *Papers on French Literature* 22 (1995): 415–29.

Burke, Peter. "The Art of Conversation in Early Modern Europe." *The Art of Conversation*, 89–122. Ithaca, N.Y.: Cornell University Press, 1993.

Crane, Mary Thomas. "'Video et Taceo': Elizabeth I and the Rhetoric of Counsel.'" *Studies in English Literature* 28 (1988): 1–15.

DeJean, Joan. *Fictions of Sappho, 1546–1937.* Chicago: University of Chicago Press, 1989.

———. "La lettre amoureuse revue et corrigée: un texte oublié de Madeleine de Scudéry." *Revue d'Histoire Littéraire de la France* 1 (1988): 17–22.

Donawerth, Jane. "'As Becomes a Rational Woman to Speak': Madeleine de Scudéry's Rhetoric of Conversation." In *Rhetorical Activities of Historical Women.* Edited by Molly Wertheimer, 305–19. Columbia, S.C.: University of South Carolina Press, 1997.

———. "Conversation and the Boundaries of Public Discourse in Rhetorical Theory by Renaissance Women." *Rhetorica* 16 (1998): 188–92.

———. "The Politics of Renaissance Rhetorical Theory by Women." In *Political Rhetoric, Power, and Renaissance Women.* Edited by Carole Levin and Patricia A. Sullivan, 256–72. Albany: State University of New York Press, 1995.

———. *Rhetorical Theory by Women before 1900.* Lanham, Md.: Rowman and Littlefield, 2002, esp. pp. 45–58.

Duchêne, Roger. "A la recherche d'une espèce rare et mêlée: les Précieuses avant Molière." *Papers on French Seventeenth-Century Literature* 43 (1995): 331–57.

———. "Le Nouveau Dictionnaire des Précieuses." *Papers on French Seventeenth-Century Literature* 50 (1990): 91–109.

———. *Les Précieuses ou comment l'esprit vint aux femmes.* Paris: Fayard, 2001.

Faderman, Lillian. *Surpassing the Love of Men: Romantic Friendship and Love between Women from the Renaissance to the Present.* New York: William Morrow and Company, 1981.

Gibson, Joan. "Educating for Silence: Renaissance Women and the Language Arts." *Hypatia* 4 (Spring 1989): 9–27.

Glenn, Cheryl. *Rhetoric Retold: Regendering the Tradition from Antiquity through the Renaissance.* Carbondale, Ill.: Southern Illinois University Press, 1997.

Goldsmith, Elizabeth. *"Exclusive Conversations": The Art of Interaction in Seventeenth-Century France.* Philadelphia: University of Pennsylvania Press, 1988.

Goldsmith, Elizabeth, ed. *Writing the Female Voice: Essays on Epistolary Literature.* Boston: Northeastern University Press, 1989.

Goodman, Dena. *The Republic of Letters: A Cultural History of the French Enlightenment.* Ithaca, N.Y.: Cornell University Press, 1994.

Grafton, Anthony, and Lisa Jardine. *From Humanism to the Humanities: Education and the Liberal Arts in Fifteenth- and Sixteenth-Century Europe.* London: Duckworth, 1986.

Grande, Nathalie. *Stratégies de romancières de Clélie à La Princesse de Clèves (1645–1678).* Paris: Honoré Champion, 1999.

Hallett, Judith P. "Sappho and Her Social Context: Sense and Sensuality." *Signs* 4 (1979): 447–71.

Hannay, Margaret, ed. *Silent but for the Word.* Kent, Ohio: Kent State University Press, 1985.

Harth, Erica. *Cartesian Women: Versions and Subversions of Rational Discourse in the Old Regime.* Ithaca, N.Y.: Cornell University Press, 1992.

———. *Ideology and Culture in Seventeenth-Century France.* Ithaca, N.Y.: Cornell University Press, 1983.

———. "The Salon Woman Goes Public . . . or Does She?" *Going Public: Women and*

Publishing in Early Modern France. Edited by Elizabeth Goldsmith and Dena Goodman, 179–93. Ithaca, N.Y.: Cornell University Press, 1995.

Hinds, Leonard. "Literary and Political Collaboration: The Prefatory Letter of Madeleine de Scudéry's *Artamène, ou le Grand Cyrus." Papers on French Seventeenth-Century Literature* 45 (1996): 491–500.

Howell, Wilbur Samuel. *Logic and Rhetoric in England 1500–1700.* 1956. Reprint New York: Russell & Russell, 1961.

Hull, Suzanne W. *Chaste, Silent and Obedient.* San Marino, Calif.: Huntington Library Press, 1982 and 1988.

Kelly, Ann Cline. "Swift's Polite Conversation: An Eschatological Vision." *Studies in Philology* 73 (April 1976): 204–24.

Krajewska, Barbara. "Du nouveau sur la Correspondence de Mlle de Scudéry." *Essays in French Literature* 25 (1988): 9–15.

Lanser, Susan S. "Befriending the Body: Female Intimacies as Class Acts." *Eighteenth-Century Studies* 32 (1998–99): 179–98.

Lazard, Madeleine. *Les avenues de Fémynie.* Paris: Fayard, 2001, esp. pp. 230–31.

Levin, Carole, and Patricia A. Sullivan, eds. *Political Rhetoric, Power, and Renaissance Women.* Albany, N.Y.: State University of New York Press, 1995.

Lougee, Carolyn. *Le Paradis des Femmes: Women, Salons, and Social Stratification in Seventeenth-Century France.* Princeton, N.J.: Princeton University Press, 1976.

Lunsford, Andrea A., ed. *Reclaiming Rhetorica: Women in the Rhetorical Tradition.* Pittsburgh: University of Pittsburgh Press, 1995.

Maclean, Ian. *The Renaissance Notion of Woman.* Cambridge: Cambridge University Press, 1980.

———. *Woman Triumphant: Feminism in French Literature 1610–1652.* Oxford: Clarendon Press, 1977.

Maître, Myriam. *Les Précieuses: Naissance des femmes de lettres en France au XVII, siècle.* Paris: Honoré Champion, 1999.

Marcus, Leah. "Shakespeare's Comic Heroines, Elizabeth I, and the Political Uses of Androgyny." *Women in the Middle Ages and the Renaissance.* Edited by Mary Beth Rose, 135–53. Syracuse: Syracuse University Press, 1986.

McDougall, Dorothy. *Madeleine de Scudéry: Her Romantic Life and Death.* London: Methuen and Co., 1938.

Niderst, Alain. *Madeleine de Scudéry, Paul Pellison et leur monde.* Paris: Presses Universitaires de France, 1976.

Norbrook, David. "Rhetoric, Ideology and the Elizabethan World Picture." *Renaissance Rhetoric.* Edited by Peter Mack, 140–64. Boston, Mass.: St. Martin's Press, 1994.

Rebhorn, Wayne. *The Emperor of Men's Minds.* Ithaca, N.Y.: Cornell University Press, 1995.

Sainte-Beuve, Charles Augustin. "Mademoiselle de Scudéry." *Portraits of the Seventeenth Century: Historic and Literary.* Translated by Katherine P. Wormeley, 55–83. New York: Frederick Ungar Publishing Co., 1964.

Skinner, Marilyn B. "Woman and Language in Archaic Greece, or Why Is Sappho a Woman?" *Feminist Theory and the Classics.* Edited by Nancy Sorkin Rabinowitz and Amy Richlin, 125–44. New York: Routledge, 1993.

Snyder, Jane. *The Woman and the Lyre: Women Writers in Classical Greece and Rome*. Carbondale: Southern Illinois University Press, 1989.

Stanton, Domna. *The Aristocrat as Art: A Study of the Honnête Homme and the Dandy in Seventeenth- and Nineteenth-Century French Literature*. New York: Columbia University Press, 1980.

Stark, Ryan John. "Margaret Cavendish and Composition Style." *Rhetoric Review* 17 (1999): 264–81.

Sutherland, Christine Mason. "Aspiring to the Rhetorical Tradition: A Study of Margaret Cavendish." *Listening to Their Voices: The Rhetorical Activities of Historical Women*. Edited by Molly Meijer Wertheimer, 255–71. Columbia, S.C.: University of South Carolina Press, 1997.

Timmermans, Linda. *L'accès des femmes à la culture (1598–1715): Un débat d'idées de Saint François de Sales à la Marquise de Lambert*. Paris: Honoré Champion, 1993.

Traub, Valerie. "The Perversion of 'Lesbian' Desire." *History Workshop Journal* no. 41 (1996): 23–49.

———. *The Renaissance of Lesbianism in Early Modern England*. New York: Cambridge University Press, 2002.

———. "The Rewards of Lesbian History." *Feminist Studies* 25(2) (1999): 363–94.

Venesoen, Constant. *Études sur la littérature féminine au XVII₍ siècle: Mademoiselle de Gournay, Mademoiselle de Scudéry, Madame de Villedieu, Madame de Lafayette*. Birmingham, Ala.: SUMMA Publications, 1990.

Vosevich, Kathi. "Tutoring the Tudors." *Women, Writing, and the Reproduction of Culture in Tudor and Stuart Britain*. Edited by Mary E. Burke, Jane Donawerth, Linda Dove, and Karen Nelson, 61–76. Syracuse: Syracuse University Press, 2000.

Wahl, Elizabeth Susan. *Invisible Relations: Representations of Female Intimacy in the Age of Enlightenment*. Stanford: Stanford University Press, 1999.

Wertheimer, Molly Meijer, ed. *Listening to Their Voices: The Rhetorical Activities of Historical Women*. Columbia, S.C.: University of South Carolina Press, 1997.

Whigham, Frank. *Ambition and Privilege: The Social Tropes of Elizabethan Courtesy Theory*. Berkeley: University of California Press, 1984.

Woodbridge, Linda. *Women and the English Renaissance: Literature and the Nature of Womankind, 1540–1620*. Urbana, Ill.: University of Illinois Press, 1986.

MODEL LETTERS FROM
"AMOROUS LETTERS" (1641)[1]

LETTER 2

She questions her about a certain very stupid man,
who is only happy because he is ignorant.

Madam,

I must discuss this man with you, the one you wrote me about. I imagine that he is happy, yet I believe that he has no reason to be [so]. He is only happy because he is ignorant and only has peace of mind because he is insensitive. It is no wonder that he has no worries, because he [also] has no knowledge. It is no great surprise that the blind are not afraid of lightning. If they don't tremble as do others, they are not [necessarily] happier; on the contrary, I think that they would prefer to have perfect sight, even on condition that it would sometimes be dazzled. You will say that I read this in the book that you admire so much and that my letter borrows from it. Think what you will; I believe that there is no more danger in taking something good from a book that we like than in picking fruit from a tree that belongs to us. We don't read simply to amuse ourselves, but also to have it benefit us.

However, returning to our man, I swear to you that I never want such a happiness. I would rather have your intelligent worries than his tranquility— I mean the noble cares that knowledge brings with it and the reasonable fears that serve to awaken the intelligence, not to trouble the mind. The happiness of these you write me about is like that of people asleep. Their minds are resting, but only because they are not capable of worrying.

I know you'll laugh at the fact that I'm ending this letter with a comparison that you'll find a little too lofty for me. It seems that it's possible to

1. All of the letters in this section are translated from Madeleine de Scudéry, *Lettres amoureuses de divers autheurs de ce temps* (Paris, 1641), 17–31, 270–78, 287–93, 417–33, 516–27, and 532–40.

avoid bouts of depression just as one avoids crashes of thunder. To evade either one, you have to be very high or very low. But although there's equal safety in both places, there's not equal glory. I would rather avoid the storm standing on Mount Olympus than hiding in a cave. And drawing on that book I'm stealing from, I would rather be above adversity than below it and would rather be incapable [of unhappiness] through reasoning than through stupidity.

I leave you then with this [thought], begging you that you will no longer speak to me in this way and no longer argue against your own interest by quitting the company of great minds. You have too large an interest to resign from their company, and if I defend them, it is in order to praise a virtue that you possess and I long for. I would love to have elegant [enough] words to say what I think since I love to serve you and to show you, whenever possible, that I am,

Madam,

Your etc.

RESPONSE 2

*She tries to prove that those who have the least amount
of wit have the least amount of worry.*

Madam,

Write what you will about great minds, it seems to me that they have more fame than happiness and that it is very difficult to have both great wisdom and little trouble. It is true that [the brilliant people] are admired and that they stand out above others; at the same time, I believe that, with all this advantage, they should still be compared to the bush in Holy Scripture, which gave off enough light but was also full of thorns.[2] There are thorns in such enlightenment: there are quite a few sorrows that knowledge increases rather than cures. Let's speak frankly and not let ourselves be charmed by beautiful appearances. Just as those who have a severe illness would prefer to feel less in order to be tortured less, so I believe that those who are miserable would want to decrease their knowledge in order to diminish their distress.

Thus we can speak of minds as [we can] senses: the most sensitive are the easiest to affect. Moreover, medicine and philosophy heal the unhappy

---

2. A reference either to Proverbs 7:6: "For as the crackling of thorns under a pot, so is the laughter of the fool: this also is vanity"; or Isaiah 33:12: "And the people shall be as the burnings of lime: as thorns cut up shall they be burned in the fire."

and sick in much the same way: the one numbs feeling, without which there is no pain, and the other tries to rid one of care, without which there is no misery. This means that the most ignorant are the least unfortunate. I don't deny that there are some who rise above misery and overcome it, but I think that people such as these are very rare. I see very few who resemble you. And to tell you the truth, I believe that those who give themselves the most grief are neither the great [minds] nor the small ones, but only the mediocre ones. It seems that disquiet takes shape in a soul just as clouds in the air: the sun raises some vapors, which it then has a hard time dissipating; and mediocre intelligences fling themselves into their troubles, which they can't seem to get rid of.[3]

While great minds overcome worry and small ones ignore it, mediocre ones burden themselves with it. Much as Christianity rejects people who couldn't care less about salvation,[4] Moral Philosophy rejects them for happiness. These are the sort of people who complain [all the time] and for whom enlightenment increases misery, since it serves only to show them the entrance to many labyrinths [of ethical quandary] from which there is no exit. Am I wrong then to believe that those who have the least intelligence have the least grief? Inasmuch as there are so few who vanquish affliction, is it not enough for me to follow the path that is most worn and to content myself with remaining below [the reach] of trouble through ignorance, since I am unable to rise above it through reason? Since the happiness of small minds is genuine, I don't care if it is less glorious than the happiness of the wise. It is for the most part as pure and as solid, even if it is not as noble. In this I am saying what I would like to be rather than what I am, because, although I am lacking in intelligence, I am not at all lacking in worry. I suffer the misery of those who have attained some enlightenment, and yet I am deprived of their advantages. You know well, and I do not at all doubt, that if you put up with my [lack of] wit, it is because of my affection and the desire that I have to be,

> Madam,
> Your etc.

3. Seventeenth-century science did not understand evaporation. This culture sees the sun as an agent causing water to change to vapors, just as the sun is an agent causing, at times, mud to turn to worms.

4. The French word "tiedes" or lukewarm, indifferent, is a scriptural allusion; cf. Revelations 3:16 (AV): "So then because thou art lukewarm, and neither cold nor hot, I will spew thee out of my mouth."

LETTER 20

She calls her her goddess—she asks her to pierce all the way to her heart
to see the affection that she cannot express.

Madam,

Although I beg you to think of me, I admit, nevertheless, that I need your judgment more than your memory in order to stay in your good graces, because your memory only shows things as they appear, while your judgment can discover them as they [truly] are. Don't be satisfied with the power to win hearts when you also might have the power to penetrate them—such is the affection that you produce there. Don't be like the sun, whose heat extends further than its light and who produces gold and metals in the earth, where the brightness of her rays will never penetrate. You will say to me that this is a language of courtship and that my friendship sounds like love. But why would [love] not have the same vocabulary, since it has the same intensity? [Love] differs only in its goal and not in its strength. Don't disapprove then if I beg you to help me make you see the extremity of my affection, and, since I call you my goddess, I pray you to show me some effect of that title, looking at my heart rather than my hands and caring more for my intention than my offering. Certainly I would be the most miserable person in the world if you judged my friendship only by its effect or by my words. I have neither power nor eloquence. But even if I had one or the other to an ideal degree, I still would not be able to demonstrate adequately to you the desire I have to serve you, and to be,

Madam,

Your etc.

RESPONSE 20

She says that she has more love than knowledge and
that, because of the influence of her affection, she
injudiciously puts her feelings into words.

Madam,

I don't believe that those who gave you their approval can forget that. Your virtues cause [in others] the desire to preserve as well as to acquire your good opinion. I have only one regret: not having enough intelligence to truly appreciate the perfections of yours. I am told that one must measure love through [deep] knowledge, and yet, although I do not know you perfectly, I can't imagine that someone could love you more. Because, if that were so, I would further regret not possessing more intelligence in order to experience even more affection. I think that I completely disagree with what you say about the sun: my heat extends farther than my light, and my love extends farther than my knowledge. Don't call me your goddess anymore, if you do not want me to call you my idol. You are mistaken to grant such honor to someone who so little merits it. Don't look any longer for words to testify that you love me: the effects on you have demonstrated that to me, and I won't see better with the light of a torch than with the light of the sun itself. Thus I make comparison of actions to words, for words do not demonstrate as clearly as actions do what kind of friendship we have. However, it is those [poor substitutes] that must serve me, since I have no other way to show you how much I am,

> Madam,
> Your etc.

LETTER 22

She sends word that nothing could stop her from writing to her, not even a fever, no matter how extreme.

Madam,

Judge the desire I have to get one of your letters by the care I take to send you mine. Having suffered a bout of fever, and seeing that the mail is ready to leave, I am resolved, despite my illness, to write to you. Needless to say, my hand trembles not from fear but from shivering. In this state I am prevented from writing you a long letter, because the messenger presses me on one side and my illness on the other. I must end then and leave what I need to tell you for another time. Perhaps I am endangering myself and the pain will become more intense, but that is not important—I will endure it patiently, since the effort I make is very commendable, to take this occasion to prove how much I am,

> Madam,
> Your etc.

RESPONSE 2 2

She is afraid that, having received a little satisfaction,
she has lost a greater one and that, by forcing herself
to write, she has only worsened her illness.

Madam,

I didn't feel the joy that I had hoped for at the return of this messenger, learning of your indisposition through the letter that you have done me the honor to write to me. I fear that the pains you took only worsened your fever and that, in giving me this gift [of writing to me], you have deprived me of a greater one that I might have had. Certainly, it's true that the two most pleasing pieces of news that I could receive are to be told that you love me and that you are in good health. Similarly, what I fear most in the world is a change [for the worse] in either your health or your friendship. The slightest fear of one or the other would make me hate my life. I swear that no letter has ever been as dear to me as the one you sent me despite your illness, but I would rather you took care to get better than to write to me. Although your news greatly reassures me, I love your health better than your letters. I beg you to believe me and offer myself to serve you in whatever you might wish, as

        Madam,
        Your etc.

LETTER 3 4

She reassures her that she has not forgotten her and hopes that
the frequency of her letters is not bothersome.

Madam,

I must admit that in my fear that I'd been wiped from your memory, I was very relieved to find out that your long silence was a result of your being so far away rather than your forgetting me. You desire that I interpret it that way, and I assure you that I share the personality of those people who readily believe what they want [to believe]. I won't look very closely to see if it's Truth or Politeness talking.

I no longer doubt that it was lack of opportunity, rather than [your] desire, that I received no letters from you. As for my letters, I have reason to hope that some are still on their way [to you], since if you had received all of them, you would not have had any reason to complain about the proofs of my remembering [you], as I have about your silence. Our complaints would have been different: you perhaps would have hoped for my letters a little less frequently and I for your letters a little more often.

But I'm sorry. I don't really believe you are angry that I write to you, and, since you tolerate my affection, your patience will result in these testimonials [to my love for you]. I only wish that I had greater ability in order to better deserve what you are to me and to more clearly show you what I am to you, which is,

> Madam,
> Your etc.

RESPONSE 34

She reassures her that her letters are never bothersome and describes the grief she feels that she has not received all of them.

Madam,

You are wrong to think that I could ever forget you, unless you could possess less worthiness or I could possess less knowledge of [your worth]. There is nothing as true as the assurance I give of my memory of you, and you have more reason to believe that than to desire it. That is more true than beneficial. You are my model and my preservation: I think of you incessantly to console myself and to guide me. You tell me that I haven't received all of your letters. If this is true I have cause to give you complaints and thanks and to think myself unhappy at the same time as I believe myself obliged to you. I would be less worthy of this favor if I felt less at this notification. I see myself forced to incorporate two opposing passions—grief and joy—resulting from the same cause. If I rejoice in the knowledge of your remembering me, I grieve at the news that I haven't received all the testimonies to it. As for my letters, you received them all on the same day from what I have learned.

However, as you can see, I wrote one after another. I am sorry that they were not delivered to you as I wanted. But since this has happened, at least I will have one grand advantage: in the future, if you don't get any at all, you may blame my bad luck for what should perhaps be blamed on my forgetfulness. [But] never doubt that I desire to honor you, and, whether I write to you or don't write to you at all, believe that I am completely,

> Madam,
> Your etc.

LETTER 3 5

She asks her to help one of her
friends with some business.

Madam,

I ask you very humbly, right at the beginning, to remember the command you gave me when I had the honor of saying goodbye to you. And it would be strange if I were motivated more by fear of bothering you with my letters than by fear of disobeying you. I can only write you very poorly composed [letters], but I still hope that you will put up with them and, after having had the patience to endure my poor conversation, that you will not deny me because of a poor letter.

What makes me hope for this favor with more confidence, especially on this occasion, is that I am writing to you on behalf of a person who has both wit and virtue. These are two qualities that you cherish and that you yourself possess to such a high degree that those who possess them only in lesser portions discover [their lack] from being near you when they happen to meet you. I am sure that the bearer [of this letter], who knows this truth only through the fame of your reputation, will soon learn it through experience once he has met you. I don't doubt at all that you will assist him, and I believe, in obliging him, that you will give me more reason to serve you and to be,

Madam,

Your etc.

LETTER 3 6

She compliments her on the
praise that she has received.

Madam,

You are offering me approbation for something that hardly even deserves toleration. I think that this results more from your affection than from your intelligence and that you have a greater desire to demonstrate your affection for me than your esteem. Be careful not to commit a sin through praising me in this way, and do not fall victim to the greatest error in the world, which would be to take me for eloquent. I defer so to your judgment that I might in this case deceive my own in order to make my belief match yours.

On another note—I think that it is neither your intention, nor mine, and when you hold me in such high esteem, it is actually Civility and not Truth speaking. I know well that you do not have less perspicuity in recognizing my faults than you have kindness in enduring them. Also, I am not asking you to remain in error for my sake.[5] I only pray that you do not lead others astray and that you don't, at times, say what you don't at all believe. It seems to me that my prayer is not at all unfair if I beg you to speak to others on my behalf as you speak on their behalf to me.

I believe that you do not want me to have a different opinion of myself, and I take your praise as a modest reprimand and believe that, in attributing such virtuous qualities to me, you [actually] want to inform me of my short-comings and [let me know] what is required in order to deserve such worthy approval as yours. This is what I must believe,

Madam,

Your etc.

LETTER 53

She praises her manner of writing and criticizes that
of others who do not have similar style and know
only a few rehearsed witticisms and no more.

Madam,

I cannot tell you how much I admire your letters. I must learn to write ones as good as yours in order to express their excellence. Whatever style you write in, they are always pleasant or useful.[6] If you write on important subjects, there is nothing as enlightening, and if they are written with more ease, there is nothing as amusing. They are serious without being pretentious and easy without being too sloppy. Your style is like those beauties who always appear fashionable and attractive whether they are dressed up or not at all.

And to describe what entirely bewitches me, it is the great consistency that one sees no less in your speech and your writing than in your manner of living. By "consistency," I don't mean that you should always do or say the same thing, but that everything should always be pleasing.

---

5. Scudéry is working out an underlying set of religious metaphors here—to be in error in terms of religion is to believe false dogma.

6. "Pleasant or useful," "agréables ou utiles," is the classical requirement for good writing, especially poetry. See Horace, *Ars poetica*, l. 343.

I admire a perfection in you that is wanting in many others. I see a great many people who learn bits and pieces from certain books and who know them by heart in order to deliver[7] them in company or write them in their letters. They sometimes carry it off, but they shouldn't show off so much if they want to attain a similar reputation. They are like those people who sell all their possessions in order to appear in the latest fashions for a week. Their discourse is dull in some places and inflated in others. It is like wearing a scarlet scarf on top of rags. [Such memorized pieces] demonstrate their stealing from others and their [intellectual] deficiency. It shows that they are not only poor [in invention] but also that they do not know how to help themselves to the wealth of others. Their fall is more deadly because they have forced themselves to fly too high. We admit that the truth about the Icaruses[8] of our sex is easy to see, although the myth shows only the truth about men. Strictly speaking, such people are dwarves in high heels and, though they want to appear grand, you can see that they are inferior. The vanity of their ambition is clear along with the inadequacy of their reach.

You know well whom I'm talking about, and I would tell you more if I had the time, but I have only enough [left] to assure you that I am,

Madam,
Your etc.

LETTER 54

She says that her letters serve as lessons for her
on how to write [well] and that she wishes she
had more wit in order to better imitate her.

Madam,

You are wrong to say that I will need more patience for your letters, since I had quite enough for your conversation. You must have a low opinion of me to think that I do not have a higher one of you. Although I don't have enough intelligence to understand the virtue of yours, that doesn't stop me from tasting its sweetness with extreme regret that I am not better educated in order to be happier.

---

7. Deliver, "debiter," also means to market or sell and so suggests a crass commercial transaction.

8. Icaruses: those with too much ambition—in Greek mythology, Icarus, son of Daedalus, the great inventor, died falling into the sea when he flew too high and the sun melted the wax that held together the feathers of his wings.

I admit that I will get more out of my acquaintance with you than you will from my approval [of you] and that I will gain more from your guidance than you will from my praise. But that doesn't matter—you have no cause to complain that I am not enlightened enough to admire the wit and refinement of your letters. At least I can show them to those who can better appreciate them and who can offer admiration more worthy than my own.

Please believe this, and do not stop writing to me, even if this person is not deserving of your letters. They will serve me as textbooks, and at least you will have this benefit: if I am lucky enough to be able to imitate you, the letters you receive from me will be more polished and more pleasing to you to the degree that they resemble your own. Maybe, little by little, I will become well educated in your school. And if I get used to calling you my beloved teacher,[9] I will have yet another reason to attribute to you this great quality and to call myself not only your pupil, but

Madam,

Your servant.

LETTER 56

She consoles her for the
death of one of her relatives.

Madam,

I just learned of the death of your good friend, which touches me greatly because she was such a worthy person and because you must be so distraught. I fear that the loss of her life will cause you to lose your sense of balance and that, by mourning her excessively, the strength of your spirit will give way to the intensity of your grief. Estimating your grief by your affection, or even more, by the unique qualities of the person you weep for, I hope, at least, that you will listen to those who try to console you. Moreover, I don't have any desire to furnish arguments [against your grief] but simply to beg you to think of the arguments that you give others when you see them suffer as you do now. Why can't you be as reasonable for yourself as you are for others? But if you have no consideration for your own interest, at least consider mine.

You had great affection for her, but must you have no more for me? Remember then that you love me and that you cannot suffer without causing me pain as well. Custom demands tears for her, but Reason demands moderation for your sake and for mine. If you continue your mourning, you will

9. "Maistresse," "teacher," and also "mistress" or "beloved"—a pun.

increase the cause for grief and you will have to weep for two instead of one. In order to put a stop to your tears, you need only realize that they won't bring her back to life and that they might make you lose me. The worry you feel for the living should be greater than the grief you feel for the dead.

If you are insensible to the arguments of Morality, don't be deaf to those of Christianity. [Your friend] requires prayers more than tears from you. Give those to her without making yourself sick. Your mourning is as useless to her as it is damaging to yourself. All the while that you sigh over her tomb, it would be better to be pouring holy water on it than your own tears. In weeping you testify to your pain, but in praying you will ease hers.[10] At the same time, I want [you to believe] that she is discharged of the debt that even the most just fear.[11] In the joy she is experiencing where she is, if she is capable of [feeling] displeasure, she will have no other cause than seeing you weep at her transformation from this life to a much better one. This being the case, try to recover your rationality, for you will not find it in an excess of grief.

You have often said that the world is full of crosses, and you have criticized the person who has escaped their share. Is this right, to weep for one of our friends who has broken out of her chains? Lamenting her death this way—isn't it like prisoners who are used to being together and cry when one of their companions is delivered [from prison]? Don't those who die leave their prison? Don't they escape captivity? Don't we believe that the righteous are happier in the other world than in this one? If this is so, compare your faith to your grief and you will see that they are inconsistent. Instead, think how it looks to shed so many tears, since they offend God and hurt your friends, since they are useless to those you mourn and destructive to your own peace.

You should consider whether you will allow yourself to be moved by our prayers, and above all, by the prayers made to you by,

        Madam,
        Your etc.

10. Seventeenth-century Roman Catholicism taught that souls usually spent time in Purgatory, paying through punishment for their sins, and Christians might shorten their dear friends' punishment by praying for them.

11. This is financial imagery for the burden of sins that must be paid for by good works, or by God's mercy (the son's death), in Roman Catholic theology.

FICTIONAL ORATIONS FROM
"FAMOUS WOMEN" (1665)[1]

MARIAM TO HEROD[2]

Argument

F ew people are unaware that Herod had his wife killed, but no one knows what she said in her defense. Of the two historians[3] who discuss her, one did not live during her time and the other was one of her husband's flatterers: therefore, it is our responsibility to look for the truth between the ignorance of the one and the malice of the other. Myself, I confess that I count myself on the side of Mariam and, whether through pity or through reason, whether blinded by her beauty or enlightened by her innocence, I say that I cannot believe that a princess descended from the illustrious and noble blood of the Maccabees[4] would have put such a blot on her reputation, and I would rather believe that Herod was always Herod, that is, unjust and bloodthirsty. Here, then, is a defense of this unfortunate beauty, who had more graciousness on her tongue than I do. Listen to her speak, I beg you, and observe her noble pride, the true characterization of the humor[5] of Mariam.

---

1. Translated from Madeleine de Scudéry, *Les femmes illustres, ou, Les harangues héroiques, de Mr de Scudéry* (Paris, 1665), 14–32.

2. The Herod of this historical speech is Herod the Great, the first of three Herods, whose sister was named Salome. It is a later Herod who kills John the Baptist and a legendary Salome who dances for his head.

3. The Renaissance knew the story of Mariam mainly through Josephus, *Jewish Wars* (69–79) and *Antiquities of the Jews* (ca. 93); another source was Joseph Ben Gorion's *Compendious . . . History of the Latter Tymes of the Jewes Commune Weale* (1558).

4. Judas Maccabeus led a rebellion of Jews against Antiochus IV of Syria in 167–166 B.C.E. Mariam is presumably descended from the rebels, the Maccabees.

5. Humor means character in this context. Greek and Renaissance science taught that people's personalities were determined by a preponderance of one of the four humors—earth or melancholy, fire or choler, air or sanguinity (blood), and water or phlegm.

Monster, who killed his innocent queen,
Monster, who loved her, bewitching and wise,
How terrible your hatred must have been
To throw away your greatest prize.[6]

MARIAM TO HEROD

It is neither fear of death nor desire for life that compels me to speak today and, were I assured that posterity would do me justice when I shall be no more, I myself would aid my accusers and my enemies, I would look on my

---

6. Literally—
      Monster, who killed this innocent queen,
      Whose heart adored this bewitching sage,
      How [terrible] the effect of your hatred
      That you put to death while loving.

last day as the beginning of my happiness, and I would await the hour of my agony with such constancy[7] that it would perhaps puzzle those who persecute me. But since they begrudge me my virtue as well as my life, it would be cowardice to suffer calumny without repelling it: innocence and renown are things so precious that they must be preserved at all cost. Be patient, then, my lord (if it is fitting for the daughter of Hircanus to so address you) while I recall to your memory, so that you may be made to see the purity of my soul, who you are and who I am, in order that, by comparing my past actions with the accusations now made against me, you may somehow prepare your spirit to believe the truths I must tell.

You have surely not forgotten that I come from that illustrious race that for many centuries has provided Judea's kings, that all my ancestors justly held the scepter you carry, that by birthright they wore the crown Fortune has placed on your head, and that, if things had gone according to accustomed order, so far from being my judge, I could have counted you among my subjects, and I might have legitimately claimed that power over you which you have usurped over me. Nevertheless, since this privileged birth enjoined me to an extraordinary virtue, Hircanus no sooner commanded me to be your wife than I, recognizing the obedience I owed to him, without considering the inequality between us, received you for my husband, and no matter how different my inclinations were from yours (thank heavens!), you know in what manner I have lived with you and whether or not you could have expected greater complacence or testimony of affection from me, even if alliance with you were just as honorable to me as mine was glorious to you.

Since then, my lord, until the loss of Hircanus, what have I done, what have I said, what have I thought against you? Nothing—unless it was that I was not able to rejoice in your conquests, because they were the funerals of my family; and [unless it was] that I have a heart as capacious as my birth is noble, so I have not been able to mount the throne without responding with tears, because I could not with justice do so, at least in the role of Herod's wife. But you know that at least I took care to hide my grief from you, even though unable to repress my sense of justice that reason and nature had given me.

I attempted during this time to justify you in my mind and, to the degree that you had ambition without cruelty, I pitied you more often than I blamed you. I termed this ambition the error of great souls and the infallible sign of a person born for great things. How many times have I said to myself

---

7. Constancy is the prime virtue of a Stoic: the ability not to be moved by emotions either negative or positive, but to take control of one's life by remaining unmoved.

that if Fortune had given you rightful enemies you would have been the greatest prince in the world? How many times have I wished that this grand and marvelous spirit you have, that this invincible courage that leads you to attempt all things, might carry you against people over whom you might be "conqueror" and not usurper? Alas! if you only knew all the wishes I have made for your glory, you would not believe me capable of having planned to tarnish it by forgetting my own! But perhaps it is for this fault that the Heavens punish me: I was not able to wish that I had not done it, and even though today I find myself in danger of losing my life, I am not able to repent preserving you by my advice, when, against all the signs, you wished to trust that traitor Barsaphane. I do not wish to reproach you with this good deed, but rather to make you remember it, to make you see that I have always done all that I have been able to. Since then, I admit, I have not always lived thus: I have no longer hidden my tears; I have no longer smothered my voice; I have wept, I have cried, I have spewed forth my complaints and my sobs. But how could the granddaughter of Hircanus do less, who went to his death by your order and your cruelty? How could the sister of young Aristobulus do less, I say, who perished because of your inhumanity, in order to confirm the scepter in your hands? Oh! No, no! Patience would have been criminal in this situation.

I was without doubt born for the throne, but I did not want to mount it since I could not do so without climbing over the corpses of my grandfather and my brother. The throne was dripping with their blood; I had to wash it at least with my tears, since I was not permitted to repay their enemy. Alas! As I remember, what a sight worthy of compassion was that, to see the successor of so many kings, that venerable old man, take his death at the hands of the man he had welcomed into alliance![8] I tremble in horror only to think of it, and I would not be capable of turning my thoughts away from it if the image of young Aristobulus did not offer itself, instead, to my eyes. What had this unfortunate [boy] done to merit his misery? He was young, he was virtuous, he was a model [young man] in all ways, and his greatest fault, no doubt, was to resemble me.

But alas! That fault should have been an advantage to him then, for if it were true that you possessed this overwhelming love for me that you have tried to persuade me was always in your heart, even if Aristobulus were not my brother, even if Aristobulus were not innocent, you should have cherished my likeness in him. A resemblance to a loved one has made weapons

8. Marriage was seen as an alliance between two men, the passing of the woman from one man to another, from father (or in this case, grandfather) to husband.

fall from the hands of the most cruel and caused them to change their intentions. But I must be out of my mind to speak in this way to him who wishes to take my own life, who, not satisfied to have overturned the throne of my fathers, to have killed my grandfather, drowned my brother, and exterminated my whole family, wishes today also to carry away my honor by accusing me unjustly of three crimes, none of which I could ever be capable!

I have been so unaccustomed to committing such practices, and I am so innocent of those I am charged with, that I doubt myself if I can correctly remember all the accusations made against me. Nevertheless, I think my enemies say that I sent my portrait to Antony, that I had too intimate a relationship with Joseph, and that I tried to make an attempt on your life. O Heavens! Is it possible that Mariam is obliged to respond to such things, and is it not enough merely to say that it is Mariam who is accused to realize that she is innocent? No, I am well aware that, without my remembering either my rank or my virtue, I must put myself in the situation of being unjustly condemned, because I am of such a class that I am unused to accounting for my actions except to God alone; nevertheless, I must justify myself before my accusers, my enemies, and my judges—[who are] all one.

You say, then, that I sent a portrait to Antony,[9] whom I do not know at all, and who had never seen me and, without noting any circumstances, even though he was at the time in Egypt, you nevertheless expect this accusation to be taken as a reliable truth.[10] But tell me a little more. Who is the painter who fashioned it? Who is the person who delivered it? Who are the people to whom Antony showed it? Where are the letters he wrote me thanking me for so great a favor—for it is unbelievable that he received such an extraordinary testimony of my affection without thanking me for it. The heart of Mariam is not a conquest so inglorious that there were not kings of the earth willing to do impossible feats to merit it. However, there remains no sign of the care Antony took to win me, or to keep me—and certainly, at that time, I would not only have had to forget my glorious reputation but also entirely to lose my reason in order even to dream of such a crime as I have been accused of. For if this were that time when you were doing everything for him, even so far as sending him all the jewels [in your treasury] and opposing the entire Roman empire in support of him, I would have been a trifle injudicious in my choice. And I cannot believe that Antony, who prides himself on his

9. Marcus Antonius, Mark Antony (83–31 B.C.E.), Roman statesman and general, co-consul with Julius Caesar, one of the triumvirate with Lepidus and Octavian, famous lover of Cleopatra, defeated by Octavian, committed suicide.

10. Antony was with Cleopatra in Egypt and therefore not with Mariam or available to her.

generosity, would have betrayed a man to whom he was so indebted for a person he did not know at all. Or, if it was when you were not allied, because of the manipulations of Cleopatra, there was even less reason to think I did it: for I would have been very ill advised to give myself into the arms of the very enemy (for during this time, your interests were still mine). And then, what likelihood was there, even if I were as wicked as I am innocent, that, during this time when the whole world echoed with the love of Antony and Cleopatra, I would have sent him my portrait? Would Rome have found [my gift] expedient to cure him of the charms of that gypsy?[11] Would the empire have needed such a remedy, or would I have wished to sacrifice myself to the vanity of that unfortunate princess, whose jealousy—do not doubt—would have exploded to the high heavens? No, Herod. None of that has happened, and the innocence of Mariam is so apparent that even her enemies cannot attribute believable crimes to her.

And yet, you know I have never prided myself on this so-called beauty of mine, and I have always taken more pains to be virtuous than beautiful. I do not deny, however, that there was a portrait of Mariam, which has passed among all the princes of the world and will perhaps be preserved there a long time. Yes, Herod, there is an invisible image of Mariam, which travels through the world, making innocent conquests, and which, without her consent, makes you secret enemies. Her high birth, her virtue, her patience, and your cruelty are the only paints that are used in this portrait, and the blood that I shall shed will without doubt fix this painting to be adored by posterity.

But, to respond to the second accusation that has been made against me, which, though false, does not prevent me from blushing because of the confusion I feel in being forced to speak of such a thing, I say with joy that, thanks be to heaven, there is no other witness against me except you, who, during the time of the supposed crime, were at Laodicea and consequently were incapable of testifying to my actions. Moreover, I am well assured that neither your eyes nor your ears could know anything to report against my innocence and that, despite your court being composed of your slaves or my enemies, despite even your sister who hates me out of envy and selfish desire for my place, who with extraordinary care has spied on the least little thing I have done or said, I am still certain, I proclaim, that she would not

---

11. The French word here is "Egyptienne," which would translate into English as "Egyptianesse"; as it carries overtones of sarcasm, we have chosen Shakespeare's word for Cleopatra, "gypsy," as an appropriate translation, since in Scudéry's time period people still believed the gypsies to be descended from Egyptians.

dare in my presence to maintain that she has heard a single word or seen a single glance that might cast suspicion on the modesty of Mariam. I know very well that she can tell a lie, but I speak with so much boldness because I know I have more virtue than she has malice and, having heaven as my protector, I am not able to believe that, even if I should die, I would not be given the grace to die in such a fashion that your injustice and my innocence will both be equally obvious.

And certainly, even now, you only have to open your eyes to see that these accusations brought against me are simply pretexts to ruin me. For what likelihood is there, even if I were capable of such a crime, that I would have chosen the confidant of Herod and the husband of Salome, my cruelest enemy? And a confidant to whom all things were confided, so that there were no wicked plots that were not communicated to him. He was a partner in all these crimes. He was the jailer and not the lover of Mariam, and, to speak frankly, it was up to him to plunge the dagger in my heart in order to obey your wishes.

O Heaven! Who ever saw such a testimony of love! Herod, how could you at parting say good-bye to me with tears? How could you look at me, as you have done, with eyes full of affection, and at the same time plan my death? Oh, if you could [do so] (which I do not at all doubt), then you also could now pretend to believe me guilty in order to see me die, despite my innocence. And please, do not tell me that this demand was a result of the overpowering passion you had for me: the death of the person you love can never be a sign of affection. Hate and love do not have the same effects: they can sometimes reign one after the other in a heart, but never together. A man who loves well is unable to live without the beloved but is perhaps able to die without her; and the thought of losing her would never be a happy one. He would regret being separated from her but not regret that she does not die with him. But you have a unique fashion of loving, and your disposition is naturally so cruel that poisons and daggers are the most agreeable gifts one can expect from you when you desire to demonstrate your love.

Tell me, please, how you are able to account for these [contradictory] things. You say that I sent my portrait to Antony and that as a consequence I have a relationship with him, and, at the same time, you accuse me also of having another one with Joseph, because, you say, you entrusted to him that which you thought most important, and since he disclosed it to me, it is therefore impossible that I would not have given myself absolutely to him in order to repay him for this revelation. Do you understand, Herod, what you are saying? Could Antony and Joseph both together occupy my heart? Were these two rivals of equal birth and merit? And Mariam, whose birth is so grand and illustrious, whose soul is so proud and so glorious that some take her noble pride for a fault rather than a virtue—would she have been capable of such a weakness for two men so different, who had no similarity to each other, other than that they were equally unable to touch my heart when they attempted it? Such a conquest is not as easy as you think—and certainly it astonishes me that you who have never been able to achieve [this conquest] would judge that it would take so little effort on the part of others.

I swear that Joseph revealed to me the evil plan you had for me, but I also swear that I did not believe it at all. I thought at first that it was the treacherous Salome[12] who (in order to make me rebel more stridently against you to hasten my fall) would have thought up such a plot—as if my own death would touch me more than those that had passed already, that of Hircanus and that of my brother. And what made me believe it even more was that I saw that he tried to persuade me that I should be infinitely obliged to you for this excessive love, which you testified to on that occasion, joined also to the fact that he told me about the plot only after you were ready to return and, far from making it a mysterious secret, he told me about it in the presence of my mother and before all my women.[13]

It is true that while I still expected something from you I doubted the truth Joseph told me. I thought that because I was the mother of your children you would have been incapable of such barbaric thoughts, and indeed, without resolving this feeling in my soul, I awaited your return. I received you then with the same melancholy I continually suffered after the loss of Hircanus and Aristobulus, without showing increased sadness; and, observing all your actions, I vowed that I always doubted the truth of Joseph's words. The evil of his wife[14] made me even more suspicious, and when I talked with you, I certainly intended more to clear things up than to reproach you. For it is true that I felt a singular affection for Joseph and that I received what he told me as purely the result of his compassion for me; I would sooner have died than he had spoken about it, and then that unfortunate man would still be alive.

But look at all the tokens of goodwill I gave him: no one says that we engaged in any very private business together; no one says that he often came to my apartments; and finally, I have done nothing for him except what his most cruel enemy could have done if she had known the same thing— certainly, I have poorly repaid him if I used him in that manner. You still say

12. See note 1. Salome was Herod's sister.
13. Ladies in waiting.
14. Salome was married to Joseph.

that hatred and vengeance made me give my favors to Joseph, after I knew your design. But you [must] realize that great souls never transgress [merely] by example. The crimes of someone else yield them such horror that they are never more strongly confirmed in virtue than when they observe the commission of evil. And for my part, I think I would have been less innocent if you had been less guilty. Finally, in conclusion, if Mariam, descended from so many illustrious kings, would have wished to give her affection to someone, it would never have been Salome's husband or Herod's favorite; and if she were capable of punishing anyone's crimes, she would not have caused the death of the one who she believed wished to preserve her life.

You know too well my astonishment when, after my speech to you was done, I understood from your response that all was true: I was so surprised that I nearly lost my ability to speak. Nevertheless, I did not foresee the accusation that today is made against me. The knowledge alone of your crime and of the innocence of Joseph, whom I exposed to your cruelty, caused all my grief. Since then, Salome, profiting from my misfortune in order to ruin me (as she has planned for a long time), has doubtless persuaded you that I wished to make an attempt on your life, and here is the only crime for which there is a witness against me. But if I am not deceived, she vindicates me more than she convicts me. For what likelihood is there that in a design of this importance I would have trusted a man of such base character? And how credible is it—if it is true that I had an understanding with Joseph—that it was by me rather than by him that this proposal was made? Have I usually consorted with such people? Would such a man come to my apartments? Have I placed him beside you? Has he been to my home? Is he the kinsman of one of my officers? In what place did I speak to him? In what fashion did I bribe him? Let him show the jewels I have given him; let him display the silver he received for this great plot—for it is not reasonable to suppose that merely on faith he would undertake to hazard his life. He will answer, perhaps, that since he did not plan to do this thing, and on the contrary he wished to warn you, he did not think of recompense. But I have to say to this impostor that, not to give me any room to suspect him, he always would have accepted what I would have offered him, and that, also, [my] not having spoken at all [with him] and [my] not having seen [him] are powerful and convincing testimonies to his lying. For, in the end, gold is the accomplice of all crimes. Hope alone is the reward of great souls, but the base and the mercenary require to be moved by the sight of a certain recompense; otherwise, that sort of people will not serve you at all—and there are far too many examples from your reign that should have taught you what I claim.

Although it is true that no one is able to make it appear that neither I myself nor any of my people have had any intercourse with that man, it is not equally so of Salome, your bosom buddy and my enemy. Quite a while ago, my women alerted me that, contrary to the propriety and decorum expected of one of the rank she holds today, he often would go to converse with her even in her boudoir. However, because I could never stoop to mount surveillance over such things, and because of [my own] excess of virtue, I did not automatically suspect others; I heard that story without considering what it meant. But if you would require them to take into account how many conversations they had together, I am certain you would find that they would not answer exactly. And then, in what place did I get the poison? Who prepared it? Where was I when I sent for it? And why, if I had this intention, was it necessary to employ this man? Was it not easy for me, during so many different occasions when we dined together, to poison you with my own hand, without confiding in anybody else? Why would I not have attempted the same thing at your return from Laodicea as someone pretends I did after your return from Rhodes, since the unhappy Joseph had revealed to me by then your cruel intentions, just as the unfortunate Soemus[15] has told me since then? Finally, Herod, all these things are beyond belief. And there is no person so lacking in intelligence who cannot well see that were I not descended from the kings of Judea and were I not virtuous, then I would have no enemies and my death would not be already determined—I would not have sent my portrait to Antony, I would not have had an understanding with Joseph, I would not have made an attempt on your life, and, consequently, my life would have been secure. But because I am descended from a bloodline too illustrious and because my soul is too proud to suffer the meannesses and cowardice of my enemies, Mariam must die. She must perish; she must be sacrificed to the hatred of her persecutors—they desire it so, and she is resolved to it.

Do not think, unjust and cruel Herod, that I consequently speak with the intention of moving you to pity; I hope to preserve my reputation and not to touch your heart. For as I said at the beginning of my speech, it is neither the fear of death nor the desire for life that makes me speak today. The former does nothing but prepare me to be crowned [in heaven]; the other has provided me nothing but torture. Thus it is not at all the hope of escaping from the danger I am in that makes me take care to justify myself; I know that my sentence is signed, that my executioners are even now ready

---

15. Soemus was a counselor of Herod who was supposed to kill Mariam if Herod failed to return from his visit to Caesar but instead warned Mariam and so was executed for disloyalty.

to strike off my head, and that my tomb is already gaping to receive me. But what moved me to speak is this purpose, that all who heard me would be able to convey to posterity that my enemies, even with all their malice, were not able to blacken Mariam's virtue or to find any plausible pretext to condemn her. If I obtain this favor from those who hear me, I die almost without pain; and I would say absolutely without regret, if the children whom I leave you were banished from their paternal home, for I do not doubt at all that because they are virtuous they will not be tainted by your hatred as I was not. The complaints they will make about my death—these will be [seen as] crimes against you: you will suppose they are plotting against your life when they complain against the loss of mine. Alas! I see them already maltreated by that slave who was your first wife; I see them subjected to the violent temper of your son Antipater, to the calumny of Salome, to the outrages of Pheroras,[16] and to your own cruelty. And perhaps those same executioners who will put me to death will spill their blood, or, more accurately, finish off spilling mine.

I already see you, unjust and cruel, at the end of so many murders; but do not hope to enjoy peaceably the fruits of so many deadly victories. You search for a peace that you will not find. You will be your own prosecutor, your own judge, and your own executioner. The ghosts of the many kings I am descended from, outraged by your [treatment of] their descendant, will surround you on all sides: those of the ancient Hircanus and of the young Aristobulus will disturb your entire life; you will always see yourself covered with the blood of your children; and the image of Mariam pursued by the executioners who await her will follow you every step you take. Whether awake or asleep, you will always see her, reproaching you for her death; you will bear in your heart repentance, shame, confusion, and despair; you will long for the death that you have given to others. Then my virtue will appear to you as pure as it is, and your crimes will seem as great as they are. But you will experience the grief of repentance without reformation. And I do not doubt, after you have broken all laws, human and divine, that someone will similarly break them—on your own head. Yes, I already see the oldest of your children—for mine would never be capable of this [atrocity]—planning to give you that poison that you have unjustly accused me of [using]. I see (I say) all the agents of your rage becoming your cruelest enemies: Salome, Pheroras, and Antipater will be most eager to destroy you. I see you hated by all your people, detested by all princes, cursed by posterity. And perhaps you will then become so odious to yourself that, after you have spilled all

16. Pheroras was Herod's brother.

the blood of your race, despair will put a dagger in your hand to deliver the world from so dangerous an enemy. But perhaps you will not be able to end it when you desire to, and you will have the misfortune to suffer in this life the torments that are prepared for you in the other. Behold, unjust and cruel Herod, the prediction that the unhappy Mariam makes for you, Mariam, dying unjustly, who on this last day regards you more as a subject revolting [against her], or as a tyrant, than as her king or her husband.

The Effect of This Oration

This beautiful and generous victim obtained all that she demanded from her husband and from posterity: for the former gave her death, and the other preserved her glory. I will think my fame great if, after so many centuries, I can contribute something to hers and if my reflections are not thought unworthy of her. I would say more if the author of the holy court[17] had not said all, but as he was too careful to leave nothing in this beautiful field, I am too vain to appear uselessly on it after him. It suffices that I behold his Triumph without his tying me to his chariot, and I prefer to give up my weapons than to see him among his trophies.

SOPHONISBA TO MASINISSA [18]

Argument

When, with the help of the Romans, Masinissa had retaken the kingdom of his forefathers and had made Syphax, who had usurped it, his prisoner, he besieged and conquered the town of Syrte, where Sophonisba, wife of the captive king, had withdrawn. The charms of this beautiful African made a strong impression on his heart, and, the Numidians being naturally of a passionate disposition, he was no sooner victorious than he felt himself vanquished. Reflecting on the stern humor of Scipio, however, Masinissa was certain that he would have the beautiful captive queen led in triumph, to

17. See note 2.

18. From *Les femmes illustres*, 64–76. Masinissa was king of the eastern Numidian Massyles and served with the Carthaginians against the Romans in Spain until won over by Scipio. Sophonisba, daughter of Hasdrubal, a Carthaginian general, was married to Syphax, chief of a Numidean tribe in northern Africa; when the Romans defeated her husband, she took poison, according to legend, sent to her by Masinissa (who had fallen in love with her) when he could find no other way to save her from capture.

prevent which he married her the same day, believing that after this no one would dare to triumph over the wife of a king allied to the Roman people. But no sooner were these hurried nuptials finished than Scipio, being informed about them, sent Laelius to order Masinissa to come to him to render an account of his victory. But Sophonisba, who naturally feared the Romans, but [feared] slavery even more, having seen something in the eyes of Laelius threatening a Triumph, spoke in this way to Masinissa when he was about to leave her.

O what a gift, my God, to take!
O what a curtain call to make!
Myself, I know no way to know
Whose punishment more bitter is:
She who takes the poison, so,

Or she who suffers what he plans.
The more I dread these choices here,
The more I see reason to fear.[19]

My Lord,

I plainly perceive by Laelius's proceedings that Fortune is not yet weary
of persecuting me: after having in one single day lost my crown, my husband,
and my liberty and, through the caprice of that inconstant one,[20] having on
that same day returned to me my liberty, a famous husband, and a crown,
I plainly perceive, I say, after such incredibly strange events, that she is yet
ready to make me lose all again.

Looking at me, Laelius has no doubt judged me sufficiently well formed
to grace Scipio's Triumph and follow his chariot. I saw in his eyes the image
of what he carries in his mind and the design that he bears in his heart. But
perhaps he has not detected what I have in mine. He does not know that the
desire for liberty is much stronger in me than [the desire] for life and that in
order to preserve the first I am capable of forfeiting the other with joy. Yes,
I clearly perceive, my dear Masinissa, that you are going to have to combat
powerful enemies: Scipio's stern humor combined with Roman severity will
without doubt provoke a strong reprimand. He will find it strange that, on
the exact day of the victory, on the exact day when you had regained the
crown that belonged to you, you would think of marriage and choose for
your wife not only the wife of your enemy but also a captive, a Carthaginian,
a daughter of Hasdrubal, and an enemy of Rome.

Nevertheless, my lord, remember that you must regard me at this time
neither as the wife of Syphax, nor a captive, nor a Carthaginian, nor the
daughter of Hasdrubal, nor an enemy of Rome—although I glory in being
so—but as the wife of the famous Masinissa. Remember also that I did not
consent to receive that honor until after you had promised that I would not

---

19. Literally—

>   O what a present to receive!
>   O good God, what an appearance to make!
>   For my part, I do not know how to know
>   Whose punishment is more bitter:
>   Whether hers who takes the poison
>   Or hers who suffers that which he devises,
>   And the more my heart considers these choices,
>   The more I suspect I have reason to fear.

Note that in French, "present" and "appearance" are the same word, *présent*, so there is an ironic
pun in the first two lines.

20. That is, Fortune.

fall under the power of the Romans. You have given your word; do not dream of failing. I do not at all ask that you risk losing the friendship of the Senate in order to save me, because your misfortune has caused you to need it; but I only desire that, according to what you have sworn to me, you prevent me from falling under the power of Scipio.

I do not doubt at all that Syphax, in his situation, will say to his conqueror that it was I who was the cause of his downfall, that it was I who loaded him with irons, that it was I who made him a friend to Carthage and an enemy to Rome. Yes, generous Masinissa, I admit all these things. And if I could steal you away from the Romans, I would count myself happy and would believe that my death were truly worthy of the daughter of Hasdrubal. Forgive me, my dear Masinissa, if I speak to you with such boldness, but since this is perhaps the last time I shall ever see you, I shall take the freedom to tell you what my sentiments have always been, so that by your knowledge of the aversion I have always had to slavery, you will more easily be induced to keep in mind my liberty.

As soon as I had opened my eyes to the light, the first thing I learned was that there was a nation that, without any right except that which the strong imposes on the weak, desired to make itself the master of all the others. And all through my childhood I heard of nothing except the Triumphs[21] of the Romans: the kings they had bound with chains, the famous captives they had taken, the misery of these unfortunate people, and all the humiliations enacted in those morbid spectacles where the pride of the Romans is defined by the noblest spoils of their victories. These images were imprinted so early in my imagination that nothing might ever drive them away.

Since then, becoming more reasonable with age, I had even more aversion to the Roman eagle, which lives only by means of the destruction it causes and which flies above the heads of kings only to carry off their crowns. You may say, perhaps, that the Romans give away as many kingdoms as they usurp and that they raise up as many kings as they chain to their chariots. But my dear Masinissa, if you would rightly consider these matters, you will find that they give scepters only in order to have more illustrious slaves and that they put crowns on the heads of their vassals only to have the pleasure of seeing them laid at their feet, for at their command [these kings] must pay them homage.

---

21. After a victory, Romans celebrated with a Triumph honoring the victorious general—he entered Rome in a parade and processed to the Temple of Jupiter on the Capitol, displaying his captives as symbols of the lands he had conquered for the Empire.

Vanity is the soul of that nation. It is the only thing that calls it into action. It is only for [vanity] that [Rome] makes conquests, that she usurps kingdoms, that she lays waste the whole world, and, not content to be absolute mistress of the large part of the universe that is her continent, she crosses the seas in order to trouble our peace. For if it was only the desire to extend her boundaries and to increase her wealth that caused her to go to war, she would be content to overturn thrones and put to death those who legitimately possessed them. But because it is pride that causes her to do these things, a simple citizen of Rome, for his glory and for the entertainment of the people, must drag kings in chains after his chariot of Triumph. O God! Is it possible that there exist conquerors as inhuman as that? And is it possible that there exist conquered kings weak enough to endure such cruel usage? Yes, no doubt. And too many examples of this kind have demonstrated that all princes are not generous. Nevertheless, it is certain that irons and crowns, scepters and chains are things that should never be seen together: a chariot drawn by elephants should not be followed by kings,[22] and kings should not be bound like criminals, deprived of any sign of royalty in order to signal their shame and the glory of their conqueror.

But what glory does he have who triumphs in this way? For if those whom he overcomes are cowards (as is suggested by the fact that they are alive), there is no reason to be proud to have surmounted them. And if these unfortunate people proved their courage in their defeat, it shows great inhumanity in him who thus treats princes who have done nothing but defend their crowns, their countries, their wives, their children, their subjects, and their household gods.

For if they wanted Triumphs for the glory of their conquerors and the pleasure of the people, it would be more glorious for them to parade with the weapons of those enemies they have killed with their own hands than to have them followed by kings whom they have not encountered in combat. Chariots, each filled with the broken weapons, the shields, the lances, the javelins, the standards seized from their adversaries, would be a spectacle less morbid and more agreeable to the eyes of the people.

But O ye gods! How is it possible that kings must be destined for something so degrading? That these same people who are diverted by fights between gladiators and wild beasts would also require this morbid ceremony and derive their pleasure from the shame and misfortune of kings? That these

---

22. In the Renaissance, the person of highest rank walked first into a room or in a parade, so a king following an elephant (or a mere Roman citizen) violates the hierarchy, the social order.

[same people] would delight in seeing four thousand men kill each other in the same day with horrible brutality and find pleasure in seeing tigers and lions devour each other—how is it possible, I say, that for these same people conquered kings must be dragged in irons?

For my part, my dear Masinissa, I find something so strange in this sort of Triumph that I question whether it is more shameful to the vanquished or the victorious, and I myself know well that I would not do either one. Judge, then, my dear Masinissa, whether a person who would not agree to enter Rome in a chariot of triumph followed by a hundred kings in chains could agree to follow in irons [the chariot] of the arrogant Scipio. No, Sophonisba possesses a soul too great for that. If I were but a Carthaginian [citizen], I would not be capable of it; if I were but Hasdrubal's daughter, I could never resolve to do it; if I were merely the wife of the unfortunate Syphax, such a weakness would never contaminate my soul; and if I were but the slave of the illustrious Masinissa, I would not follow any other conqueror.

But since I am all of these—a Carthaginian, the daughter of Hasdrubal, the wife of Syphax and of Masinissa, and queen of two great kingdoms—let Scipio not expect to triumph over Sophonisba. No, generous Masinissa, even if the chains given me were diamonds and my irons all glittered with gold and gems, even if I were assured to be restored to my throne as soon as I was detached from the triumphal chariot, I would choose death over royalty. And if my hand had carried irons, I would no longer consider it worthy to carry a scepter. Indeed, I have so strong an aversion to servitude and slavery, and my soul is so sensitive in such matters, that if I thought Scipio would have even my portrait carried in the Triumph, I would pray you to put to death all the painters in Numidia. But no, I condemn myself for that thought. For if the insensitive Scipio did carry my portrait in his entrance into Rome, it would proclaim my glory more than his—anyone would be able to see that I knew how to die when I could no longer live with honor, and [anyone would be able to see] that the courage of a woman may surpass the vanity of Rome.

I do not doubt at all, generous Masinissa, that if you do not with all your force oppose Scipio's severity, you will be forced to grant me death in order to keep your promise, for besides the public interest, there is also a particular interest of his own. He remembers that his father and his uncle were killed in Africa; he regards me as a suitable sacrifice to appease the spirits of the dead. Moreover, the glory of Rome and his vengeance joining together in his heart make it unbelievable that the daughter of Hasdrubal could obtain her freedom. It seems to me, however, generous Masinissa, that it would be entirely unjust if, on the same day that you recovered the crown of Numidia, your wife should be tied to the triumphal chariot. It seems to me that that would make you at the same time king and slave. If it is true (as you have told me) that my misery and my tears, joined to the little beauty I have, have touched your soul and forced you to love me as much as yourself, then that would be as much a triumph over you as over me. Consider well, Masinissa, if you would be able to be a spectator on that day, and if you doubt me worthy of the honor you have done me in marrying me, whether I would be capable of bringing you such shame.

But do not fear that I will expose you to such suffering. If Scipio is inexorable, and if you keep your word that you have given me, my death will justify the choice you have made.[23] Nevertheless, before resorting to such an extreme remedy, do everything that you can to touch the heart of that unfeeling [Scipio]. Tell him that I have given myself wholly to you; that of all the booty your valor has acquired for the Roman people, you ask only one slave from him.

But if his injustice should oblige you to deliver me into his hands, as if you were the basest soldier of his legions, tell him then that this slave is your wife, that no one can triumph over her without triumphing over you, and that the blood you have shed in service of the Republic deserves the gift of permitting her to live in freedom. Explain to him that you have placed her in your kingdom, in your palace, on your throne; that she belongs to you with good reason; and that she cannot be taken away from you without injustice. If these powerful reasons do not touch him, tenderly plead with him, but finally, if you are not able to sway him to pity, remember your word, and do not allow me to be taken.

I see clearly in your eyes, my dearest Masinissa, that it will grieve you to give me such a morbid gift. I see clearly, I say, that it will pain you to send poison to the same person to whom you have given a diadem, your heart, and freedom. I know well that it is a chilling thought, and that it will be very difficult to see the same torches that lighted our marriage service light my funeral, and this same hand that you gave me as pledge of your faith open a tomb for me. But in the end you will find all these things more bearable (if you are as generous as I believe) than to see me loaded with chains.

Those who say that true generosity consists in suffering fatal accidents with constancy and that to quit life in order to avoid misfortune (according to their opinion) is yielding victory to Fortune, these people, I say, do not know the true glory of princes. Such sentiments are suitable for philosophers but not for kings, whose every action should be a heroic example

23. That is, Sophonisba would prove worthy of Masinissa's choosing her as his wife by committing suicide to prevent his dishonor.

of courage. But if departing from life is allowed (which I do not doubt), it must certainly be when one can avoid the shame of being led in triumph.

It is a great misfortune to a king when his subjects revolt, but if he then would dream of taking his life, I would judge him a coward, because he might yet fight and punish them. It is a great misfortune to a prince to have lost a battle, but because it is often seen that those who are vanquished today are tomorrow victorious, it is necessary to hold firm and not abandon oneself to despair. Indeed, all misfortunes that can have an honorable remedy should not impel us to take refuge in the tomb. But when all is lost and there remains no other choice but chains or death, we must break the bonds that attach us to life in order to escape those of bondage.

There you have it, my dear Masinissa, all that I had to say to you. Remember what I have said, I beg you, and do not listen so much to what Scipio will say to you that you forget your promise and what I have just told you. It is so just and reasonable (if I am not mistaken) that you cannot disapprove. Go, then, my dear, beloved Masinissa. Go fight for my liberty and for your glory against the unfeeling Scipio. Ask his pardon if, after refusing to look at the beautiful prisoners he made in his most recent conquests, he would wish to see tied to his chariot a woman whose looks had the power to conquer Masinissa. Let him fear that I will be his conqueror rather than he mine, and let him know that the stern virtue of his profession will help him to refrain from the desire to triumph over me.

You may easily see, my dear Masinissa, that my mind is not confused and that I speak to you with great calm. I assure you that in the situation I find myself in I regret nothing except being forced to be separated from you so soon. That is the only thing, without doubt, that can still touch my heart, for after having seen my country laid waste, Syphax made a prisoner, the crown fallen from my head, and what is still worse, Sophonisba about to be Scipio's captive—after all these things, I say, a tomb would be refuge and resting place to me, could I but enter there without abandoning you.

But I have this consolation in my misery, that having ever maintained irreconcilable hatred to Roman tyranny, I have at least this advantage: to have been the captive of a Numidian and not a Roman, and more, a Numidian who is my husband and my liberator, whose slave I no sooner was than I became absolute mistress of his soul. Go, then, my dear Masinissa, and do not fail to keep your word to the unfortunate Sophonisba, who will be waiting with great impatience either for freedom or for poison.

The Effect of This Speech

This beautiful and pitiable queen obtained what she asked, because Masinissa obtained nothing from Scipio. Masinissa sent her to death because he could not preserve her freedom without danger [to himself]. And this coward preferred his own interest, and his alliance with the Romans, to the life of this generous person! I would have tolerated his having sacrificed her to preserve his glory if he could not have done otherwise. But this gallant man lived eighty years after this loss and remained a Roman ally. This is what makes me angry at him every time I read about this in history, and it is also what now silences me, for if I write any more I will be forced to insult him. Pity Sophonisba with me, my dear reader, and since I am trying to amuse you, be obliging and do not approve the action of the unfeeling and entirely too prudent Masinissa.

ZENOBIA TO HER DAUGHTERS[24]

Argument

You may easily see, in this speech and the preceding one, that there are two sides to everything and that through different paths you arrive at the same end—I mean at virtue. Sophonisba chooses to die, the valiant Zenobia chooses to live: and both live and die by the principles of generosity. The one regards liberty as the chief good, the other believes that the chief good is sovereign wisdom. The one could not endure the idea of a chariot because she believed it shameful to those who followed it; the other followed the chariot almost without suffering because she believed nothing to be shameful except crime. The one saw the triumph of a conqueror with despair as the supreme disgrace; the other considered it with disdain as the caprice of Fortune. The one died; the other lived. The one sought glory where the other saw ignominy, and yet, as I have said, both took virtue as their object: so true is it that there are different sides to everything, depending on the bias with which one views them. You have heard the reasons of the one; now listen to those of the other, and judge them both.

24. From *Les femmes illustres*, 77–94. On the death of her husband, protecting her young son's right to the throne, Zenobia took over rule of Palmyra in 267 C.E. In 270, she conquered Egypt and much of Asia Minor. Aurelian attacked her in 272, and it is likely that she was paraded in Aurelian's Triumph.

To follow the chariot without fainting, as if crowned;
To see scepter and irons, without perishing from hate;
To teach constancy to the one who offers shame;
That is to vanquish Fortune and triumph o'er Fate.[25]

ZENOBIA TO HER DAUGHTERS

It has been a long time, dear and unfortunate princesses, that I have been
seeing these useless tears falling; it has been in vain that my constancy has
demonstrated that great spirits are able to endure great grief without despair:
the images of the throne you lost and of the chariot you followed haunt your
memory, rendering my example impotent and lending all the days of your

---

25. The literal translation follows:
>   To follow a chariot without fainting, with a crown;
>   To see a scepter and irons, without perishing from worry;
>   To teach constancy, to the one who offers these things;
>   That is to vanquish Fortune and triumph over her.

lives renewed affliction. You still carry on your hearts the chains you carried on your hands that fatal day when you entered Rome, and without losing any of that noble pride that illustrious birth inspires in those who are born with that advantage, Aurelian triumphs over you every time you remember his Triumph.[26] I am very distressed, O my daughters, that, having caused you to be companions in my disgrace, I have been unable to pass on to you the constancy necessary to endure it. That is, however, the only inheritance that I am able to leave you as I die, and I wish with all my affection that this virtue might pass from my heart to yours, so that, being unable to live as queens, you might yet reign over your selves.

If anyone ought with good reason to despair because of an excess of adversity, it is certain that Zenobia could have, for just as she has possessed more glory than any of her sex had ever before obtained, so also her misfortune has been more lamentable than anyone has ever before heard of. You know that on my side you may count the Ptolemies,[27] the kings of Egypt, among your ancestors, and ultimately I am descended from the illustrious blood of Cleopatra.[28] But alas! You might say that the chariot of triumph that Augustus[29] designed for her has passed on to me by right of succession and that I am simply following [the chariot] that was prepared for her.

Yet Fortune has treated me with greater inhumanity, for, as you well know, I followed a chariot that I considered mine to guide, and I had had it made with the plan to triumph over him who triumphed over me. You know as well that the beginning of my life was full of bliss: the valiant Odenatus, your father and my dear lord,[30] after having given me the crown of Palmyra,[31] wished also for me to share with him in the glory of his conquests. And I can say without arrogance and without wronging that great man that, if he gave to Zenobia the crown she wore, she also with her own hand added leaves to the wreath of laurel[32] that Victory had placed on her head. Yes, my

26. Lucius Domitius Aurelianus, Roman emperor, 270–275 C.E.

27. Ptolemy is the family name of all the Macedonian kings of ancient Egypt.

28. Cleopatra VII of Egypt (69–30 B.C.E.), ally of Pompey who expelled her, reinstated and supported by Julius Caesar, eventually partner with Mark Antony, to whom she bore several children, attacked by Augustus Caesar in 31 B.C.E., and committed suicide after Antony's death—supposedly the most beautiful woman in the world, loved by both Julius Caesar and Mark Antony.

29. C. Octavius Augustus (63 B.C.E.—14 C.E.), great-nephew of Julius Caesar and his heir, one of the triumvirate with Lepidus and Mark Antony, he overthrew Antony and became sole emperor after Lepidus's downfall.

30. Polite term for husband.

31. Palmyra was an oasis between Syria and Babylonia and thus guarded trade routes; it ruled the East under Zenobia and was made part of the Roman Empire by Aurelian.

32. A crown of laurel signified a conqueror in Roman celebrations.

daughters, I am able to say, without offending the memory of Odenatus, that we would have conquered the whole East. And fired by a legitimate anger, we undertook to take revenge on the Persians for the indignities suffered by the Emperor Valerian,[33] whom Sapor[34] held prisoner, while the infamous Gallienus,[35] his son, abandoned himself to all sorts of licentiousness.

Nevertheless, Odenatus did not fail to send him all the prisoners we took in this war. We took the greatest towns of Mesopotamia—Carrhae and Nisibis surrendered to my dear lord, and, pursuing victory, near Ctesiphon we defeated an innumerable multitude of Persians. We took many satraps[36] prisoner, and their king took flight.

And continuing almost always victorious in all the encounters we happened into, the fame of the valor of Odenatus made such a stir that at last it woke Gallienus. Then, provoked by fear rather than gratitude, he made him his partner in the empire and, to honor him yet further, he had made, as you know, medallions on which my dear Odenatus [was pictured] dragging the Persian captives.[37] Up until this point I experienced nothing but happiness: I was equally the favorite of Victory and Fortune. But alas! Can I speak it? My dear Odenatus was assassinated along with my oldest child. I passed from one extreme to the other, and I was now as unfortunate as I had been blessed. Then, O my daughters, I had need of all my virtue to endure such misery, and the loss of Odenatus without doubt made the loss of my liberty appear less harsh. It was more painful to follow my lord to his tomb[38] than to follow the chariot of Aurelian. And the funeral ceremony made me shed more tears than all the magnificence of the Triumph where I was displayed. But though my grief was immense, I did not remain long in tears. I dreamed of preserving our empire for my children and of paying back the blood he lost with the blood of his enemies. And since it is said that valor was the soul of this great man, I vowed to pass my whole life scooping up palms[39] to lay

33. Publius Licinius Valerianus, Roman emperor 253–260 C.E.; faced with increasing attacks from hostile forces in the East, he was eventually captured by the Persians in 260.

34. Sapor was king of Persia who reigned 241–272 C.E; he was successful in expanding the Persian Empire through aggressive attacks on Roman territory.

35. Publius Licinius Egnatius Gallienus, son of Valerian, ruled with his father from 253 to 260 C.E. and then by himself until 268 C.E.; he held together much of the Roman empire but lost much ground in multiple attacks and in Scudéry's time was condemned as a failure.

36. Satraps are lords or governors of provinces in ancient Persia.

37. In Roman and Renaissance times, victories, achievements, and anniversaries for rulers, nobles, and scholars were often commemorated by a publicly distributed medallion, one side showing a bust portrait of the person honored, the other recording an appropriate symbol and motto.

38. That is, in the funeral procession.

39. Palms were signs of victory to be waved in Triumphs.

on his tomb, that it might one day be said that by my hand alone I revenged his death, preserved the empire for his children, and erected a monument to his fame. I believed, I say, that it was better to hang on his coffin the spoils of his enemies whom I would overcome than to dampen his ashes with my tears. And with this resolve, I took in one hand the arms and in the other the reins of the empire. I have always believed, my daughters, that virtues are not incompatible with one another, that it is not impossible for the same person to possess them all, that those of men could be practiced by women, that true virtue is not limited by sex, that one could be both chaste and valiant, demonstrate great courage on one occasion and humility on another, be severe and merciful in diverse situations, be able to command and obey, and know how to bear chains and crown with the same composure.[40] It is by means of this opinion, my daughters, that I have undergone experiences so seemingly different, because I have always remained the same as I am today.[41] But to finish up this account of my life to you, you know that death, which carried away my dear Odenatus, did not take away the pleasure of his arms.[42] On the contrary, it seemed to me that his valor joined itself to mine. I defeated the army that Gallienus sent against me under the leadership of Heraclianus and, not content with this first victory, I passed into Egypt and made myself absolute mistress of the kingdom of my ancestors. From there I went all the way to Ancyra, the principal city of Galatia; I led my armies through all Bithynia as far as Chalcedon and all over the territory beneath the Bosporus; and after having vanquished the Persians in a multitude of encounters and spread the fame of my victories throughout the universe, Aurelian, guided by Fortune, and much more capable of using a sword than Gallienus was, finally arrived in person to put a stop to my career.

I would exhaustively recount my misfortunes to you, as I have done my successes, if I did not well know that you remember them all too well. And I would not have undertaken to review my victories had not your extreme melancholy made me believe that your imagination, overwhelmed by nothing but sorrowful images, had made you forget them. You are not unaware by what road Aurelian conducted me to Rome; you remember, no doubt, how the perfidy of Heraclianus led him to take the city of Theanea; how, despite my leadership and valor, the artifice of Aurelian caused him to win the battle before Antioch; how the ingenuity of Zabdas brought me to safety; how I retired to Emesa; how I rallied my troops; how a second time I

40. In philosophy, the Stoic is able to escape slavery to fortune by refusing to react with extreme emotions to either good or bad events.

41. Constancy is the main virtue to a Stoic. See note 6.

42. "Arms" is a pun: it means both "embrace," and "arms, weapons, protection."

engaged in battle with Aurelian, who, after we thought he was lost, gained
at last the victory despite all my efforts. You know as well that I abandoned
Emesa and went into retirement at Palmyra, waiting for the reinforcements
that the Persians, the Saracens, and the Armenians had promised me. You
know, I say, that Aurelian came to besiege me there with a strong army
he put together of Pannonians, Dalmatians, Misenians, Celts, a multitude
of Moors, and a great number of other troops drawn from Asia, Theanea,
Mesopotamia, Syria, Phoenicia, and Palestine. You know, I say, that I then
faced as great a preparation for war against me as it would take to conquer
the entire world.

Nevertheless, I did not lose heart on that occasion. You know that I
defended the walls of Palmyra with as much courage as leadership, that Aurelian himself was dangerously wounded there, struck by an arrow that was
probably launched by my hand, for the gods know whether or not I spared
myself in trying to preserve your freedom. And furthermore I know, since
I have been in Rome, that posterity will recognize that I did not abandon
the throne that belonged to you without defending it. Aurelian wrote in his
own hand to his friend Mecapor that "it is true that I fought this war against
a woman, but a woman who had more archers on her payroll than if she
had been a man, a woman who faced peril with prudence and who by her
foresight had made such strong preparation for war to oppose his attacks
that it was impossible to imagine what prodigious numbers of spears and
stones she had provided." In the end, he said, speaking of me, "there was
no place along the walls of Palmyra that was not defended by engines [of
war]. Her people threw fireworks on our soldiers at all hours and, in a few
words, [though] like a woman she is fearful, she fights like a person to be
feared." There, my daughters, that is my enemy who said this about me, and
certainly he had no reason to say I was afraid, because when he offered me
my life and a pardon (for his letter was written in those terms) provided I
would surrender the place to him and deliver into his hands all my jewels and
treasures, I answered him with such resolution that Aurelian was offended.

I remember that, among other things I said, I told him that no person
ever before him asked such a thing of me. "Remember," I said to him, "that
virtue should govern the affairs of war just as well as those of peace. Furthermore, I tell you[43] that the aid from the Persians we are waiting for will
not fail us; we also have on our side the Armenians and the Saracens, and
Aurelian, since the robbers of Syria conquered your army, what will happen

43. Zenobia uses "tu" to address Aurelian, the familiar form of address in French, which positions him as her friend or her inferior, not as her ruler.

when we have the forces we are waiting for from all over? Surely you will take that immense pride down a peg, [the pride] with which you command me to surrender, as if you were already victorious." You see, my daughters, that while you were at the temples praying to the gods, I was doing all things possible to preserve you and nothing to damage my glory.

You know, finally, how Aurelian defeated the Persians who were coming to our aid; and, seeing that it was absolutely impossible to save that place, I wished at least to get myself to safety. But Fate, which was determined on my ruin, arranged at last that Aurelian should be my conqueror and I should be his prisoner. He no sooner saw me than he asked me where I got "the audacity to attack Roman emperors and scorn their forces." "Aurelian," I said, "I acknowledge you as a legitimate emperor because you know how to vanquish [your enemies], but as for Gallienus and such as him, I never recognized them as such."

Up until now, my daughters, you could not accuse me of lacking heart. I once wore a crown without arrogance; I had a hand sufficiently steady to hold both a scepter and a sword at the same time. I mastered the art of ruling and the art of fighting; I knew how to conquer, and, what is more, I knew well how to make use of victory. I welcomed good fortune with moderation. And even during the time when my youth and the weakness of my sex might have made me take some pride in the little beauty I enjoyed, I listened without pleasure to all the flatterers of the court painting me in their verses with lilies and roses, claiming that my teeth were oriental pearls, that my eyes, black though they were, appeared brighter than the sun, and that Venus herself was not as beautiful as I was.

My daughters, I have told you all these things and elaborated them more than I ought in order to make you understand that in all the actions of my life I was never guilty of weakness. Do not think, then, that in this, the most important action of all, and in which I should have shown the most courage, that I lacked it, since I possessed enough all the other times. No, my daughters, I have done nothing in all my life that gives me greater satisfaction than following a triumphal chariot with equanimity. It is truly at such times that it is necessary to have a heroic soul, and never let it be said to me that in such encounters despair is a virtue and constancy a weakness. No, vice can never be virtue and virtue can never be vicious.

Also, let no one tell me that this sort of constancy is more appropriate to philosophers than to kings. And you must recognize, my daughters, that there is no difference between philosophers and kings, except that the one teaches true wisdom and the others should practice it. After all, sovereigns ought to be examples to their subjects and, because they are on display before all the world, there is no virtue that they ought not to pursue. Nevertheless, among all those [virtues] that are most necessary to princes, constancy is the most illustrious because it is the most difficult.

As for despair, which puts a dagger in the hand of those who would avoid slavery, it is more a weakness than a virtue—they cannot bear to look at Fortune when she is angry; she no sooner attacks them than they veer away from fighting her; she no sooner wishes to destroy them than they themselves aid her in her plans. Through a weakness unworthy of them, they yield the victory to this fickle one, and through a hasty action, often without knowing what they are doing, they escape their chains [only] by quitting life, loving solely its sweetness without being able to endure its bitterness.

For my part, my daughters who think otherwise, I hold that those who would live with glory should die as reluctantly as possible. And to speak reasonably, untimely death is more a mark of remorse, repentance, and weakness than of grandeur and courage. Someone might perhaps say to me that I am born of blood that ought never to be encompassed with chains—because Cleopatra was not willing to follow the chariot of Augustus, I should never have followed that of Aurelian. But there is this difference between that great Queen and me: that all her glory consisted in her death, while I made mine consist in my life. Her reputation would not have benefited had she not suffered death by her own hand, and mine would never have reached the height it has if I had deprived myself of the glory of knowing how to bear chains with such courageous grandeur, as if I had triumphed over Aurelian as he had triumphed over me. If Cleopatra had followed Augustus's chariot, she would have seen a hundred rude things while trudging through Rome that would have reproached her for her past indiscretions. The people would have no doubt made her understand by their mutterings the failures in her conduct.

But for my part, I was very certain that I would see nothing around the chariot I followed except the men whom I had once vanquished and witnesses to my valor and my virtue. I was sure (I say) that I would hear nothing rude and that I would hear nothing spoken except [sympathy] for my present unhappiness and my past victories. "Behold," said the people, "the valiant Zenobia! Behold this woman who has won so many victories! Admire her constancy on this occasion. Tell me, is it not as if the chains of diamonds she wears were fastened on her by a family member, as if she guides the chariot she follows?" After all, my daughters, while I was burdened like a noble slave with those chains of iron, or to name them more accurately, those chains of gold and precious stones, during all the magnificence of this Triumph, which was without doubt the most unfortunate day of my servitude, I was yet free in my heart, and I possessed a soul tranquil enough to see with pleasure that my constancy drew tears from some of my enemies. Yes, my daughters, virtue evinces such strong charms that the austerity of the Romans could not resist it, and I saw many among them crying over the victory of Aurelian and my misfortune.

Moreover, no one who is truly wise should allow cowardice to trouble the mind with matters that do not at all concern it. All this great preparation made for the Triumph should not frighten a rational spirit. All these chariots of gold, [all] these chains of diamonds, all these trophies of arms, and this crowd of people who gather to see this sorrowful ceremony should not at all bring fear to a noble person. It is true that my chains were heavy, but when they do not harm the spirit they scarcely bother the arms that carry them. And for my part, in that lamentable state, I thought more than one time that while Fortune had made me follow a chariot, yet I had made myself triumph over it.

By the same revolution that happens to all things of this world, it is possible that one day you will have scepters made out of the same chains that I bore. But at last, if this should not come to pass, do not torment yourselves immoderately. Take more care to make yourselves worthy of the throne than to regain it, for in the humor I am in I have a higher opinion of a simple slave who is faithful than of the mightiest king of the world who is not noble. Imagine this, my daughters, in order to endure your servitude with more equanimity, and certainly believe that if I have been conquered by Aurelian, my equanimity has [nevertheless] conquered Fortune.

It is clear through all the course of my life that death did not frighten me at all, for she is able to make me glorious; I have seen it a hundred times under a more terrible aspect than all who despair ever have seen it. The dagger of Cato, the sword of Brutus, the burning coals of Portia, the poison of Mithridates, the asp of Cleopatra[44] —none of these is as frightening. I have endured a hail of spears and arrows falling on my head; I have seen a hundred javelins with points turned toward my heart; and all that did not frighten me.

44. Marcus Porcius Cato (234–149 B.C.E.) was a famous Stoic but did not commit suicide, so perhaps Scudéry has confused him with Gaius Longinus Cassius, who committed suicide in 42 C.E. under the impression that he and Brutus had lost the crucial battle to Mark Antony and Augustus Caesar. Marcus Iunius Brutus (85–42 B.C.E.) fell on his sword after being defeated by Augustus Caesar and Mark Antony. Portia, daughter of Cato, married to Brutus, swallowed coals or inhaled fumes from a brazier to commit suicide after becoming ill while Brutus was in exile. Mithridates VI (120–163 C.E.), King of Pontus, after being defeated committed suicide by a guard's sword when poison failed him. Cleopatra (69–30 B.C.E.) escaped being led in Augustus Caesar's Triumph by an asp's bite.

Do not imagine, then, that if I had believed Death could make me glorious I would not have found her by my own hand. She is accustomed to conquering others. She would have broken my chains if I had desired it, but I believed that it was more glorious to bear them without shedding tears than to pour out my blood in weakness or despair. Those who think their gratification consists in themselves leave a throne with less regret than others who never find anything in their souls that contents them and are forced to find their happiness in things outside themselves.

You will ask me, perhaps, what is left to accomplish for princesses who have lost empire and freedom. And I would answer you with this argument: since the gods wished to give you a nobler test of your courage, you are obligated to endure it well and to make known to all the earth, by your patience and your virtue, that you are worthy of the scepter that you have been deprived of and that the chains given you are unworthy of you. There it is, my daughters, what is left for you to accomplish. And if you will let yourselves be moved by my example and arguments, you will find that your lives can once again be sweet and glorious.

At least you have this benefit, that the current state of your fortune cannot possibly get worse than it is, so if you are able to accustom yourselves to it at all, nothing will be able ever after to trouble your tranquility. Remember that out of the many millions of people in the world, there are not a hundred who wear crowns. Do you believe, my daughters, that all these people are unhappy and that without a throne there is no sweetness in life? If that is the case, how you are deceived! There is no condition of life that has not its pains and pleasures, and true wisdom is knowing how to take advantage of them if Fortune brings you both. Those who take their own lives do not realize that as long as we are living we are able to acquire glory. There is no tyrant who is able to keep me from continuing to immortalize my name for always, provided that he lets me live and I am virtuous; even my silence itself will speak for me as long as I endure any suffering with fortitude.

Let us live, then, my daughters, because we may do so with honor and because we have the means left us to give evidence of our virtue. The scepter, the throne, and the empire that we have lost were given us by Fortune, but our constancy comes directly from the gods. It was from their hands that I received it and for that reason you should imitate it. [Constancy] is the true mark of heroes, just as despair is [the mark] of the weak or the thoughtless. Do not worry then about what posterity will say about me, and do not fear that the day of Aurelian's Triumph will obscure all my victories, for as I have said, it is the most glorious day of my life. Moreover, I know that when he spoke in the Senate, Aurelian made a portrait of me that will make me well known to our descendants. Preserve it, my daughters, so that when I shall be no more, the remembrance of [all] that I was may obligate you to be always what you should be.

Here are the paints with which Aurelian prepared this painting: "I have learned," he said, "that I have been reproached for doing one thing unworthy of a person possessing greatness of soul, triumphing over Zenobia. But those who blame me would know what praise they should be giving me if they knew what kind of woman she was, how well advised she was in her councils, how courageously she proved herself, how scrupulously she kept order [in her troops], how imperious and grave she appeared among the soldiers, how generously she fulfilled her obligations, and how severe and exact she was when compelled by necessity. I might point out that it was by her means that Odenatus vanquished the Persians and pursued King Sapor all the way to Ctesiphon. I can assure you that this woman had so filled the East and Egypt with terror of her weapons that neither the Arabians nor the Saracens nor the Armenians dared to move [against her]. Thus, let those be silent who are displeased with [my actions], for if there is no honor in conquering and triumphing over a woman, what must we say about Gallienus, in contempt of whom she maintained her empire? And what must we say about Claudius,[45] a saintly and venerable prince who, occupied by war with the Goths, through a laudable prudence, tolerated her reign so that this princess might keep others' armies busy and he might more easily achieve success in his other enterprises?"

There, my daughters, that is what my conqueror said about me, even though I followed his chariot. Be as just [in your judgment as he was], I beg you, and believe that whoever lives in this manner does not need to commit suicide to immortalize her name.

The Effect of This Oration

This oration lets us see that an orator who is convinced may easily convince others: the princesses lived, like their mother, and did not wish for death. The gardens that Aurelian gave them for their dwelling place, which today are called the Tivoli, seemed more attractive to them than the tomb. History testifies that this noble queen was throughout her life highly esteemed

---

45. Marcus Aurelius Claudius II succeeded Gallienus as emperor in 268 C.E.

among the Roman matrons and that her daughters were married into the
most illustrious families. That was hardly because of their birth, but more
because of their misfortune, especially because these same people believed
that Antony and Titus[46] were married unworthily, even though they were
joined to queens. Such an opinion is prideful, but it [is understandably so],
coming from those who triumphed over the world. And she who says that
says it all.

SAPPHO TO ERINNA[47]

Argument

You are going to hear speak that famous woman who has been the talk of
all ages, who was admired by Plato himself, whose image was engraved like
that of famous people, who bequeathed to us a kind of verse that is called
"sapphics"[48] because she invented the meter, and who was called "The Tenth
Muse" by two great men of Greek and Roman antiquity.[49] I am giving her the
opportunity to exhort her friend to compose verses just as she did, in order
to make us see that women are capable of it and that they are wrong to
neglect such an agreeable occupation. Such is the argument of this speech,
which I dedicate in particular to the glory of the fair sex, as in general I have
dedicated the entire volume to them.

46. Scudéry seems to imagine Antony as Cleopatra's legal husband, and he is accused of being
married unworthily because Cleopatra was infamous for her multiple liaisons. Titus Flavius Vespasianus, Roman emperor 79–81 C.E., lover of Berenice (who was married to her uncle Herod,
king of Chalcis, and involved in an incestuous relationship with her brother, Agrippa II); again,
Scudéry imagines Titus married to Berenice, which he was not, because of her unpopularity in
Rome.

47. From *Les femmes illustres*, 306–20. "Sapho" (French spelling) was the name Scudéry took for
herself in the renaming that was part of salon culture. The most common form of the story of
Sappho in the seventeenth century was Ovid's and that of other Romans; they saw Sappho as a
forlorn, aging, heterosexual woman, in unrequited love with a young man, a woman who eventually committed suicide. It is currently much debated to what extent in the seventeenth century
the other version of Sappho's story circulated, which emphasized the love-longing expressed
for women in her poetry and, sometimes, her role as a teacher of young women. Although the
Romans did not realize this, Erinna was a fourth-century B.C.E. poet, not a contemporary of
Sappho; she was famous for her epigrams and her long hexameter poem, *The Distaff*.

48. Sapphics is a kind of verse form in Greek poetry named for Sappho, a four-line strophe
(choral stanza) that she used in most of her poems.

49. More than two great men called Sappho "the tenth muse"—the title dates back at least as
far as the *Anthologia Palatina* (940 C.E.), which attributes the title to the ancients.

Within this lovely medal closed
The wonder of the universe:
But please remember that this prose
Is not as lovely as her verse.[50]

SAPPHO TO ERINNA

Today Erinna, I must, indeed I must, overcome this distrust of yourself deep
in your soul and this false modesty that keeps you from employing your

50. A literal translation of the poem follows:
     Come to see in this beautiful item
     The wonder of the universe:
     But remember that this prose
     Is not as beautiful as her verses.

intellect in matters it is capable of. But before I speak to you of your worth in particular, I must make you see [the worth] of our sex in general so that through that knowledge I may more easily persuade you to my point of view.

Those who say that beauty is women's share and that fine arts, great literature, and all the sublime and exalted sciences fall under the dominion of men, without our having the right to claim any part of them, are far from both justice and truth. If this were so, all women would be born with beauty and all men with a strong disposition to become learned; otherwise, Nature would be unfair in her allotment of these gifts. Nevertheless, we see every day that ugliness can be found in our sex and stupidity in the other. If it were true that beauty were the sole advantage we might receive from Heaven, not only would all women be beautiful, but I believe that they would be so until death, that Time would spare in them what he is every moment destroying and that, being sent into the world for no other reason than to let their beauty be seen, they would be beautiful as long as they were on earth. Indeed, that would be a strange fate, to outlive by a century the one thing that could make us commendable, and out of that huge number of years that move us towards the tomb, to pass only five or six in [a state of] glory.

Those things that Nature seems to have made for no purpose but to ornament the universe hardly ever lose the beauty that she once gave them. Gold, pearls, diamonds preserve their brilliance as long as their existence, and the phoenix likewise, it is said, dies with its beauty in order to be re-born with it. Let us infer, then, because we see no roses and lilies in the complexion of the loveliest women that the rigor of a few winters does not fade and because we see no eyes more sparkling than the sun which are not [eventually] shadowed over and which, after having made a hundred brilliant conquests, find themselves [reduced] to the position of merely watching the conquests of others, let us infer, I say, because we see that (despite us and our worries) each instant of our lives strips us of the loveliest traits we have, that Time carries away our youth, that the golden filaments in which so many hearts have been ensnared will one day be no more than silver threads, and that, finally, this beauteous air that unites so agreeably all the individual features of a lovely face, in which one sees a glimmer of divinity appear, is yet not strong enough to conquer diseases, time, and old age.[51] Let us conclude, I say, that we must possess other advantages than just this one.

---

51. This sentence is a good example of a periodic sentence; Scudéry is showing off her rhetorical skill by constructing in French this Latinate structure, where sense is suspended until the end of a long sentence.

And to approach this reasonably, beauty is among our sex what valor is among men; but just as bravery does not prevent men from loving the study of belles lettres, so beauty in no way prevents us from understanding and studying these arts either. If there is a difference between men and women, it should only be in affairs of war: the beauty of my sex conquers hearts, and the valor and strength of men conquers kingdoms.[52] Nature's intention appears so clear in this respect that one cannot deny it: I consent, then, that we shall leave taking towns, giving battle, and leading armies to those who were born for that. But for those things that require only imagination, vivacity of wit, memory, and judgment—I cannot bear us to be deprived of these.

As you know, men are almost all either our slaves or our enemies, and when the chains we make them wear seem to them too heavy or they break them, they are most irritated with us; so let us not quarrel over the beauty of imagination, the vivacity of spirit, the force of memory.[53] But regarding judgment, some of them unfairly claim that they have more than we do. Still, I think that the moderation and modesty of our sex are [proof] enough that we lack nothing in this area; and, if it is true that we possess to a high degree the abilities [I have listed] previously, then it is almost impossible that we do not possess the other.[54] For if our imagination shows us things as they are, if our reason understands them perfectly, and if our memory serves us as it should, how is it possible for our judgment to err? Imagination, when it is vivid, is such a faithful mirror; reason, when it is enlightened, penetrates so profoundly into things; and memory, when it is healthy and cultivated, instructs so powerfully by example, that it would be impossible for judgment not to develop.

Believe me, Erinna, that when the sea is calm, it is difficult to cause a shipwreck; the worst pilot is able to get into the harbor, and there are no reefs that are not able to be avoided when one can see them and the waves are not excited. On my part, I acknowledge that I do not understand how those who relegate to us imagination, wit, and memory as our portion can boast about having more judgment than we do. If their imagination does not show them things as they are, if their wit does not understand things

---

52. Could Scudéry have known Sappho's Fragment 16, which was not available in French translation by 1642, when *Les femmes illustres* was first published? It begins, "Some say that the most beautiful thing / upon the black earth is an army / . . . but I say it is what one loves" (see Jane McIntosh Snyder, *The Woman and the Lyre* [Carbondale, Ill.: Southern Illinois University Press, 1989], 22).

53. That is, let men and women be judged equal in these minor things.

54. The first advantages are imagination, wit, and memory, and so the other is judgment.

perfectly, and if their memory is not faithful, the means of thinking being based on false reports, how can their judgment operate fairly? No, Erinna, it is not possible.

But to be more reasonable than those few men, we may say that, among them and among us, there are people who possess imagination, wit, memory, and judgment all at once. And, if I would wish to do so, I would be able to show, through a firm and powerful process of reasoning, that our sex can boast of being richer than men in the treasures of the mind. For consider, Erinna, the almost universal order that one may observe among all the animals who inhabit woods and caves: you will see that those who are born with strength and courage are often not very skilled and not very clever and the weak ordinarily have a stronger instinct and are more reasonable than those to whom Nature has given other advantages. You may well conclude, following this pattern, that since Nature has given more strength and courage to men than to women, she must also have given us more wit and more judgment.

But once more, Erinna, let us grant that they possess as much as we do, provided they will agree also that we possess as much as they do. You will tell me, perhaps, that even if I obtained the consent of all men to this declaration, I still could not persuade them that knowledge of belles lettres is beneficial in a woman, for through a custom established by men, for fear perhaps of being surpassed by us, study is as much forbidden to us as battle. Making verses is the same as making war, if we wish to believe them, and to wrap it up, it seems that we are permitted nothing except that which should be instead forbidden us.

Why, Erinna, do we possess fine imagination, perceptive wit, capable memory, solid judgment and yet employ all these talents only to curl our hair and search for decorations that will add to our beauty? No, Erinna, that would be a useless abuse of the gifts we have received from Heaven. Those who are born with eyes to make conquests have only to add artifice to the natural graces—and that is to give unworthy employment to the mind, to give it nothing to do all our life but such tasks.

One might likewise say that, if things were arranged as they should be, the study of belles lettres should be permitted to women more often than to men, for because men must manage the whole universe, some being kings, others governors of provinces, some priests, others magistrates, and all heads of their families and, consequently, occupied with public affairs or their private business, they certainly have little time to give to this sort of study. They have to steal the time from their subjects, their family, or themselves. But for us, our leisure and our retirement give us every opportunity that we could hope for. We steal nothing from the public or from ourselves. On the contrary, we enrich ourselves without impoverishing others; we bring honor to our country by bringing honor to ourselves; and without wronging anyone, we acquire great glory. It is only fair, I think, since we allow men to dominate, that they should allow us at least the freedom to know everything that our minds can encompass. The desire for virtue should not be forbidden us, and consequently, it is no crime to practice it.

The gods have made nothing useless in all of Nature; each thing follows the assigned plan: the sun brightens and warms the universe; the earth continues to give us flowers and fruits; the sea grants us all its riches; the rivers water our meadows; the woods provide us shade; and, indeed, all things are useful to the commonwealth. This being the case, why then would anyone want us to be the only ones rebellious and ungrateful to the gods? Why then, I say, would anyone want our minds to be unworthily employed or eternally useless? What use would it be to scorn someone who is reasonable? And how can it be logical that a person who is infinitely commendable as an individual should become wicked and damnable as soon as she belongs to our group?

Those who own slaves instruct them for their [own] convenience; and yet they whom Nature or custom has given us as masters would have us extinguish in our minds all the brilliance that Heaven has put there and would have us live in the heaviest shadows of ignorance. If this is to obtain our admiration more easily, they do not achieve their aim, for we cannot admire anything that we do not understand. And if it is also to make us more subservient, this is not a noble motive. And if it is true that they possess some authority over us, it makes their dominion less glorious to reign only over the stupid and ignorant.

You may say to me, perhaps, that all men are not so harsh and some even agree that women may use their minds in learning belles lettres, as long as they do not get caught up in the desire to compose their own works. But let those who are of this opinion remember that if Mercury and Apollo are of their sex, Minerva and the Muses are of ours.[55] Nevertheless, I confess that, having received so much from Heaven as we have, we should not lightly attempt such an endeavor. For example, it is not shameful to make verses, but only to make them poorly, and if mine had not the good fortune of pleasing, I would never have made them public a second time. Such shame is not particular to us, and whoever does poorly something that he voluntarily

---

55. Mercury is the god of eloquence and Apollo of poetry, while Minerva is the goddess of wisdom and of arts and crafts, and the nine Muses preside over song, poetry, and the arts and sciences.

undertakes no doubt merits blame, no matter what sex he is. A poor male orator, a poor male philosopher, a poor male poet acquires no more glory than a woman who attempts all these things with little success; and whatever sex one is, one deserves reproof when one does poorly, and great esteem when one does well. But because the custom and the depravity of the age requires it, Erinna, leave those thorny sciences to those who do not like to seek glory except in difficult paths.

I do not wish to lead you in places where you will see nothing agreeable. I do not want you to pass your entire life in tiresome research into mysteries that no one will solve. I do not wish you to employ all your intelligence uselessly, to find out where the winds go after they have caused shipwrecks. And, finally, I do not wish you to consume the rest of your days in philosophizing indifferently about everything. I love your [air of] tranquility, your noble character, and your beauty all together: I do not at all desire for you the kind of studies that make your complexion yellow, your eyes sunken, your visage pale, that put wrinkles in your forehead and make your humor somber and anxious. I do not wish at all for you to avoid the daylight or society. Rather, I only wish you to follow me to the borders of Parnassus.[56] It is there, Erinna, that I would lead you; it is there that you will surpass me as soon as you arrive; it is there that you will acquire a beauty of which neither time, nor years, nor seasons, nor old age, nor even death will be able to rob you; and finally, it is there that you will fully understand that our sex is capable of anything we would attempt.

You will say to me, perhaps, that, in wishing you to be transported to the land of poetry, I do not keep my word, for in descriptions of those who make verses, it seems that beauty cannot compete with the grimaces that [making verses] causes. But understand, Erinna, that that is nothing but the fabrication of men who wanted to make us think that; just as those who speak oracles are agitated by the presence of the god who makes them speak, so likewise, poetry, being wholly divine, agitates those who practice it.[57] But even if that were so, your eyes would not be less bright, for just as after the oracle is pronounced, the priest recovers his original tranquility, so you will no sooner put down your pen than you will recover your original graces. And furthermore, I do not think that you will ever fill up your mind with such morbid images that they will spout forth, provoking morbidity in your eyes.

56. Parnassus is a mountain in ancient Greece sacred to Apollo and the Muses.
57. Scudéry is referring to the "divine fury" that in Plato's theory is supposed to take over and inspire poets.

You will be absolute mistress over the topics that you will treat, and from all the beauties of Nature you will be able to choose that which most pleases your fancy. The description of a forest or a fountain, the complaints of a lover and a mistress, or praise for some virtue—you will have enough subjects to make clear the talents that Heaven has given you. You were born with such glorious advantages that you would be ungrateful to those who gave them to you if you did not learn how to use them well.

You will ask me, perhaps, if it is not glorious enough to be a beautiful woman to whom all the great minds of the age dedicate verses in order to praise her, without meddling herself in making her own portrait. You will ask me, I say, if her glory is not better established in this fashion than in the other. But I answer you, whatever praise can be given to you, it would bring you more glory to have composed verses for all the famous people of your century, if well done, than if they had each composed them for you. Believe me, Erinna, it is better to give immortality to others than to receive it from others and to find that same glory in yourself than to wait for it from others. The portraits that others make of you in this way might not ever descend to posterity, except as paintings made for pleasure. People will admire the imagination of the poets more than your beauty and these copies, indeed, will be taken for the original. But if from your own hand you leave some mark of who you are, you will live always with honor in the memory of all men. Those of your age who have praised you will be taken at their word, and those who have not will be seen as stupid and envious.

Nevertheless, I do not mean that you should draw your own portrait, that you should speak of your own beauty, of your own virtue, and of all the rare qualities that are in you. No, I do not wish to require something so difficult of your modesty. Poetry has other potentials: you only have to speak to make yourself known to posterity; you only have to speak elegantly and you will be well enough known. Yes, Erinna, if you employ your pen to no other end than to blame the vices of your time, people will never stop praising you.[58]

Consider once again then, I beg you—how feeble and of short duration is the reputation that is based on beauty. Out of all the infinite number of beautiful women who without doubt lived in previous centuries, scarcely two or three are still spoken of. And in these same centuries, we see the

---

58. In Scudéry's time, poetry was often admired for its moral purpose. Exposing the vices of the times is thus a worthy purpose of the poet.

glory of numerous men solidly established through the writings that they have left behind. Erinna, let not time, old age, [and] death rob you of these roses and take away your beauty. Triumph over these enemies of all things beautiful! Put yourself in a position to uphold by your example the glory of our sex. Make it known to our common enemies that it is as easy for us to conquer through the force of our intelligence as through the beauty of our eyes. Make clear your judgment through contempt for those aspersions that the vulgar will cast on your resolve. Make the whole world see, from the beautiful paintings of your imagination, from the noble endeavors of your mind, from the lovely achievements of your memory,[59] and from the stunning signs of your judgment that you alone will offer the benefit of reestablishing the glory of all women. Do not scorn what I am telling you. For if through a false modesty you resolve never to follow me and to make your whole glory consist of your beauty, you will mourn your whole life the loss of this beauty. You will be spoken of as if you were of another century, and you will find that indeed I had good reason to tell you today what I think I have said formerly in some of my verses:

> Your looks, and all that charming grace
> Of rose and lily in your face,
> Your heavenly orbs, so clear and bright,
> Though emblems of eternal light,
> Must all decay, your beauty wither;
> Death makes you both forgot together.
> But learning will your fame extend
> O'er Death and Hell in your last end.[60]

---

59. Memory is very important to theories of poetry in Scudéry's time, for a poet is required to have broad knowledge and because in the new empiricist view, sense impressions from experience lodged in the memory are drawn on to make poetry vivid.

60. The rhymed translation is that of James Innes, who translated Scudéry's collection of speeches as *Les femmes illustres; or, The Heroick Harangues of the Illustrious Women* (Edinburgh, 1681), 435. A literal translation is,

> The lilies, the carnations, the roses
> And all lovely qualities
> With which your face is painted,
> The brilliance of eyes and complexion,
> All will be lost, form and matter,
> And you will die entirely.
> If you would conquer confinement and mortality,
> You must reach eternity through learning.

The Effect of This Oration

It cannot be said that this oration had no effect, if we take it literally, for it seems that that [young woman] whom Sappho addressed allowed herself to be transported where [Sappho] desired [her to be], because a Greek epigram told us that just as Sappho surpassed Erinna in lyric poetry, so Erinna surpassed Sappho in hexameter verse. But if we stray from the literal sense, to more closely approach my intentions, I will be very happy if I can persuade our ladies of that which this lovely Lesbian persuaded her beloved friend,[61] and more so if I might persuade the whole world that this lovely sex is worthy of our adoration, so that one day temples and altars might be consecrated to them, just as I now consecrate to them the triumphal arch[62] that I have erected to their glory.

61. "Amie" means both friend and lover.

62. In the Renaissance, triumphal arches of great artistic complexity were often erected in cities to welcome new rulers, to celebrate political triumphs, and to commemorate important people. Sor Juana Inez de la Cruz, for example, in Mexico designed such an arch and wrote verses for it.

RHETORICAL DIALOGUES

CONVERSATIONS ON DIVERSE SUBJECTS (1680)

On Conversation[1]

"Since conversation is the bond of society for all humanity, the greatest pleasure of discriminating people,[2] and the most ordinary method to introduce into the world not only civility, but also the purest morals and the love of glory and virtue, it appears to me that the company cannot be entertained more agreeably, nor more usefully," said Cilénie, "than to examine what we call 'conversation.' For when men speak only about the requirements of their business affairs, one cannot call it [conversation]."

"In fact," said Amilcar, "a lawyer who pleads his cause before judges, a merchant who negotiates with another, a military general who gives orders, a king who discusses politics in his Council—all this ought not to be called 'conversation.' All these people may be able to speak well about their interests and affairs, and yet not have that agreeable talent of conversation, which is the sweetest pleasure of life, and perhaps more rare than one may think."

1. Based on Madeleine de Scudéry, "De la conversation," from *Conversations sur divers sujets* (Paris, 1980), as edited by Delphine Denis in *De l'air galant et autres conversations* (Paris: Honoré Champion, 1998), 67–75, 305–11, and with thanks to the students of Professor Donawerth's fall 1993 English 489B, "Gender and the History of Rhetorical Theory," who edited a seventeenth-century translation of this dialogue as a class project; special thanks to Stephanie Lenkey for her expert assistance in French translation. A version of this dialogue appears first in Scudéry's novel, *Artamène, ou, Le grand Cyrus* (Paris, 1653), vol. 10, book 2, 712–32, in the episode known as "The History of Sappho." See Madeleine de Scudéry, *The Story of Sapho*, ed. and trans. Karen Newman (Chicago: University of Chicago Press, 2003).

2. *Honnêtes gens* are discriminating, honest, decent, polite middle- and upper-class people; "honesty" in seventeenth-century France and England combines virtue and elegance as a standard of taste for polite society.

"For my part, I do not doubt you at all," replied Cilénie, "but it seems to me that before it can be decided wherein principally consists the charm and beauty of conversation, all the people who compose this company should recall those boring conversations that they found the most irritating."

"You have a good point," said Cérinte, "for by observing all that is tiresome, one may better understand what is enjoyable; and to show [you] an example," she added, "I made a family visit yesterday, during which I was so overcome with boredom that I thought I would die of it. Indeed, imagine—I found myself in the midst of ten or twelve women, who spoke of nothing else but all their little domestic cares, of the faults of their servants,[3] of the good qualities or vices of their children; and there was one woman among the rest, who spent more than an hour recounting syllable by syllable the first stammerings of a son of hers, who is just three years old. You may judge after that, if I did not pass my time in a pitiable manner."

"I assure you," responded Nicanor, "that I spent my time little better than yourself, since I found myself engaged against my will with a troop of women (you may easily guess who I mean), who employed the whole day in nothing but speaking well or ill of their clothes and in lying continually about what they paid for them. For some, out of vanity, said much more than was correct, as I was informed by the least silly of them all; and others, to be thought clever, said much less [than it cost] to make their clothes—so much so that I passed the entire day in hearing such shallow and senseless matters that it still makes me a little vexed."

"On my part," said the lovely Athis, "fifteen days ago I found myself with some ladies who, although they had wit enough, strangely wearied me. For in short, to tell things as they are, these are women who are flirts by profession, who have at least one affair each, and an affair that so possesses them that they think of nothing else[4]—so much so that when you are not a part of their intrigues, and find yourself in their company, you become quite embarrassed yourself, and also greatly embarrass them. And indeed, the whole time I was with these women I'm speaking about, I heard them talking continually without understanding what they were saying. For there was one on my right who, speaking to one who sat next to her, said she knew from very good sources that such a gentleman had broken off with such a

---

3. *Esclaves* might be either "servants" or "slaves." We have translated it as "servants" here because in France in the seventeenth century there were no slaves and slaves brought in from the colonies were entitled to their freedom on entry into the country.

4. In the novel, this clause continues with "but how to remove one another's gallants through all sorts of ways."

lady and that this one had consequently renewed [her amour] with such another. And another on my left, speaking passionately to one lady among her friends, told her the most foolish stuff in the world. 'After all,' she said to her, in a fret, 'you-know-who ought not to boast that she has deprived me of a gallant, since the man she believes she has wrenched from me is someone I have driven away. But if the fancy strikes me to recall him, I will do it so well that she will never get any for the rest of her life.' On the other hand, I heard some giving an account of a collation[5] they were treated to, affectedly saying that it was paltry, as if they thought they would diminish the beauty of the lady in whose honor it was given by saying that her lover was not magnificent enough. In short, I must confess that in my life I never felt so much impatience as I did that day."

"On my part," replied Cilénie, "if I had been in your place, I would have found a means of diverting myself at the expense of the very ones who bored me. But I could not find a way to escape boredom three days ago, with a man and a woman who make conversation on two subjects only: that is to say, the complete genealogies of all the families of Mytilene and all the possessions of these families. For indeed, except on certain occasions, how entertaining is it to hear such gossip for a whole day long: Xenocrates was the son of Tryphon, Clidemus descended from Zenophanes, Zenophanes was the issue of Tyrtaeus, and so of the rest? And what diversion is there, likewise, to hear that such a house in which you have no interest, which you never visited, and where you'll never go as long as you live, was built by this man, bought by that one, traded by another, and is at present owned by a man you do not know?"

"This is certainly not very agreeable," answered Alcé, "but it is not nearly as annoying as encountering people who are engaged in some troublesome business and can speak of nothing else. And in truth, a while ago I met a sea captain, who claims that Pittacus ought to recompense him for a ship.[6] He kept me three hours, telling me not only the reasons he claimed to have for being reimbursed, but also what someone might say in response to his [claim] and what he could reply. And to make me the better comprehend the losses caused him, he set about telling me in detail what his ship cost him. For that purpose, he told me the names of those who built it and specified to me all the parts of his ship, one after the other, unnecessarily, to make me understand it was one of the best and dearest of ships and he had suffered a great injustice."

5. A collation is a light meal, or lunch.
6. The version in the novel continues, "which was lost."

"It's true," said Amithone, "that one feels persecuted encountering that sort of person. But to tell you the truth, those grave and serious conversations where no enjoyment is permitted have something so depressing that I never happen into them without being taken with a headache. For the talk is always on the same note. They never laugh, and all is as formal as if one were at church."

"I agree with what you say," replied Athis, "but I must say, to the shame of our sex, that the men have a great advantage over us as to conversation. And to prove it, I need only tell the company that, going to Lycidice's house, I found her in her mother's chamber, where there was so great a number of women that I could barely find a place for myself, but there was not one single man. I cannot tell you in what manner all those ladies had their wits addled that day, though some of them were very witty. But I am forced to tell you that the conversation was not very entertaining. For in fact, they spoke only of tedious trifles, and I may say that in my life I never heard so much talking that said so little.

"But happening to be near Lycidice, I could easily observe the annoyance she felt. It's true that I observed it with delight, since it made her say a hundred amusing things. While she was very much bored with this noisy conversation, which went so much against the grain with her, one of her kinsmen arrived. And this is remarkable, that though this man had not that elevated wit rarely to be found, and though he was but of the rank of ordinary well-bred people, the conversation changed all of a sudden and became more ordered, more witty, and more agreeable, though there was no other change in the company than the arrival of a man who spoke very little. But indeed, without being able to tell you the true reason, they began talking of other things, they talked much better, and those same persons who bored me, as well as Lycidice, amused me extremely.

"When the company was gone, I remained alone with Lycidice. She was no sooner free than, passing from her humor of annoyance to cheerfulness, she said to me, 'Well Athis, will you still condemn me for preferring the conversation of men to that of women? And are you not forced to acknowledge that whoever would write what fifteen or twenty women say together would make the worst book in the world?' 'I confess,' said I to her, laughing, 'that if the person wrote all that I have heard spoken today, it would be a bizarre account.' 'For my part,' she said, 'some days I am so irritated by my sex that I despair that I am a woman, especially when I find myself in one of those conversations composed entirely of dresses, furniture, jewels, and similar things. Not that I am opposed to ever speaking of such things,' she added, 'for indeed, sometimes my hair is well enough arranged that I am happy to have someone tell me so, and sometimes my clothes are beautiful enough and well enough made for me to think it good that someone should praise them. But I would wish us to speak very little of these sorts of things, only out of courtesy, only in passing and nonchalantly, only without eagerness, and not as some women do of my acquaintance, who spend their whole lives speaking and thinking of nothing else and whose thoughts of those things are likewise so full of indecision that, in my opinion, at the end of their days they will still not have determined to their satisfaction if carnation becomes them better than blue or if yellow is more advantageous to them than green.'

"I must confess that Lycidice made me laugh, and I found it even more pleasant since it is true that there is a lady of my acquaintance who employs her whole intelligence only in such things, who never talks of anything else, and who makes her greatest glory consist only in what is piled up around her—that is to say, in the gilding of her palace, in the magnificence of her furniture, in the beauty of her clothes, and in the richness of her jewels.

"After having laughed at what Lycidice said, I wished to defend women in general and told her I was persuaded there are as many men as ladies whose conversation is scarcely agreeable. 'There are some of them without a doubt,' she replied, 'whose company is unbearable. But there is this advantage, that one can more easily get rid of them and one is not obliged to treat them with so exact a civility. But Athis, it is not this that I'm concerned about. For what I am telling you is that the most amiable women in the world, when they are together in a great number, and without any men, say hardly anything of value and are more bored than if they were alone. But it is not the same for men who are well-bred. Their conversation is, without doubt, less enjoyable when there are no ladies than when there are. But commonly, though it is more serious, it is not irrational, and they can more easily be without us than we without them. Meanwhile, this vexes me more than I can tell you.'

" 'For my part,' I answered, 'it seems to me that I could live without being bored, even if I never saw anyone but my female friends, provided they were all like Lycidice.' 'I'll tell you, if you like,' she responded, 'to requite your civility, I would be as little bored as you, if all my friends were like you. But I must at least add, provided I might see them but one, two, or three at the most together. For to see twelve of them at a time! I would rather see nobody. Yes,' she pursued, with the most pleasing gloominess in the world, 'though there were twelve Athises in the world, I would not wish to see them all together every day, unless they had two or three men with them. For though you never say anything inappropriate, I am sure that if there were twelve of you, you would; or at least, you would speak like the rest, of the sorts of things that are meaningless, and make the conversation so tedious and so boring. In the end,' she continued, 'what would you have me say more than that? Unless you are a great hypocrite, you must confess, that this I-don't-know-what, which I am incapable of explaining, makes a well-bred man delight and divert a company of ladies more than the most amiable woman on earth would know how to. I'll say more,' she added, 'for I maintain that when there are but two women together, if they are not intimate friends with one another, they will amuse themselves less than if each of them talked with a man of wit, though they had never seen him before. Judge after this if I do not have reason to grumble about my sex in general.'"

"Those conversations are without doubt very annoying," replied Amilcar, "but there is another kind that also troubles me in a strange way. For I happened to be one day at Syracuse with five or six women and two or three men who had it in their heads that, for a conversation to be agreeable laughing is required all the time—insomuch that as long as those persons are together, they do nothing but laugh at everything they say to one another, even if it is not very amusing. And they make so great a noise that often they are no longer listening to what they are saying, and then they laugh only because the rest laugh, without knowing the reason. However, they do it as heartily as if they knew what was said. But it is strange—their laughter is sometimes so contagious that one cannot help but be taken with their malady. And I found myself one day with those perpetual laughers, who inspired me so compellingly with their laughter that I laughed until I almost cried, without knowing why I did so. But to speak the truth, I was so much ashamed of it fifteen minutes later that all my joy turned, in a moment, into vexation."

"Though there is a great deal of folly in laughing without reason," responded Valeria, "I am not so uncomfortable in the company of these sorts of people as I am when I meet with those people whose conversation consists of nothing but long, sad, and lamentable stories, which are extremely tedious. For example, I am acquainted with a woman who knows all the latest tragic adventures[7] and who spends entire days in deploring the misfortunes of life and in relating lamentable events with a sad and doleful voice, as if she were paid for bewailing all the calamities of the world."

"Let us not pass over so quickly," said Plotine, "the fault of never-ending stories. For in my opinion, one ought to guard against becoming accustomed to perpetually telling stories, as I know some who never speak but of what is past and are always telling what they have seen, never what they see."

---

7. This clause was translated with the wonderful comparison, "whose daily discourse is a book of martyrs" by the seventeenth-century translator Ferrand Spence.

"It is true," said Amilcar, "that sometimes those eternal storytellers are very much to be dreaded! Some of them are confused; others [talk] too long; some are so troublesome that they will never let themselves be interrupted; others, on the contrary, interrupt themselves, and at the end do not know either what they have said or what they want to say. But those who stick to things that no one cares about, and which of themselves are not very amusing, are the most annoying of all the tale-telling tribe."

"I know likewise a family," resumed Cérinte, "where the conversation is very irritating; for they never discuss anything but the trivial news of their neighborhood—which courtly people, who come there by chance, are not interested in and have no understanding of. And I remember well, one day I heard them talk of a hundred little intrigues that did not concern me at all, the fame of which extended no farther than the street where they happened to be, and which, besides, were so little amusing in themselves that I was extremely bored."

"It is also a great agony," said Nicanor, "to find oneself in a large company where everyone has a secret—principally when you have none—and you have nothing more to do than to listen to the little murmur made by those who converse with each other in whispers. And yet, if they were truly secrets," added she, "I would have patience. But it very often happens that these things which are said with so much mystery are nothing but trifles."

"Likewise, I know other people," joined in Alcé, "who, to my mind, possess a trait at once very irritating and also very agreeable. For they have such a fancy for earthshaking news in their heads that they never speak unless it concerns battles, or some siege of an important city, or some great revolution in the world; and you would say to hear them [talk] that the gods change the face of the universe only to furnish them with conversation. For unless it concerns such grand and important occurrences they never speak and cannot bear [discussing] any other kind. So that without knowing how to sift to the bottom of politics and without being well versed in history, a person cannot discuss any subject whatsoever with them."

"It is true," replied Nicanor, "that what you describe is not always agreeable. But likewise very irritating are those other people, who, without troubling themselves about the major events in the world, want to know nothing except that particular [piece of] news you just finished discussing. For you see them always as busy as if they had a thousand affairs [to attend to], though they have none of any sort except knowing all those of everyone else, in order to go repeat them from house to house like public spies, who are neither here nor there, for they tell the news from here to those over there as the occasion presents itself, without getting any benefit from it.

Thus, they do not even aim to know things in order to know them, but only to repeat them to others."

"It is also a great fault," said Cérinte, "to always show off all your wit. And I know a man who, in the first few visits he makes in places where he wants to please, passes continually from one subject to another without going deeply into any; and I can assure you without exaggeration that in an hour I have heard him speak on all possible subjects, since not only did he tell all that happened at court but also all that happened in town. Then he related all that he had done that day. He even recounted what was said in the places where he had been and asked Arpasia what she had done. After that, he teased Melinta about her silence and then spoke of music and painting. He proposed several different excursions and said so many different things that a man in the company, taking notice of this great diversity, made others likewise observe it with the intention of praising him. 'For indeed,' said he, after causing it to be noticed, 'there is nothing more tiresome than to find oneself in a conversation with the sort of people who get stuck on the first thing that is discussed and go so deeply into it that in a whole afternoon they never change the subject. For since conversation ought to be free and natural and all those who compose the company ought to have an equal right to change it as they see fit, it is an irritating thing to meet with those opinionated people who leave nothing to say on a subject and who are ever harping upon it, no matter what care is taken to interrupt them.'"

"For my part," said Cilénie, "I am perplexed to hear you all talk as you do. For, after all, if it is not fitting always to talk of science like Damophilus; if it is tedious to converse about all the little cares of a family; if it is not appropriate to speak often of clothes; if it is not judicious to do nothing but gossip about love affairs; if it is not entertaining to speak only of genealogies; if it is too vulgar to discuss lands sold or exchanged; if it be likewise forbidden to speak too much of our own business dealings; if too great a gravity is not diverting in conversation; if there is folly in laughing too often and in laughing without cause; if stories of morbid and extraordinary events are not engaging; if the little tidings of the neighborhood are boring to those who are not concerned with them; if these conversations of little things that are whispered in the ear are irritating; if people who converse only of great events are wrong [to do so]; if those indefatigable seekers after private tidbits[8] are not justified;

8. We have translated "nouvelles de cabinet" as "private tidbits": news of the cabinet would be the gossip or secrets one could only tell one's most intimate friends, since they were the ones in French aristocratic society who were admitted to the cabinet, the most private of rooms. We still have in English a form of this expression in "cabinet secrets," although now it means the secrets that only the great political leaders share with their counselors.

of what can we speak, and of what must the conversation be composed, to make it both rational and pleasing?"

"It must be composed of all that we have rejected," Valeria agreeably replied with a smile, "but it must be conducted with judgment. For in the end, although all those people we have mentioned are bothersome, I boldly maintain that one cannot speak except about what they do and that one can speak agreeably on such subjects, even though they don't."

"I well understand that what Valeria says is true," replied Amilcar, "though it doesn't seem so at first. For I am so persuaded that all sorts of things may properly be included in conversation that I do not exclude any."

"Indeed," added Valeria, "one must not imagine there are things that are impossible to include. For it is true that there are certain encounters where it is quite proper to say what would be ridiculous on any other occasion."

"For my part," said Amithone, "I confess that I would prefer there to be some rules for conversation, as there are for many other things."

"The principal rule," replied Valeria, "is never to say anything that offends the judgment."

"But still," added Nicanor, "I would like to know more precisely what you conceive a conversation ought to be."

"I conceive," she responded, "that in general, it ought to more often concern the subjects of ordinary polite conversation rather than great events. However, I think that nothing is precluded; that conversation ought to be free and diverse, according to the times, places, and persons with whom we find ourselves; and that the secret is to always speak nobly of small things, fairly simply of great things, and very graciously concerning the subjects of polite society, without haste or affectation. Thus, although conversation ought always to be both natural and also reasonable, I must not fail to say that on some occasions the sciences themselves may be brought in with a good grace and that an agreeable silliness may also find its place, provided it be clever, modest, and courteous. So that, to speak sensibly, we may say in all honesty that there is nothing that cannot be said in conversation, provided it is managed with wit and judgment and one considers well where one is, to whom one speaks, and who one is oneself. Notwithstanding that judgment is absolutely necessary in order never to say anything inappropriate, yet the conversation must appear [to be] so free as if we rejected not a single one of our thoughts and all is said that comes into the fancy without any affected design of speaking more often of one thing than another. For there is nothing more ridiculous than those people who have certain subjects on which they speak brilliantly and otherwise say nothing but foolishness. I believe that you should speak spontaneously, and yet you should always know what you're talking about. For if this course is taken, women will not be inappropriately learned nor ignorant to excess and everyone will say only what ought to be said to make the conversation agreeable. But what is most necessary to make it sweet and entertaining is that it must have a certain air of civility, which absolutely precludes all bitter retorts, as well as anything that might offend decency. And, finally, I want you to know so well the art of conversation that one is able to flirt with the strictest woman in the world; to speak a little foolishness to grave and serious people; to discuss science appropriately with the ignorant (if forced); and, in sum, to adapt his or her wit to whatever is discussed and whoever is the company. But besides all I have now said, I would have a certain spirit of joy reign [over conversation], which, without partaking of the folly of those eternal laughers who make so great a noise over so small a matter, does, however, inspire in the hearts of all the company a disposition to enjoy everything and to be bored with nothing. And I would have both trivial and important things discussed as long as they are discussed well and, without compulsion, have nothing spoken but what is necessary to be said."

"In the end," added Amilcar, "without giving you the trouble of speaking any more on conversation or making rules for it, it is enough to admire your [conversation] and to act as you do in order to merit the admiration of all the earth. For I assure you that I will be rebuked by no one when I say that I never heard you say anything but what was agreeable, courteous, and judicious; and no one knows so well as you the art of pleasing, charming, and entertaining."

"I wish," she replied, blushing, "that all you said were true and that I could believe you rather than myself. But to show you I cannot believe you and that I know I am often wrong, I declare ingenuously that I sense I have now said too much and, instead of telling all that I think about conversation, I should have contented myself with telling each one of the company what you have just said of me."

After this, everyone in turn combating the modesty of Valeria, we gave her so much praise that we almost made her angry. And afterwards we conducted so civil and enjoyable a conversation that it lasted almost until evening, when this charming company separated.

On Speaking Too Much or Too Little, and How to Speak Well[9]

Facing four rivals around his mistress at the same time, Amilcar was not without employment. He conducted himself, however, much better than another could have with such an encumbrance and thus contributed to making the conversation much more agreeable than usual. For one of Plotine's lovers, named Acrise, was a man who talked more than any other person ever talked. Sicinius hardly spoke at all, Telane talked agreeably about everything, and Damon loved to talk only about the sect to which he belonged. Consequently, whenever Amilcar found all these rivals around Plotine, there was not one who did not make for interesting talk by the manner in which Amilcar turned the conversation, and when they were not there he amused himself even more admirably, sometimes through counterfeiting the silence of the one, sometimes through talking too much like the other, and other times through humorously examining all the beliefs of the new sect of Pythagoras. And so, by this course, he prejudiced his rivals, diverted his mistress, and was never bored himself.

One day, among others, Acrise spoke so much and said so many useless things and Sicinius spoke so little that the two together were impossible pests. Because they had come one after another to Plotine's house, she sweetly complained to Amilcar, who arrived at Plotine's just after they left. "Please," she said, as soon as she saw him, "promise me two things that I have to ask you. First, that you will never talk so much that I can't get one word in if I wish to, and the other, that I will not be required to do all the talking and that you will once in a while join in the conversation with me. For I have seen two men today—one who would not let me say a word, and the other who did not even say four [words]."

"I can easily guess," replied Amilcar, "that Acrise and Sicinius have been to see you. But, my amiable Plotine," he added, "since you disapprove of both these faults, tell me which is the most intolerable, so that I may know which I ought most to avoid."

"I assure you," she answered, "that I have been gravely irritated by both of them. For it is very bothersome to see the conversation on the point of expiring every moment. On my part," she added laughing, "I would rather have the burden of overseeing the sacred fire of the Vestals than to have to entertain these people who contribute nothing to the conversation, to whom

9. The text we translated for this dialogue is "De parler trop ou trop peu et comment il faut parler" from *Conversations sur divers sujets* (Paris, 1680), vol. 1, as edited in *Choix de conversations de Mlle de Scudéry*, ed. Phillip J. Wolfe (Ravenna: Longo Editore, 1977), 25–39. Our thanks to the students of Professor Donawerth's fall 1995 course in English 489, "Gender and the History of Rhetorical Theory," who did an edition of this dialogue from the Ferrand Spence translation. A version of this dialogue was first published as part of Scudéry's novel *Clélie* (Paris, 1658), vol. 8, part 4, book 2, 637–75.

you must always say something new, who are enemies of long speeches, who hardly ever say anything but 'yes' or 'no,' and who, to spare themselves even the trouble of uttering a syllable, give only a little nod to signify they have heard you. In good earnest," pursued Plotine, "I know nothing more tedious than this type of profound silence between two persons, which recurs from time to time when one of them speaks too little. Silence on any other occasion has something sweet about it. But in this case it is annoying, and there is no noise, no matter how bothersome, that does not please me more."

"Seriously though," continued Amilcar, "the clatter of those who talk too much is just as irritating as the silence of those who hardly ever talk, and if you would carefully consider it, you would find it at least as bothersome. For, after all, is there anything more overwhelming than to hear the vast number of false and useless things that these great talkers say? For I confidently imagine that those who talk a great deal surely speak fallacious and worthless things. And what is most disturbing is that these people, at the same time as they make long recitations which one could do without, also hinder others from saying things which the company would be glad to know about. In fact," continued Amilcar, "Acrise, Sicinius, Telane, and myself were together yesterday on the banks of the Tiber. And as Telane, who is inquisitive, asked me in precisely what place the founders of Rome had marked out the first boundary of their city, when I wished to answer him and had begun to speak, saying 'Romulus,' Acrise interrupted me. And seven more times, like the best pupil[10] in the world, I recommended to speak and to say 'Romulus,' without succeeding in finishing my answer to Telane, who could not forbear laughing at my patience and perseverance. But at length I was forced to yield to Acrise and to resign myself to listen to him, though he said a hundred trifles that one might be content never to hear in one's whole life. For besides talking too much on fabricated or unproductive subjects, which I have already said, they likewise take up many disagreeable topics. And how can it be otherwise when they do not have judgment enough either to let those around them speak or to know that society ought to be a free [exchange], that there ought to be no tyranny in conversation, that each person has a role and a right to speak in turn, and, finally, that this [ideal] will never be [achieved] except through the attention of those who listen, so that those who speak well have the privilege of speaking more than others."

10. Amilcar is imagining himself a pupil in Renaissance fashion, called upon by the teacher to stand up and recite his lesson.

Valerie and Cesonie came in a moment after Amilcar had said these words. Emile, Horace, and Zenocrate also arrived. Seeing so many discriminating people capable of arbitrating concerning the subject of the conversation with Amilcar, Plotine told them about the boredom she underwent in the company of Acrise, who talked too much, and of Sicinius, who talked too little—then entreated them to give their opinions of these two defects.

"As for me, being lazy," said Valerie, "I think that I would rather speak too little than too much."

"You have a good point," added Cesonie, "for although women are generally accused of loving to speak too much, I find a great chatteress much more irritating than a great chatterer. Indeed, when women speak too much, ordinarily their conversation is nothing but a torrent of trivialities and superfluous words that weary all who have a mind even a little rational."

"In my opinion," returned Amilcar smiling, "I disagree. For when a magnificent talkative woman is young and beautiful, and makes no grimaces while speaking, but, on the contrary, shows her lovely white teeth and scarlet lips, I listen to her with much less pain than to one of those big talkative men, whose audacious and insolent demeanor is as tiresome to the eyes as to the ears."

"According to this individual," said Emile, who was not greatly averse to saying nothing at times, "I confess that I would not wish to be a great talker. But in someone else, I would be more comfortable with a man who always talked a lot than with a man who always required lots of talking to."

"I assure you," replied Horace, "that although all the world speaks, few people know how to speak [eloquently]."

"You have a good point, without doubt," responded Emile, "and I also maintain that there is hardly anything on which all people agree, unless it be that health is a blessing. Even beauty is not without dispute. Wealth is sometimes regarded as something injurious. The sciences are placed by some in the rank of doubtful. And medicine, which has no purpose but to give health and prolong life, is, however, considered by certain people as a dangerous practice, causing more bad than good. So the only truth is that there is uncertainty in the minds of men. Some approve what others condemn, and there is hardly anything that is commended by someone without being blamed by another. Thus some believe that to speak very little is a defect; others that to speak a great deal is perfection; some that to speak eloquently is to use big words; others that to speak well is to speak naturally and precisely; some that choice words are requisite; others that negligence is required, to avoid affectation—without realizing that affected negligence is the greatest fault of all. Similarly, there are those who believe that to speak well one must sound like a book; and there are those one finds who, to avoid this defect—which is, without doubt, a very great one—speak as vulgarly as the masses, without considering that all excess is equally bad and that, if it is perilous to speak too well, it is likewise to speak too ill. But in my opinion, there is one thing in language that is universally condemned by everyone, and that is obscurity and pompous nonsense, since truly whoever is listening desires to understand what is told to them and whoever is speaking is obligated to make himself understood."

"Emile is obviously right," Zenocrate acknowledged, "in saying that those who speak nonsense are condemned by everyone."

"However, there are a lot of them," replied Plotine, "but what surprises me the most is that I know several specific persons who are capable of this fault, and yet I also know that one could not say that they are totally without intelligence."

"There are such people, without question," rejoined Emile, "and the reason is that there are several kinds of pompous nonsense."

"But can you tell me clearly," responded Plotine, "why these good folk, who have some degree of intelligence, do not explain themselves distinctly and without confusion?"

"Undoubtedly, they are people who now and then conceive more or less appropriate things," answered Emile, "but whose words so completely tangle their thoughts that one cannot guess what they wished their listeners to grasp."

"There are others," countered Zenocrate, "who only explain themselves poorly because they do not themselves understand [what they are talking about]. Thus not only are they searching for the words they wish to say, but also for the ideas they wish to think!"[11]

"You see very well, then," replied Emile, "that I have reason to maintain that there are many forms of pompous nonsense. In effect, the people I first spoke about are obscure in their discourse because they do not choose the words well that might express their thoughts; and the second, of whom Zenocrate has just now spoken, are so because their ideas are so confused that there aren't words available to express such confused thoughts or to make them comprehensible. Similarly, there are many other sorts of speakers of obscurities, some of which are amendable. Indeed, I know some

11. This distinction between words and ideas, *res et verba,* the matter of a discourse and the form of expression, was popularized during the Renaissance through study of Aristotle's *Sophistical Refutations,* which divides problems of clarity into those based on form of expression and those based on reasoning, and Erasmus's *On Copia of Words and Things,* a textbook on style.

people who, in order to show that they have a lively and ready imagination, never give those with whom they speak time to finish what they wish to say. So that, impertinently undertaking to divine their meaning, they interrupt those who are speaking and, talking precipitantly themselves, they reply, one could say, before anything has been proposed to them. For, to consider rationally, a person who has not finished speaking has not yet said anything that a proper answer could be founded on, because very often the last words of an utterance reverse the beginning. Thus it almost always happens that those people who so brusquely interrupt others and like to prematurely guess [their meaning] say senseless things themselves and make a strange gallimaufry,[12] even if otherwise they are well enough stocked with intelligence."

"For my part," said Valerie, "I know speakers who speak nonsense, who only do so because they are distracted and are not listening closely to what is being said to them. Yet mechanically answering, they respond very improperly."

"There are some speakers of nonsense," replied Horace, "who speak so only out of a desire to be elegant, and they imagine that, to be known as clever, they must never speak clearly."

"For my part," said Amilcar, "I know that there are men and women whom one hears saying nonsensical things only because they wish to be the first to use certain fashionable words—words that chance has introduced, that the caprice of the *beau monde* accepts, and that time and usage sometimes authorize. Not knowing their true meaning, these people bring the words in inappropriately and very often say the opposite of what they mean."

"There are yet others," responded Emile, "who do not know anything about what they are speaking. For, being resolved to speak boldly about everything, though they know nothing, they venture, with a very mediocre intelligence, to discuss those subjects about which you can hardly speak well if you haven't studied them. Yet there is much more shame in pretending to such a capacity inappropriately than in being judiciously silent and in acknowledging that we know nothing of the things that are being discussed."

"For heaven's sake," said Plotine then, "let's leave these speakers of pompous nonsense, who are not worthy of occupying the heads of so many people who speak so lucidly, and let's discuss, I beseech you, only those who talk too much or too little. Now, I must confess, in my opinion, it seems to me that the latter are so dull themselves while also extremely boring to

12. A gallimaufry is a hash or stew, so by metaphor a nonsensical jumble.

others that I would rather speak too much than speak too little, for then, though troubling my friends, I would at least entertain myself."

"While it seems scarcely possible to be of an opinion contrary to yours without being on the wrong side," Emile demurred, "I cannot keep from saying once more that I prefer to speak too little than to speak too much; and yet, I sometimes prefer the conversation of a great talker than that of a person who talks hardly at all. Although it is common that a person who speaks hardly anything possesses good judgment, it almost never happens that a person who speaks too much possesses good judgment."

"That's a good point," replied Amilcar, "but also, it doesn't happen very often that those people who speak hardly anything have a great deal of intelligence; and quite often it does happen that those people who talk too much are very well stocked. Now, on my part, I am persuaded that wit is like fire and that, if there is any there, it will have to show itself in some way or other."

"Yet great men there have been," countered Horace, "who did not love to speak."

"That's true," responded Emile, "but they made their intelligence apparent in their writings or their actions, though they did not show it in their speech. For I am as convinced as Amilcar that wit cannot be completely concealed and must necessarily show itself. One is able, of course, to find great princes, great philosophers, great poets, great painters, and excellent artificers[13] who speak little. But their actions or their works speak for them and demonstrate that their silence is not an effect of stupidity. It is not the same with those people whose wit resides only in words and who never employ themselves except in speaking, seeing that, ordinarily, their actions, I am sure, speak nothing to their advantage."

"But," retorted Zenocrate, "not all people of judgment are such great friends of silence."

"I'm not saying," responded Emile, "that all who talk a lot lack judgment entirely—for I should do injustice to too many educated people. [I'm] only [saying] that they who speak too much must not have any [judgment]."

"Believe me," asserted Plotine, "there is a very fine line between speaking a great deal and speaking too much."

"Liberality and prodigality resemble each other in some ways," replied Emile, "yet we can distinguish quite well that the one is a virtue and the other

---

13. Artificers are skilled artistic workers or craftsmen; those who practice any art or applied science.

a vice. Thus we may easily distinguish those who speak a great deal and well from those who talk too much and poorly, or at least inappropriately."

"But," resumed Valeria, "are there not some people who speak too much and yet do not fail to speak well?"

"There are some, without a doubt," answered Amilcar, "and I know a Greek in Sicily who spoke with all the Attic[14] purity and yet never failed to be annoying because he spoke more than he ought. For to define the person who speaks too much, one recognizes him principally by the tiny number of ideas expressed in the great number of words, by his inane urge to speak without ceasing, by his eagerness to give an opinion about everything, to cut everyone else off, to exhaust any subject he treats, to continue speaking without thinking, sometimes whether or not anyone is listening, [and] to be unable to keep quiet even when among people of higher quality[15] and more ability than himself. I do not deny that those who speak a lot are sometimes revealed, even though they speak well, to be annoying—to people who love to speak as much as they do. But indeed, as you do not come across that every day, we must not, for the convenience of a few people, condemn the people who speak a great deal and well, and who offer a thousand pleasures through conversation because they never say anything but what is necessary or agreeable. Indeed, when someone loves to have the discourse all to himself, because Nature has given him the ability to express himself, because he has an agile wit and a lively imagination [and] a memory filled with a thousand well-selected and reasonable things, because his judgment is master of his wit and his fancy, and because his conversation has the true air of sophistication, he may unquestionably speak a great deal without speaking too much.

"And I am sure that if this man is such as I have described him, he will know how to be silent when he desires to be, will let others speak who desire to do so, and will not behave like the great jabberer I met when I arrived at Syracuse,[16] to whom I had begun to describe the great peril I had run into at sea when a tempest arose—a danger that he had begged me to tell about. But I had hardly begun to tell him that the sea grew troubled all of a sudden, when he interrupted, saying, 'That reminds me of a time when I was traveling at sea and something similar happened to me. And just imagine,' he

14. By analogy to the preferred ancient Greek dialect, "Attic" means marked by simple and refined elegance, pure, classical, witty.

15. Rank, status, social position.

16. A city in ancient times on the east coast of Sicily, founded by the Greeks, later the center of a Roman province.

added, without remembering what he had requested of me, 'that after having embarked at Tarentum[17] in a very good ship (whose pilot was from Cumae[18] and which was loaded with all kinds of merchandise because Tarentum is a rich and powerful city where there is great commerce in all sorts of goods), the wind changing all of a sudden, the ship was constrained to stay fifteen days longer in the port of Tarentum, where I had quite a pleasant adventure. For, when I went on board, I said goodbye to quite a pretty woman, whom I had courted for some time and who, in consideration for me, had banished from her house a lover she had before me. But she thought I had departed the night before, so when I landed the next day and went to her house to let her know I would still have the pleasure of seeing her for several days, I found her laughing with an unbroken heart in the company of my old rival, although she had just taken leave of me with tears. Anger took such strong hold of me that I quarreled with both my rival and my mistress. The anger cured me of my passion[19] and, after parting from this visit, I made another one, where I fell in love with a pretty young lady, with whom I flirted shamelessly and for whom I experienced so much love that I let the ship go that I was already embarked on with the intention of departing.' 'But,' I said to him, interrupting him in turn, 'when you interrupted me, I thought it was to recount some tempest to me, which resembled the one you asked me to describe. And yet, though you embarked, I see you are again on land, engaged in making love.' 'Have patience,' said he to me, 'we aren't there yet.' And indeed, I had need of patience.

"For through that prodigious desire he had to be always talking and never to let anyone else talk, he related to me all the remarkable things that had happened to him in his new amour. He showed me his mistress's letters, he recited songs, he embarked again and made a voyage without a tempest— all before he came to the story of that voyage where he really thought he might perish. So this man, who wished to know how I had almost drowned, knew nothing of it, and told me a hundred things that I didn't know what to do with. Yet he spoke elegantly and, I suppose, if it had been appropriate at the time to acquaint me with every little thing he knew, one might say that this man spoke eloquently. But as I could make nothing of what he told me, and as I had only once or twice recounted the danger I had run, and as it is pretty natural for all people to love relating a storm they have just escaped

17. An important city and harbor in southern Italy on the gulf also named Tarentum.

18. An ancient city on the Italian coast near Naples, founded by the Greeks.

19. In the Renaissance, natural philosophy taught that passions were the result of physical humors that coursed through the body and that a new passion could thus drive an old one out.

from, I suffered more than you can well imagine. And his eloquence upset me so much that, if I had not taken the course of ridiculing him in secret while he was speaking, I would have been extremely displeased."

"You have recited this story so amusingly," resumed Plotine, laughing, "that it would have been a shame if there had never been people who talked too much. And what I find good in it," she added, teasing, "is that, in counterfeiting a man who speaks too much, you restrained yourself no more than anyone else."

"That's true," replied Amilcar with a smile. "Sometimes I hold forth willingly enough. But to prove to all the company that I know how to keep from talking when I wish to, I need only inform them that I have loved you more than eight days without telling you, even though each and every moment I wanted to."

"Pray," said Plotine, "let us not so soon change the topic, nor amuse ourselves speaking foolishness, which is as irrelevant to the company as your Greek's recital of his adventures was to you. For since I am not an enemy of speaking too much, and since it is one of the most common things in the world, I would not be sorry to have someone explain to me how one should speak in order to speak well."

"First of all," said Amilcar, smiling, "you must have a good portion of wit, a fair amount of memory, and a great deal of judgment. Then it is necessary to adopt the language of well-bred people of that nation and to avoid equally the language of low-class, vulgar people, of silly wits, and of those people who intermingle a little of the court, a little of the vulgar, a little of the past century, a little of the present, and a great deal of the urbane—making their language the most bizarre of all."

"But still," said Plotine, "I don't find this sufficient. For you say well how not to speak, but not precisely how to speak well."

"I assure you," replied Horace, "to speak elegantly and agreeably, nothing more is needed than to speak as you do."

"And indeed," added Emile, "the charming Plotine speaks as a rational woman should speak—agreeably. For all her expressions are at once noble and natural; she does not hunt around for something to say; there is no hesitation in her words; her discourse is clear and easy; there is a gentle turn in her manner of speaking, no affectation in the sound of her voice, a great deal of freedom in her movement, and a wonderful coherence between her eyes and her words that contributes a great deal to making her speech more agreeable."

"But how can I, who hardly ever think about what I say," retorted Plotine, "possess all that which you describe?"

"If you paid more heed to it," answered Zenocrate, "you would not speak as agreeably as you do. For people who think so much about what they are going to say never say anything worthwhile."

"But," interrupted Cesonie, "I would also like to know what the difference is between a man who speaks well and a woman who speaks well. For though I know for a certainty that there ought to be a distinction, I don't know precisely of what it consists. They make use of the same words, they speak at times of the same things, and they even quite often have thoughts that are alike. Yet, as I have already said, an educated woman should not always speak like an educated man, and there are certain expressions which the one may properly make use of that yet would be very unbecoming in the other."

"Indeed," responded Plotine, "there are some things that are altogether bizarre in the mouth of a woman which are not shocking in that of a man. For example, if I should swear by the sacred fire or by Jupiter, I would startle those I spoke to. If I should undertake to pronounce decisively concerning a difficult question, I would pass for ridiculous. If I even affirmed what I said with too boisterous and confident a tone, people would doubt if I deserved to be called a maid. If I spoke of war like a military tribune, all my friends would laugh at me. While it is necessary to speak modestly, it is also necessary to guard against succumbing to another defect, which is that of speaking with a certain affected simplicity, like a child—very unbecoming. Nor must we speak foolishly. But we also must not always be listening to ourselves speak, as certain women do who really attend to the sound of each word they utter, as they would to the sound of a harp they wish to tune, and who, with an affected tone of gravity, speak often very stupid things in very pretty words."

"What the wonderful Plotine says," replied Amilcar, "is wonderfully well said. But let us speak of a fault equally common among both men and women: it is this, that we must carefully avoid a vulgar accent, which renders the finest topics disagreeable. For I contend that it is without comparison much better if I have a little African accent when speaking the language of Rome than if I have a peculiar accent like that of the basest craftsman. And indeed, I hold that there is absolutely no place in the world where there is not a difference between the accent of well-bred persons and that of common people. And I must add that a foreigner is much less blamable for keeping the accent of his own country than a man or woman of quality who speaks like their servants. And I, for my part, who am very picky about all these things, am quite touched by the sound of a voice with a sweet, pure accent, and by a certain nobility that I find in the pronunciation of some of the people I know and principally in that of the charming Plotine."

"But pray," said Cesonie then, "tell me what those who do not speak like Plotine can do to acquire her graces and to lose their deformities."

"Frequent the company of well-bred people," replied Emile, "and see few others. For, after all, it is not the role of books to teach speaking; and those who content themselves with reading in order to be fit for conversation are strangely mistaken and do not know what reading is good for. Reading is necessary to refine intelligence, regulate morals, and strengthen judgment. It may also serve to teach a language; but conversation alone is capable of lending gracefulness to language. And yet it is necessary that it be a conversation of people of good society, in which women have the greatest share. Otherwise, the language of those who regulate their speech by what they read might be a little too elevated, too erudite, too dry, too uncouth, or too affected. For just as ordinary books do not speak as people speak in conversation, neither must we speak in conversation like books."

"All the same," said Plotine, "I am amazed that the whole world does not dream of speaking well, since it seems to me that there is nothing easier than always to be with well-bred people. But it is not like learning other things. On the contrary, it is quite often difficult to heed those who teach singing, painting, or dancing. But since to speak well you need nothing more than to frequent the company of gentlefolk and people who speak agreeably, I make a vow to study how to speak all my life and never willingly to see any other sort of people."

"Others should be courting your company," countered Zenocrate, "rather than you seeking the company of others."

"That's right," said Amilcar, "but there is something else that the lovely Plotine needs to learn, which is to listen a little more favorably to what I sometimes say to her."

"As for that," she answered, "one learns that all too soon with you. But there is something else that I would like for those who do not know it to learn—which is to pay attention to what is being said to them and not to fall to daydreaming inappropriately in company. A little absentmindedness," added she, "I forgive. But a succession of constant daydreams, in which certain people indulge, who are never entirely there and who are not, indeed, anywhere—I think it is best to reform such [absences]. And when we have so many things to consider that are more worthwhile than what is spoken around us, we ought to stay in our closets and keep ourselves company since, without question, it is an incivility not to listen to what is said where we are and to slight all the rest of the company where we find ourselves. For my part, I am persuaded that nothing but the murmur of a river and the noise of a fountain can we listen to sociably while dreaming."

"Notwithstanding all you can say," replied Amilcar, "the freedom to dream is a sweet thing, and you should be aware that everywhere may be found houses more agreeable solely because the hosts don't restrain anybody there. And indeed, there one may daydream, talk, laugh, sing, and converse with whomever one wishes; one may come and go without saying a word and enjoy a freedom that is so sweet that [such houses] are preferred before many others."

"Be that as it may," said Plotine, "I stick to what Emile said. For, even without learning so many things, it will be much more convenient for me to converse only with well-educated people. And really, I am resolved to see no other if possible."

"You did well to add those last words," responded Amilcar. "Because, the way the world is made, it is pretty difficult to find only such people as are worthy of that name."

On Wit[20]

Since you want me to inform you in detail about a conversation, Madame, that you have been curious about, I consent, because it was the most agreeable adventure in the course of a little trip I made with a small number of my friends, male and female, to satisfy the desire I had to view the sea. Since I had never seen anything except rivers, I admit that I did not understand very well all the wondrous descriptions of shipwrecks that I had read, some in verse, some in prose, and I was very curious to see what occasioned them. And I will not conceal the fact, Madame, that one of my relatives who was on the voyage helped me write this account of it for you—an account that will be less boring if fictitious names are substituted for the true ones.

Our company was composed of two of my close kin, people of taste,[20] and two ladies of quality, very beautiful and extremely witty. The lord of the wilderness where we went to view the sea was a very rich and worthy gentleman who had renounced the world out of grief that he had lost an only son, eighteen years old, who, in an adventure in which love and glory played

20. Based on "De la raillerie," in *Les conversations sur divers sujets* (Paris, 1680), vol. 2, 523–614, as edited in *"De l'air galant" et autres conversations*, ed. Delphine Denis (Paris: Honoré Champion, 1998), 99–114, 313–28. Our thanks to Lillian Doherty, who started translating this dialogue with us but had to turn to other scholarly pursuits. A version of this dialogue was first published in Scudéry's novel, *Artamène; ou, Le grand Cyrus* (Paris, 1653), vol. 9, book 3, 960–88.

20. *Honnête gens* we have translated here as "people of taste," and "ésprit" as "wit." In Scudéry's usage "ésprit" seems to mean something in between the English word "wit" and the Italian word "sprezzatura" or gallant spirit, with perhaps also the connotations of "fire" or "soul" and "style."

a great part, of which you will hear another day, was taken by pirates—[and the father] had heard nothing of him for ten years.

The manor we visited was very beautiful. One can view the expanse of sea from all the rooms, but especially well from a large summerhouse that stands at the end of a long terrace [carved by] nature and extending from the chateau to the edge of the cliffs overlooking the sea. The waves breaking against the rocks on which the summerhouse is built make a very agreeable spectacle, although there is something terrible about them because of the roaring noise, which one is scarcely able to imagine without having heard it.

Antigene (which is the name I shall call the person whom we went to see), warned ahead of time that we would arrive one morning at his home (since we were to stay overnight three leagues from there), had prepared everything that he thought appropriate to entertain us. And since several days previously he had received the news of the general armistice that the king had granted to his people and his enemies, he had waited for us in order to make a small party to celebrate—such was his great zeal for his king and for his country. He had even invited some very beautiful ladies who for reasons other than ours were in the neighborhood, and this select gathering was assuredly a choice one.

He received us at the end of this large terrace, which led to the summerhouse that I've already told you about. Antigene conducted us there and showed me the sea in all its expansiveness, which amazed me and filled me with admiration. We perceived a vessel approaching a nearby beach; and soon we saw two gentlemen who jumped into a small boat with some of their men [and], arriving on land, took the road [leading] to the chateau. They were goodlooking, although of different ages. But they were so far away that Antigene did not recognize them. Without lingering over things I will tell you about at length another time, Antigene, seized by a presentiment, asked permission from us to go to see who these strangers were, one of whom had come to ask to speak with him. A half hour later he returned to us transported with joy and presented to us a Spaniard of very handsome appearance, although a man of mature years: "Help me to thank the generous Don Alvarez, with whom long ago in my youth I made a six-month voyage," he said, addressing his words to me, since I was his relative, "for he has brought back my son, whom I believed lost all these years." Saying this, he presented to us his son, named Clearchus, who is very handsome, and whose air and lovely grace pleased the whole company and fully reflected the wit that we were afterwards to find in him.

This [lucky] adventure, which seemed straight out of a romance, caused us [great] joy and made the party [even] more pleasant. And since in the summerhouse was a portrait of Clearchus's mother represented as Venus rising from the sea, it was easy to recognize that Clearchus was her son, since he had the same look and the same features. Antigene had loved her deeply, and he had not been able to bring himself to remarry, although he was still rather young.

Because the dinner hour was approaching, after Antigene had explained in a few words that Don Alvarez and Clearchus had come all the way from the oriental Indies and, through various chances, had nearly made a circuit of the world, he led us into the house between two rows of orange trees in great boxes, so large that they almost formed an arbor. And to make the meal more magnificent, and to make it include something reminiscent of the sea, the courses were mixed, and there were fish of a prodigious size and a lovely appearance.

Since Don Alvarez spoke French very well because his mother was French, and since he had an inexhaustible wit, he contributed a great deal to the company's conversation. He very quickly made clear his great joy in seeing peace between France and Spain. Because he was born of a Spaniard acclimated to the Indies through extensive assignments, and of a French-woman, whom the caprice of Fortune had conducted there with her rela-tions, he was delighted to have arrived at a time when the war was over between the two nations.

During the dinner party there was an excellent symphony, which brought an atmosphere of celebration to the company. We drank the health of the king to the sound of trumpets and the roar of the cannon, for this manor was fortified with many [artillery] pieces. On leaving the table, we passed through a magnificent chamber where fine little caskets had perfumed the air. After the company was seated, there arose a fairly pleasant dispute between two ladies. For there was one who passionately loved to listen to the tales of a traveling gentleman of wit and, strangely enough, another who completely dreaded them. "Please," said Clarice to Antigene, "let us know all the particulars of the voyage of Don Alvarez and Clearchus."

"For my part," replied Clearchus, "I find myself such a stranger in my [own] country that it seems to me I no longer know how to speak the lan-guage any more, so much so that I must be given time to relearn it, as if I had never known it, before I agree to tell a long story."

"As far as I'm concerned," said Don Alvarez, "I do not wish to be liable to incredulity, for almost all travelers are suspected of adding to the truth. And then, since it was the caprice of Fortune that took us to such different countries, neither Clearchus nor myself is prepared to tell those long stories that bore most of those who listen to them."

"Ah, Don Alvarez," replied Melinta agreeably, who especially disliked those long stories that Clarice desired, "how much joy I take in discovering that you are not at all one of these prodigious liars like those I've unwillingly encountered too often on social occasions, who spend entire days telling you that in such a place there is a river that plunges into an abyss and that goes ten leagues beyond that, and that in another [place] are cloud-covered mountains—who amuse themselves with describing frightful animals, extravagant customs and, what is most rare, still ignore all that surrounds them and only know what doesn't concern them. Indeed," she added, laughing, "I know a man who made a census of the monsters of the Nile, who spoke of the phoenix and the halcyons as if he were talking about nightingales and warblers, and who nevertheless did not know half of the trees of our own forests."

I could tell by the expression of Don Alvarez and Clearchus that they listened to this raillery with admiration: I fueled this debate instead of resolving it. The rest of the company felt the same way. And taking her at her word, looking at Melinta, whose humor is playful and charming, I said to her, "I assure you that if I ever made a voyage of even a little length I would be careful to keep myself from seeing you until I was tired of telling others all I had seen."

"You would do me a great favor," she replied, "for when I am in a humor to know these sorts of things, I get a book that helps me understand them, and I stop [reading] when it pleases me, which I cannot do when a gentleman takes pains to tell twenty years' worth of experience in one day."

"You are right, Madame," Don Alvarez said to her, smiling, "for if I attempted to tell you all that I had seen, you would without fail die of boredom, and perhaps I would be just as sick [of it] as you."

Everyone laughed at what Don Alvarez said. "You are awfully obliging to Melinta," replied Clarice, somewhat disappointed. "However, this kindness [to her] deprives the company of a very great pleasure."

"Since I don't wish to incur your hatred," answered Melinta in a pleasant manner, "I'll acquiesce, if Don Alvarez and Clearchus will consent to tell us something about their travels, until the time for our walk. But if I accommodate you," she continued, "you must also somewhat accommodate my humor, and we will agree on the nature of the questions that we will ask Don Alvarez and Clearchus. For I declare to you that I do not care at all, as I already said, about bizarre customs of foreign peoples or about all the peculiarities of seas, great rivers, mines, and a thousand similar things."

"For my part," replied Clarice, "I love [to hear] anything that a witty traveler can tell me, as long as whatever he tells me is something new, and the more exotic the more to my taste [do I find them]. But," she added, "I am willing to give you the choice [of what to tell]."

"I confess to you," answered Melinta, "that what I find the most agreeable is the character of extraordinary persons, and I don't doubt that if I were born during the time of Caesar or Alexander and had seen any traveler who had met them, I would have felt great curiosity to inquire into what made them tick."

"Very well," said Clarice, "we must beg Don Alvarez and Clearchus to search their memories for anything of this sort to tell us."

Don Alvarez responded that he could not make himself bore such an elegant person in order to satisfy another one. Clearchus excused himself also more strongly for the same reason. Everyone jumped into the discussion with pleasure, inventively mocking the excessive curiosity of Clarice, whose impatience was apparent to everyone.

"For my part," I said, "I have a desire to know in what place during your voyages the ladies were most amiable."

"You've got to be kidding!" interrupted Melinta; "you are fishing for compliments."

"For myself," said Arpasia, "I am curious to know if wit occurs in all times and all countries."

"No doubt about that—" interrupted Clarice, who was not satisfied with what Arpasia asked, "this is no question to ask a traveler, and I still would prefer [to hear] about the character of some great prince, which Melinta claims to desire."

"I find Arpasia's query so thoughtful," said Climene, "that I join her [in her request], in order to oblige Don Alvarez and Clearchus to tell us whether or not they really found wit in the most distant and most savage lands."

"This question won't take a long answer," said Don Alvarez, "for I think I can say that wit exists in all times and all countries. But it varies according to the diversity of nations, of temperaments, and of customs. In general, wit is a type of seasoning that gives a spicier flavor to conversation, and it is rightly a natural result of the human spirit."

"But," added Clarice, who wished to break off this conversation, "I know people who do not joke."

"That does not mean," responded Clearchus, "that they are not able to joke."

"But if they are not able to," said Melinta laughing, "that doesn't prove anything. For are there not people who have no judgment? And yet, speaking of people in general, one still says that human beings have the ability to reason. So I believe that it's not wrong to say that wit is universal and that it is like mineral springs that absorb the qualities of the earth and the mineral veins that they pass through. For according to the temperament of a people and the customs of nations, wit is rude or tactful, nasty or agreeable; it is mocking among some people and among others a simple playfulness that makes society more pleasant."

"I assure you," said Don Alvarez, "that what the beautiful Melinta has said is better than anything that I would be able to say about my travels."

"Indeed, wit is practically an inseparable companion of Melinta," said Clarice, "and she is so well acquainted with it that she could not fail to speak agreeably [on the subject]. She often carries it to the point of injustice. For," [Clarice] added, "she doesn't hesitate to amuse herself at the expense of a man who spends his [whole] life admiring her, and that's all I'm going to say about it."

"In truth," answered Melinta laughing, "you are more unjust than I am to desire to be mean to both Theocrites, of whom you were speaking, and me at the same time. For indeed, I tell you that if I were not permitted to laugh in his absence about the many [funny] things he does, I would not suffer him near me at all. And that is why, if you believe that he cares for me and that my presence is a pleasure to him, you must put up with my making fun of his melancholy. That doesn't stop me from saying that Theocrites is very much a gentleman. But to desire that I should see him grave from morning to night and that I must listen seriously to his sighs for entire days, and after that not amuse myself as a result, that is to be a friend neither of Theocrites nor of myself, because you wish to cause him great sadness and to deny me a very great pleasure."

"For myself," said Polemon then, "I think that the beautiful Melinta is right."

"Personally," I added, "I share Clarice's opinion, and it seems to me that it is too inhumane to make fun of a lover."

"To speak sincerely," said Euridamia next, "I think that there is no such thing as innocent teasing."

"I am then often guilty," answered Melinta, "for I vow that I never find a conversation as pleasant as when there is some agreeable malice mixed in, which makes it more amusing and more animated. Besides, to speak truthfully, if there were ever an innocent teasing, it is that done to a serious and solemn lover. For it is true that gallantry without playfulness is a thing so unreasonable that I do not know how you can find it unpleasant that I joke about such a thing."

"Since you joke with such good grace," answered Euridamia, "you almost persuade me that one should not have qualms about teasing the way you do, and I am sure that you believe completely that anything said pleasantly in the spirit of teasing is permissible, without exception."

"Ah, Euridamia," she answered, "you go too far there. It is, however, true," she added, correcting herself, "that it is difficult enough to keep locked up in your mind a thing that you have found amusing and that you know would not be too terrible to tell. For indeed, to be honest, I am convinced that it takes a more refined wit to jest delicately than it takes to do many things that appear much more difficult."

"It's important to admit," added Polemon, "that it requires an infinite stock [of wit] to joke about things as you joke about them, whenever you please, and that it is sometimes more of a pleasure to be teased by you than to be praised by someone else."

"It is certain," I added, "that Melinta is admirable when she wants to be. But it is also true that there are thousands of people who take part in teasing who should never have done so."

"For myself," said Euridamia, "I will go even further and say again that there is scarcely any innocent teasing, and that whoever makes much of a habit of it risks giving up friendship, integrity, and virtue."

"Oh, honestly!" cried Melinta laughing. "You are being very cruel to me."

"To appease you," replied Euridamia, "I will confess that there is a kind of gallant teasing that has less malice in it than other kinds [do]. But what I maintain is that such wit is not really amusing unless it stings a little. To make a habit of teasing is like walking along a precipice: it is the most difficult thing in the world to do it completely right, without offending friendship, or decency, or integrity, or virtue, or without doing yourself an injury. For indeed, it is nearly impossible to make a profession of joking without causing dislike, or at least fear. To be reasonable, too, there is almost no one that it's appropriate to make fun of. Indeed," she added, "I know scarcely any people who rightly deserve to be the subject of joking."

"What!" cried Melinta, "you want to protect everyone in the world [from teasing]?"

"I assure you," replied Euridamia, "that there is scarcely anyone whom I would leave to your mercy. First of all," she continued, "I think that not only should you never make fun of your particular friends but also never of your acquaintances. For indeed, as carefully as you single them out and as delicately as you amuse yourself, you are still singling them out. But when you have once singled them out, I do not think that you should again make fun of them. And I will never be like those people who do not spare those who, of all the world, they like the best, for my opinion is that it is very dangerous to amuse oneself at the expense of one's friends."

"But at least," said Clearchus, "may we not abandon to Melinta her enemies, if she has any?"

"In truth," replied Euridamia, "I hardly find it more attractive to make fun of enemies than of friends. For when you hate someone, no vengeance is weaker than insulting someone who can return the favor, and there is a certain cowardliness in all jokes that are inspired purely by a spirit of revenge. I also think that it is very dangerous to make fun of your social superiors, that it is spiteful to make fun of people much lower [in class status] than you, and that a gentleman should use moderation with ladies, and that ladies should not be too quick to tease gentlemen for fear of discovering someone who does not respect such rules."

"In short," said Melinta, "from the way you talk, I infer that you will hardly let me make fun of myself."

"I assure you," answered Euridamia, "even though it is the most innocent mockery that it is possible to make, if it is not done with great judgment it will not be too entertaining, and it is certainly much more difficult to speak amusingly about oneself than about others, except on those occasions when making fun of yourself first prevents mockery by others, for that is one way to disarm them.

"Moreover," she added, "I find that it is never proper to mock people who possess no merit, because such mockery almost never seems elegant. And I also think that we should never make fun of those who do possess [merit], because such mockery also almost never seems elegant. And I also think that we should never make fun of those who do possess it, because [it would be] a great injustice to fix on a slight fault to the disparagement of a thousand good qualities, since it is certain that mockery often recoils upon the one who makes it. And for that reason, it's necessary to consider carefully whom you are mocking, the place where you are, and before whom you speak.

"I likewise boldly maintain that we should never make fun of crimes, because we ought to detest them; nor misfortunes, because we ought to pity them; nor imperfections of the body that one can't get rid of; nor old age, since it is an unavoidable evil unless one dies young; nor foreigners just because they are foreign, for a Persian, for example, can't help being a Persian, just as you can't help being French.

"At the very least," she added, "I think that if you wish to mock someone, you must do so while speaking to that person and never say things that are really offensive, but only such things as will enliven the conversation a little. For in that case I admit that it is allowable to make war on one's best friends. But Melinta, there are very few people who know how to tease either agreeably or innocently. And truly I'm not astonished by this. For in the end, birth [alone] can give [you] this talent, for it is certain that art is not able to give it, and whoever would try to force Nature has such poor success in amusing others that that person actually provides ample material for mockery, while imagining that he or she is mocking them. It is different from all other agreeable qualities of the intellect," she continued, "for there is no other that cannot be acquired by study. But this one alone must be given by Nature and must be managed by Judgment.

"Finally, it is not enough to think funny things; it is also necessary that you must have a certain trick of expression that makes these ideas amusing.[21] And the expression on your face, the tone of your voice, and generally the whole person must contribute to making amusing that which by itself is not so enjoyable."

"I would never have believed," said Antigene then, "that a person as serious as Euridamia could speak so well on something she never does."

"On the contrary," she replied, "it is because I do not tease at all that I am an authority on the topic of teasing. For, since I have no interest in it whatsoever, I speak about it objectively, and I examine all the different [styles of] teasing of those I am acquainted with without being unfair to anyone. But to tell you the truth, except for one of my friends, who has an admirable delicacy of wit and a sophisticated, malicious imagination that pleases on all occasions, I know no one besides Melinta whose mockery I excuse."

"It's true," I said then, "there is nothing more intolerable than the sort of people who, without [stopping to] think, say terrible things about each other while imagining that they are teasing and who believe that, since they are speaking about others' faults in rude language, they are joking."

"There is another group of people," responded Polemon, "who make me despair when I discover them. For they make their jokes consist entirely of a vulgar and low-class way of speaking, which fills the imagination with disgusting matter [and] their mouths with the expressions of the coarsest people, demonstrating that, in order to learn that way of speaking, they must have spent most of their lives in the worst company on earth."

"Hey, Polemon," cried Melinta, "you please me immensely by hating that sort of people you're talking about. And though I defend teasing in general, I exclude almost all joking and that sort in particular, if I may be permitted [that distinction]. For I want teasing to be elegant, even if a little

---

21. Like "ésprit" and "honnête gens," "agréable" encompasses a set of related meanings. Here we have translated it as "amusing," but it could be translated as "delightful," or "agreeable to the audience."

malicious. But I would like it also to be modest and gentle, so that it offends neither the ears nor the imagination and so that it never makes anyone blush or fret.

"And truly," she added, "the teasing of a well-bred man ought not to be that of any profession except gentleman. For there are [kinds of] joking among low-class people, among middle-class people, in the army, in the law courts, at the university, in the country, and also at court, which is almost always the best kind. But if the courtly is the kind I mean, then you cannot distinguish it from others because it is like an accent—to have the best accent is to have none at all."

"What Melinta says is admirable," resumed Euridamia, "but there is still another group of jokers who exasperate me whenever I meet them any place, because they imagine that they have to make a joke out of everything, so much so that, since they are always wracking their brains to find what they are looking for, they speak a thousand dull things for every amusing one. Thus it turns out that for the three or four decent jokes they will make during their whole lives, one must endure listening to a thousand rotten ones."

"For my part," I spoke up, "sometimes I come across this one man who drives me to despair by continually repeating something he has said that he thinks is amusing, and I swear to you that I have heard him repeat one of his jokes more than a thousand times."

"I also can't stand those," added Don Alvarez, "who tell mean stories and laugh at them first themselves and would laugh at them all alone if I were the only one listening."

"After all," said Euridamia, "there is also another sort that is the most boring of all, since, in my opinion, I know nothing more annoying than a certain tasteless and stale teasing that is never appropriate. For when we see those who speak trying [too hard] to be amusing and failing completely, nothing is more tiresome."

"Those grand tellers of lengthy 'funny' stories," I repeated, "who say a thousand unnecessary things before getting to one amusing item are not very funny either, even though they think they are. Moreover, it's so difficult to tell neither too much nor too little in the case of stories, whether funny or serious, that few people in the world do it well."

"These people who unload a ton of proverbs," replied Euridamia, "are also the sort of person to be dreaded even more. When they cite a proverb at just the right moment, it can be very pleasant, but when it's the wrong time, the effect is terrible, and it would be better to say something stupid of their own creation than to pick a proverb and put it in at the wrong time."

"I know some others," put in Melinta, "who, as silly as they are, do amuse me for a quarter of an hour. For when I come across people who think that in order to be wits all they have to do is be very gay, talk a lot, laugh at everything they say and at everything they think up, make a big uproar, and abruptly say rude things, I cannot keep from laughing at them as heartily as if they were the most amusing folk in the world."

"But what makes you laugh at them," responded Euridamia, "is that you are naturally malicious, and you are able to find a lot of material for amusing jokes in those who joke in bad taste."

"However," added Antigene, "without noticing it, we have come to share Euridamia's opinion. For since joking is such a difficult thing to do well, I [now] believe that she is right to say that it's dangerous to get involved with it."

"I quite agree," said Melinta, "when she condemns hurtful joking and when she can't stand anything satirical or crass or dull or foolish. But as for the gallant and the sweet [kind of teasing], I couldn't be more opposed [to her opinion]. Euridamia must indeed share my opinion, or else she must explain precisely what kind of joking remains for me to take pleasure in."

"I've already told you," replied Euridamia, "that I don't approve of any of them, even though there are some that amuse me."

"Tell us those that amuse you, at least," said Antigene, "for in my opinion there are very few things that amuse you that would not also amuse everyone else. And if only to cure Melinta of her maliciousness," he added smiling, "I implore you to establish Laws for Teasing, swearing that I will follow them more exactly than anyone ever kept the Laws of Solon."[22]

"Hah! If you ask me," interrupted Melinta, laughing, "I don't promise any such thing, and I am very much mistaken if anyone at all is able to say of the laws she's going to make what Anacharsis[23] said about the laws of that [great] lawmaker."

"Whatever!" said Euridamia. "Since Antigene will follow them, that[24] won't stop me from making them."

22. Solon was a sixth-century B.C.E. Athenian statesman who freed serfs from their land-bondage debts, revised the constitution to distribute political power across a broader range of classes, and established a more humane law code (replacing the ordinances of Draco—the draconian laws).

23. Anacharsis was a sixth-century B.C.E. Scythian prince who traveled in Greece and met Solon; many pithy sayings are attributed to him, as well as letters actually written in the third century B.C.E. but which the seventeenth century took for authentic and which served as the model for Montesquieu's *Lettres Persanes*. In her edition of some of the *Conversations*, Denis explains that the allusion Anacharsis makes to the laws of Solon is repeated in book 9 of Scudéry's *Cyrus* (1656), 535.

24. "That" refers to Melinta's comment that no one will follow the laws Euridamia makes.

"I also promise you never to violate them," I said, "as long as you give them to us right now."

"In that case, the word 'Laws' so frightens me," said Euridamia, "that I don't dare open my mouth. So to speak more modestly, I wish only to tell you my opinion and to submit it to your judgment.

"I will tell you then," she continued, "that I allow none but those who are born to tease, not any who must force themselves to it. Likewise, I think that no one should have to strain for it. For certainly if it does not come by itself and without trouble, it will never come out well. In addition, teasing must be so different from satire that the one may never be taken for the other. I know very well that some say that teasing that doesn't sting amuses no one. But for me, I think otherwise. Indeed, I like teasing that is surprising and even hits the person addressed where it hurts. But I will not allow pricking too deep or any that pierces the heart deeper than the thorns felt by someone picking roses while daydreaming.

"Indeed, I think that [good] teasing is born of a lively imagination and a spirit full of fire and that, taking something from its origins, it is as brilliant as those flashes of lightning that dazzle but yet do not burn. In addition, I also think that you should not joke all the time. For besides the fact that long jokes are boring, furthermore, the minds of those who are to be amused must not get too used to the joking or else there will be no more surprise.

"But what I principally decree—for I have insensibly fallen into the habit of making laws as you ordered me to—is that people should each know their talent and be content with that. That is why I think that those to whom Nature has given a certain [delightful] naïveté, whether in their gestures or in the expressions on their faces or in their manner of speaking, should not desire to attempt anything more, for it is true that the art that might perfect [such talent][25] could also sometimes spoil it. Thus we must simply follow our own genius without envying that of others, it being certain that teasing is not like painting.[26] For it is possible to make a copy of a painting so exact that even experts doubt whether or not it is the original. But imitating someone else's [style of] joking can only be done poorly, and so it should never be attempted.

"However, to go over again the list of unamusing wits that we have already criticized, if my memory doesn't fail me, I decree that those who tell

25. Scudéry is playing with and denying the commonplace that art perfects nature.
26. Here Scudéry wittily parodies the centuries-old doctrine of "*ut pictura poesis,*" the comparison of poetry to painting, often part of a debate between poetry and painting; see Horace, *De arte poetica*, l. 361.

a story may not announce that it's amusing ahead of time. In addition, I think it should be either ingenuous or else full of wit, that the beginning should not be funnier than the ending, and, above all, that it should be original and very brief. I also decree that those who tell a long story do it with so much art and so much charm that they captivate the minds of those who hear it, and if possible, that they trick them by telling them something at the end of their tale that they couldn't foresee. But principally, I pronounce that they must not say anything unnecessary and that their eloquence must not be forced or confusing, and, on the contrary, that they must move from one thing to the next without difficulty or confusion, and that they must not interrupt themselves too often with 'oh, I forgot!' or 'I didn't tell you,' or 'I should have said,' and a thousand other similar things repeated by those who do not have their thoughts in order and whose memory deserts them when they tell a long story.

"Furthermore, I decree that, when joking, no person may stop speaking the language of well-bred people,[27] as someone has so judiciously complained, except for those people who have the ability to impersonate others, and these should not precisely be placed in the category of wits, for in the case where someone wants to imitate an angry servant who is complaining, it would be wrong to speak like the master, since imitation is the goal, and the closer one comes to achieving it the more the impersonator merits praise.

"In addition, I think that those who make jokes shouldn't be too in love with their own inventions and that they should be careful not to repeat what they've said before. As for those who make use of proverbs while being witty, I've already said that they must be appropriately placed, and I say again that they should come up so naturally when someone applies them to the topic, that those who hear them will wonder why they didn't think of them themselves—for in this case, the more commonly known, the better.

"But finally, to speak of what is properly called wit, I say that to be truly good at it requires a fiery spirit, a very lively imagination, an extremely sensitive judgment, and a memory full of a thousand different things appropriate for every occasion. Furthermore, it is necessary to know the world[28] and to take delight in it, and it's requisite to possess a sort of gallant and yet natural turn of wit and a sort of bold familiarity, which, without any audacity, has something that pleases and that silences others."

27. By this "law" Euridamia excludes dialect jokes in poor taste, and also off-color stories, as vulgar.
28. "To know the world" suggests not only that the wit must not be too spiritual or morally superior, but also that the wit will move in the best society—the *beau monde.*

"Aha, Euridamia! A person has to have a lot of wit to say what you've said," spoke up Clearchus.

"I myself believe," said Melinta, "that if she would give up her grave humor, no one else would tease so charmingly as she."

"Gravity," responded Euridamia, "is not so great an obstacle as you think to ingenious wit, and I know a man who is now no more, who, with a sad and mournful air and a naive and drooping expression, said more pleasant things and made more courtly jokes than any other person will [ever] say or make [again].

"Nevertheless," she added, "though I have made you see that I know quite a lot about how to be witty, I must again repeat what I said [before] and what I still maintain, that you must be especially careful how you make fun of your friends. However, there's a general rule to be followed," she continued, "with which you can't go wrong, [and] that is, never say anything that you wouldn't want them to hear and never say anything so cutting that it would prevent them from enjoying it. For it's never proper to say anything to your friends that amuses others [around you] more than them or that would force them to say to you what would amuse you less than any others who are listening. For indeed, friendship is so delicate [a relationship] that you can never be too careful not to endanger it.

"Besides, to speak sensibly, the best wit is not composed of cutting remarks. The pleasure taken in such words by those who are amused assuredly comes more from their spiteful nature than from the teasing. For it is certain that an absolute trifle, humorously turned, makes a much more properly amusing joke than a satirical accusation of someone, even if called by the name of wit. Moreover, even if you are less entertaining when you joke less cruelly, you still should do so. For, after all, it is not a fault to be ignorant of how to tease, as long as you understand [others'] teasing. But it is a very great [fault] not to be scrupulously [careful] in your friendships and to prefer to risk making a friend angry than to lose the opportunity for a joke."

"What you say is so wise," replied Melinta, "that I am ashamed of myself."

"Be that as it may," said Antigene, "she has said nothing that is not common sense."

"Unfortunately, I know it all too well!" responded Melinta. "For if I were to guide my wit by what she has just said, I would never be able to speak again in my life!"

"However, it would be too great a loss to require you to be silent," I answered, "for there are very few people who speak as agreeably as you [do]."

"But it seems to me," said Antigene, "in examining wit, we have forgotten to point out how useful it is among the [great] people of the world, for it gives them a way to tell the truth up to a certain point, without [anyone] having the right to take offense at it."

"That's a good point," responded Melinta.

"Also, it seems to me," said Don Alvarez, " that we haven't discussed that sort of wit that consists of packing a great deal of meaning into a few words—whether funny or serious. For there is a concise and compact way of speaking called 'bons mots,' which has quite a different character."

"For my part," said Antigene, "I think that these serious ones are a kind of maxim. But whether serious or amusing, they must surprise and delight and never offend. Such strokes of wit may be applied appropriately in any great public event and on a hundred other occasions. But mediocrity in this gains nothing. If it is not done exceptionally well, it should not be done at all. And not too often."

"If we follow this rule," Clarice interrupted, who despaired at the length of this conversation, "wouldn't it be proper to put wit aside, a conversation topic that has overjoyed Melinta, and in order to satisfy me in my turn, to have Don Alvarez give us the character of some great foreigner, so that we may change the topic of the conversation?"

"Please permit me to add something further on this subject," said Antigene, "for what I have to say is worth knowing."

Euridamia asked him to say what it was.

"It is," he said, "the word of a very great king on [the subject of] wit."

"Permit me, at least," interrupted Clarice, "to ask you if this is the word of a dead prince or a living prince, and if it is some faraway prince or one of our European princes."

"That doesn't matter, Madam," answered Antigene with a smile, knowing that Clarice wasn't interested in anything that wasn't exotic. "For what I have to relate would apply in the Indies as well as in France."

"Tell it then," replied Clarice, "so that we can finish up with wit."

"All right," said Antigene, "and here is what I have to say. A lady of marvelous wit and quite extraordinary merit, having observed that the great prince I was speaking about had a natural inclination for wit, asked him one day, on an appropriate occasion, how it was that he never indulged himself in it. He replied, with admirable wisdom, that it was because he thought it unfair to tease [others] without being teased himself, something a king should never expose himself to and, furthermore, that the mockery of a king, even the least cutting, is never forgotten, either by those who suffer it or those who hear it."

"I must confess," said Clarice, "that it would have been a pity to deprive the company of such an excellent response, and if the prince who said it reigned in any country where Don Alvarez traveled, he would give me great pleasure were he to make him better known to us. For I would be overjoyed if he would sketch for us the character of some great foreigner."

Don Alvarez and Clearchus gave their excuses so pleasantly that Clarice might have been offended, not understanding that they were teasing, so much so that Antigene took the lead, after the whole company had admired their gracious responses: "I see then," said Antigene, smiling, "that it is up to me to do the honors at my house. But, fortunately, I can do so without much trouble. For, since Melinta will endure [the description of] a character,[29] provided it is a person of high rank and merit, and since Clarice wishes [to hear about] only something a little distant from us in time or place, I have just the one to satisfy both, by telling you about the prince whose elegant and judicious thoughts on wit you were just admiring.

"The same Consul of Alexandria of whom I told you not long ago, and who sent me a [speech in] praise of the king, composed in Arabic by the Patriarch of Mount Libanus,[30] has added it to a French translation of an Arabic manuscript that is supposed to be a remnant of those writings that the Egyptian priests kept for their kings. I took my words from this [source] and, according to the reckoning of the manuscript that I'm referring to, the prince in question lived about 15,660 years ago."

Everyone laughed at a date so long ago.

"Do not laugh at this," answered Antigene frostily, "for manuscripts and even printed books sometimes lie. But, in truth, the most ancient Greek historian we have, he who is called the 'Father of History,'[31] reckons 15,000 years [to have passed] between their Hercules[32] and Amasis.[33] Now, according to our manuscript, this prince lived about 13,400 years before Amasis. And according to the most precise chronology [that we have], more than 2050 years [have passed] between Amasis and us. So, adding this time to

---

29. In the seventeenth century, the "character," or literary sketch of a particular social type of person, was very popular; it was presented as part of a narrative or collected in a volume of portraits of types of people.

30. The mountain seems to be invented.

31. Herodotus (484?—425 B.C.E.), famous for his *History* of the ancient world and the conflicts between Greece and Persia, is known as the "father of history."

32. A legendary Greek hero, noted for achieving twelve heroic labors imposed on him by Hera.

33. Amasis, pharaoh of Egypt ca. 569–524 B.C.E., was remembered as bringing peace and prosperity shortly before Egypt came under Persian rule.

the 13,300 years before Amasis gives us about the number of years I told you, with the understanding that, in a calculation of this sort, 500 or 600 years, more or less, is no big deal, and, after arguing five or six hours about it, you conclude that you would have been just as well off to know nothing about it."

"You see," said Melinta, "antiquity is well established, and distance, too. I think that Clarice will be satisfied by this. But take care that I be [also satisfied] by a king so far away. For, if all he has done was to build the pyramids that everyone talks so much about, I could easily be content with knowing nothing further."

"And for my part," said Clarice, "before you go any further, I'd like to know his name, and also, if that manuscript describes him, I would prefer if you would begin there, for that kind of portrait makes all that comes after much more pleasing and easier to fix in the mind."

"I'll tell you," replied Antigene, "everything I know about him. He was named Sesostris the Great,[34] to distinguish him from that other Sesostris known to our historians of Greek and Latin, who was a mighty prince, but much inferior (as our Arab claims), to this former Sesostris the Great, so much so that they gave him, he says, the name of Sesostris only because in his virtues he faintly resembled this earlier Sesostris.[35] And the earlier one, according to everything said about him, was so perfect that people might suspect him to be the complete Idea[36] of a prince, rather than a [real] prince himself, as some say about the first Cyrus of Xenophon."[37]

"This is very promising," said Clarice, "but what did he look like?"

"The book not only says," answered Antigene, "that he was the handsomest man in the kingdom, but it also adds that no statue or portrait could do him justice, so that if a stranger who had [just] arrived at his court found him disguised and hidden in the throng of his courtiers, he would not have failed to pick him out by a certain majestic air that told the whole world that he was the king. Nevertheless, that air was not an unnatural or strained gravity, always frowning, as was that of most of the oriental monarchs, who could hardly be distinguished from their statues whenever they showed themselves

34. Sesostris, a mythical Egyptian king, was reputed by Herodotus to have made great conquests in Africa and Asia.

35. The verb here is *pretendre*, "pretend," so perhaps a clue that the prince is a fiction.

36. In Platonic epistemology, the mind remembers rather than invents Ideas, or the universal forms that make up reality rather than the material world, which only seems to be reality.

37. Xenophon, prolific Athenian writer (ca. 427–354 B.C.E.), was most famous for his historical novel about Cyrus (557–530 B.C.E.), the Persian emperor, which offered Cyrus's rule as a model for government.

in public. On the contrary, you saw in him and his manners all the ease of a perfect gentleman and [at the same time] all the dignity and authority of a great prince. And his manner, particularly when he was with his officers, or among ladies, or with those who served him, to whom he gave his commands in many different ways, mixed a kind of civility and a heroic familiarity with such grandeur that, rather than only revering him, they could not help loving him."

"It's a good thing for us," said Melinta, "that this prince lived 15,000 years ago, for if he were now living, we would hardly be able to resist going to see him, even if we had to travel as far as Don Alvarez did. And who knows but that we might even be overwhelmed by a desire to become his subjects."

"Am I right in understanding," asked Clarice, "that this grandeur that appeared in the least of his gestures resulted from his having performed great acts,[38] which, captivating people's minds, reinforced their perception of greatness?"

"That's true," said Antigene, "but, in particular, he had a certain greatness of soul and a largeness of heart and spirit that was almost without bounds and that both embraced and enclosed all that might make a king esteemed and admired.

"The manuscript notes that many times he merited the title of 'Conqueror' and might have liked it better, by his inclination, than any other. The public preferred to call him 'the Great,' because there have been famous conquerors falling short in other qualities, whereas he towered over others.

"For many centuries after his reign, the Egyptians said that their nation derived from him all that made them superior to others and that the times were good or bad depending on whether the princes deviated from or came near to his conduct, that he had restored the authority of the royal government, before him badly shaken, [that he had] caused justice to reign, transformed the morals of his subjects, reformed the laws, straightened out and supported religion, brought order to [the country's] finances, and nourished and promoted the arts and sciences.

"On the other hand, he had changed the whole method of warfare and taught his successors all that his predecessors had been ignorant of in that art, which is the master of all other [arts]. His wisdom and his foresight were equal to his courage and his valor, and those who could not see the hidden

---

38. *Res gesta*, "great acts": Europeans of the late Middle Ages and the Renaissance loved romances or tragedies featuring the great acts of great rulers or heroes. The phrase came to stand for that kind of heroic story.

source of them took for unbelievable good luck and for miracles of blind Fortune [what were actually] the surprising results of all these virtues joined together to such a great degree. Places before impregnable were taken almost as soon as they were attacked. The Euphrates and the Tigris[39] were crossed as if they were streams. The desolation of war fell only on their enemies. Abundance marched with his armies. The year had but one harvest, even though he waged many campaigns.[40] The winter that stops others' [campaigns] often began his. One might almost say that he commanded the seasons, or at least that through his example alone he made all those he commanded act like armies above and beyond human power. Because he took for himself all the glory of these expeditions so extraordinary and so laborious, he also took upon himself a great part of the toil.

"Amid all this, the least interval of rest at his court had all the advantages of a long peace. The previously mentioned high pyramids (to observe the movements of the stars), obelisks, triumphal arches, palaces, gardens almost like those of fairy tales—he built them [all]. But these were the recreations of his mind and the least of his cares. His festivals and spectacles corresponded to this same grandeur. But the customary magnificence of his household, of his court, and of the troops maintained for his [personal] guard, his immense wealth, which was sufficient for all his wishes, and the prodigious accumulation of rare and precious things of all sorts, which were displayed in his treasury, were a continual exhibition which charmed strangers and attracted them from all corners of the earth; and those who were able to see up close the lord of all these goods found them to be far inferior to their master himself. Each person discovered in him their own gifts but to a greater and more surprising degree. The remarks on wit, which the ladies have so much commended, he tossed off in passing to a lady of infinite merit, with a superior wit and intelligence, whom he had chosen out of the whole court as the most suitable to shape the early years of the prince who would succeed him. She said that it was a wonderful lesson for herself and that she would consider herself lucky if she were able to teach the son all that she herself was always learning from the father.

"They say that he left this same prince, his son, other instructions in writing, which the Egyptians guarded among their sacred objects, and that they were required to be solemnly read to their new kings on the throne before crowning them."

39. The Euphrates and the Tigris are famous large rivers of the Middle East.
40. A pun on "campagnes," both fields (to fit the metaphor of harvest) and military campaigns.

"This is what I find charming—" said Clarice, "it seems to me that this is a description of an [ideal] character [who is] twenty kings in one. But at what age did he do such great things?"

"He began," said Antigene, "at twenty-four years old and was not yet forty when he dictated them and wrote them down. He had inherited the crown at the age of five, and it was noted as an omen that the first days of his reign were marked by a victory in battle. But the Heavens, which often mold great men and great princes through adversity, decided to give it to him at an age when no one would be able to blame him [for it].[41] His minority, as was the custom in Egypt, was troubled by civil and foreign wars, and the state seemed to be on the verge of being toppled. [But] as he grew up, civil war died down. The foreign war was ended through new conquests and his marriage.[42] Then he himself began to steer the ship [of state] in which he had been until then a passenger, and contrary to the inveterate practices of rulers during his time, who were nothing but the instruments of their ministers, he made all his ministers his instruments. He wanted to [over]see everything and know everything. He listened to all his subjects, who (up to that point) had had hardly any access to their amiable lord. He did not call for diversions except as respite from his work. He assigned hours each day for all the royal responsibilities and [special] days for each sort of business, and what was even more marvelous, he allowed his reason to govern more often than his desire. However impatient he was at his age to extend his reputation in warfare, he applied himself as if [he were] a king of sixty years, to regulate and to reform the interior of the state, wherever this was absolutely necessary, and as the foundation for all the great [things] he could do in the future.

"He was lucky not to have long to wait for a just and natural opportunity to declare war. Then he passed like lightning through the countries of his enemies and made them see by the speed of his conquests that they [ended up] giving him all that was theirs by refusing to grant him what was his own by legitimate succession. Because of his moderation,[43] he restored to them at the first peace these conquests that he might have justly kept.

41. Renaissance peoples generally believed that national adversities might be God's punishment of a ruler for his sins.

42. Since ancient times, it was the custom of European aristocrats and royals to end war and make peace through marrying the heirs to hostile camps to each other.

43. Moderation, or temperance, the mean between two extremes, was considered an ideal virtue for a monarch in the Renaissance (and throughout the ancient world as well). See Aristotle's *Ethics*.

"The envy that resulted from so great renown caused all the rest of Africa and a part of Asia to join together against him. The number of his enemies only increased his triumphs, and solely for the love of his people, and for the general good, he did not offer, to speak accurately, but rather once more donated to the world a peace such as he had himself determined. From his retirement in a dreadful desert,[44] an intelligent man, who was regarded as a prophet in Egypt at this time, predicted by the first two or three years of his reign what the others would produce, and wrote in an exalted kind of poetry about the king's conquests to come, concluding with these verses:

Through all the universe this glorious prince
More happy, halcyon days will so dispense,
His goodness with his justice will combine,
And in one league all nations firmly join.
Yield, Romans, yield, I as a prophet say,
This is the dawn of a much vaster sway."[45]

"O Antigene," cried [Don] Alvarez then, "you mean there were Romans fifteen or twenty thousand years ago?"

"It's not that," said Melinta, "but as the proverb says, 'to be a good liar one must have a good memory,' and Antigene has forgotten, without realizing it, the pleasant fiction that we all understood, I imagine, and the pleasure it gave us, which hindered us from interrupting him, when he put this King of Egypt in place of our own king."

"I confess it," admitted Antigene, "[but] if I hadn't talked about the Consul of Alexandria, the Patriarch of Mount Libanus, the Arabic manuscript, the first Sesostris, and 15,000 years, Clarice would never have listened to me."

44. "Solitude" or "desert" in the seventeenth century referred to any wild and uncultivated place, not just to barren ones.

45. This translation of the verse is taken from the late—seventeenth-century English translation: *Conversations upon Several Subjects Written in French by Mademoiselle de Scudéry*, trans. Ferrand Spence (London, 1683), book 2, 112; my thanks to the Folger Shakespeare Library. A literal translation of this verse goes like this:

> I see another Peace following this last, and yet another one,
> That this all-victorious King will restore to the world,
> Whose justice and magnanimity alone
> Will join together and make a treaty.
> Yield, Romans, yield, if I have any gift of prediction—
> For now begins a much greater and much happier Empire [than yours was].

"You're wrong," said Clarice, "for I listened with even greater attention when I understood that the subject was really Louis XIV,[46] and no one hears his praises with greater pleasure than I do."

"You must at least admit," said Antigene, "that only in this one instance you prefer what is present and nearby to what is ancient and far away."

"I'm too good a person to deny it," said Clarice.

"And we're too good," said Antigene "not to acknowledge that your preference here is the preference of almost all the world. Indeed, we admire, with a great deal of justice, the dialogues of Plato and Xenophon.[47] But if they were to come again into the world and publish conversations, it might be in vain that they put all the wit and wisdom of their Socrates into them, for it is a great question whether or not they would [even] be read. And I'm much deceived if at least some people would not find them too long and tedious. Even a clever man, who, taking great pains, fills his memoirs with all he has discovered from Plutarch and Seneca[48] about what is proper for the civil life, if he should come upon a book in which the natural manner of living of well-bred people is painted and the best advice that it's possible to receive is given, especially for courtiers and ladies (the best people in the world), he could hardly be made to open the volume; he would no sooner find out from the first page that it was printed at the Barbin or Courbé publishers,[49] but he would categorize it forever among the useless works of our century."

"And look at us!" said Polemon, "who have listened with such [intense] curiosity to what is said about the gardens of Semiramis and who would see [the Gardens] of Tivoli[50] with so much pleasure, [but] because we are in [the gardens] of Antigene, we have been happy for two hours on this beautiful and pleasing terrace without seeing anything of the rest."

46. Louis XIV (1638–1715), king of France, was Scudéry's own monarch. He came to the throne under his mother's regency, guided by the counselor Cardinal Mazarin, and had little power until 1660. He built a strong central bureaucracy, waged several successful wars that nevertheless depleted national resources, and supported the arts but enforced religious conformity.

47. Almost all of the philosophic works of Plato (429–347 B.C.E.) are published as dialogues between Socrates and his pupils—among the most famous are the *Symposium* and the *Phaedrus*. Xenophon (427–354 B.C.E.) also published dialogues on economics and on the unhappiness of the tyrant, which featured Socrates.

48. Scudéry is probably referring to the short treatises on moral philosophy and the *Parallel Lives* of the Greek and Roman rulers by Plutarch (50–120 C.E.) and the philosophical dialogues and the letters by Seneca the Younger (ca. 4 B.C.E.—65 C.E.).

49. Claude Barbin was Scudéry's printer for the many volumes of the *Conversations*. Augustin Corbé was Scudéry's printer for *Amorous Letters, Famous Women*, and most of her novels. The "clever man" may be an allusion to Nicolas Boileau-Desprèaux; Boileau was a relentless critic of Scudéry and her heroic fiction.

50. The gardens in Tivoli, a summer resort for ancient Romans, were famous for their beauty.

"You're right," said Antigene, "and even though the rest will not meet your expectations, it is only fair to show it to you, such as it is."

Then, leading the way, he conducted us through bowers of jasmine and honeysuckle, through alleys of chestnuts and acacia, lined with rows of little fountains in the shape of balustrades, through very lovely gardens, and all the way to a little grove of fir trees at the end, which had a great oval space in the middle.

Then we were quite surprised to discover in a leafy parlor a short opera of his own invention, and with a very ingenious plot, on the subject of peace, which could not have been better suited to all that we had just been talking about. For there were gods and goddesses debating with each other who should have the largest share in that great event of praising the king, for arms, for laws, for religion, for sciences, for arts, for buildings, and for [public] entertainments. Everyone remembered those twenty kings within one king, as Clarice had put it. We praised Antigene's magnificence and especially his wit, for having known so well how to satisfy the opposite tastes of Melinta and Clarice, who [for once] agreed with all the rest of the company in giving him compliments and the praise he deserved.

NEW CONVERSATIONS ON DIVERSE SUBJECTS (1684)

CONVERSATION ON THE MANNER OF WRITING LETTERS[52]

A lady who greatly loved to read, and who was very lazy about writing to her male and female friends, requested one of her cousins to send her some books to entertain her in the country. This cousin, whom I shall call "Cléante," thinking to reproach her courteously concerning her perpetual silence, sent her nothing but collections of letters, for she had said to him in parting that, until her return she would not thank him for the books he would send, because she did not like to write, being persuaded that she wrote much worse than she spoke, adding modestly that she did not wish her letters to injure her friend's regard for her in her absence.

Cléante therefore wished to persuade her that people have always written and received [letters]. For this purpose, he sent her all [sorts of] collections of letters, beginning with Malherbe, Balzac, Costar, Voiture, and, to be

---

52. Based on Madeleine de Scudéry, "Conversation de la manière d'ecrire des lettres," in *Conversations nouvelles sur divers sujets, dedie'es au roy* (Paris, 1684), book 2, as edited by Delphine Denis in *"De l'air galant" et autres conversations* (Paris: Honoré Champion, 1998) 141–58 and 336–44. Our thanks to Stephanie Lenkey for her expert assistance in French. A version of this dialogue first was published as part of Scudéry's novel *Clélie* (Paris, 1655), vol. 4, 1122–49.

brief, all the dead authors, without neglecting the epistles of the ancients. He even added letters by Don Guevar the Spaniard, Cardinal Bembo, Cardinal Bentivoglio and, above all, those of Annibale Caro, whom Montaigne in his time and the wise and famous Chapelain in ours placed above all the other Italian authors.[53] In short, Cléante put together a little library of letters, which he sent to her by one of his servants.

Since Aminte possessed infinite wit, she well understood this joke, but she kept her word and did not thank Cléante with a note, contenting herself with sending him this poem:

> To Cléante
> No! I will not stoop to recant—
> The more I read, the more I revere,
> The more I wish not to reply,
> For one should never indite
> Unless always the best to write.[54]

Cléante found it extremely amusing that Aminte found it easier to reply in verse than in prose, to the extent that he showed this poem to Bérise, their mutual friend, who was full of wit. And since Aminte was not more than half a day away from them, they decided to form a party to go to see her and

53. François de Malherbe (1555–1628), French poet and critic, official poet of Henry IV and Louis XIII, advocated classical ideals of clarity and precision of language. Jean Louis Guez de Balzac (1597?–1654), a French writer, greatly influenced French prose style with his Latinate sentence structure in *Lettres* (1624). Pierre Costar (1603–1660) defended Voiture and his letters. Vincent Voiture (1597–1648), a French man of letters, wrote in the *precieux* style of Scudéry's circle. The "epistles of the ancients" must have included Cicero's letters, Ovid's and Horace's verse epistles, and perhaps Seneca's and Pliny's letters. Don Guevar the Spaniard, was Antonio Guevaro (1480?—1545), Spanish moralist, novelist, historian, and bishop. Pietro Bembo (1470–1547), Italian humanist and Cardinal in the Roman Catholic Church, wrote in many genres, promoted a classical style and the Tuscan vernacular as a standard for Italian, and established Petrarch and Dante as national poets. Guido Bentivoglio (1577–1644), cardinal of the Catholic Church, was famous for his histories and letters. Annibale Caro (1507–1566), Italian poet and friend of Bembo, translated the *Aeneid* and was noted for his letters. Michel Eyquem de Montaigne (1533–1592) is still famous for his *Essais*, first published in 1580, in a complete edition in 1595. Jean Chapelain (1595–1674), French critic and poet, founding member of the French Academy, wrote an epic poem on Joan of Arc (*Pucelle* 1656) and attacked Pierre Corneille's *Le Cid* on grounds of taste.

54. A literal translation follows:
> No, I will not stoop to take this back
> The more I read, the more I admire,
> The more I wish to write nothing;
> For one should never write
> Unless one writes always well.

to combat her slothful reluctance to write.[55] They brought with them a very amiable woman (whom I shall name "Clariste") of a humor quite different from Aminte's, for she often wrote two or three notes a day to her special friends. And this group made their trip two days later.

Aminte received these three very agreeably. "If our visit is importunate," Bérise said to her, while embracing her with an elegant and playful air, "blame yourself, because if you had written us, perhaps we would not have come to see you."

"I assure you," replied Aminte after greeting them and inviting them into her study, "I do not repent my silence, for after having read the enormous number of beautiful letters that Cléante maliciously sent to me, I am confirmed in my resolution not to write unless absolutely necessary. And out of all the different styles that I have observed in all these collections of letters, I did not find one that I would be capable of or that suited me or that I could imitate. Without doubt, I saw a thousand elegant phrases, but except for the letters of Voiture, all the rest were written for the public, and Balzac and Costar and all the others thought more about posterity than about those to whom they were writing. The greatest number of the love letters by these excellent men," she added, "are scarcely suitable to inspire love, and Voiture himself was a thousand times more admirable in his letters of gallantry than in his actual love letters."

"I assure you," responded Bérise, "that you would write better than anyone else, if you wanted to take the pains to do so, and I find it perfectly amusing that you had to send verses to Cléante rather than thank him in prose."

"The reason," replied Aminte, "is very easy to find, for nothing is easier than to compose a wicked little poem, and nothing is more difficult than to write a pleasant little note; and, in my view, it's all right for a lady to make mediocre verses without shame, but not a miserable letter in prose."

Since this party existed only to persuade Aminte to write occasionally to her friends, Clariste told her that the whole world wrote letters, either well or not so well, and that it appeared very strange that she alone never wrote to anyone.

"I think," answered Aminte, smiling, "that I shall prove to you the opposite of what you have just said."

"You'll be embarrassed," said Bérise.

---

55. The friends' trip is thus like the modern-day "intervention," where family and friends get together to urge someone to stop drinking or doing drugs!

"Do you not see," replied Aminte, "that in the works of Sarrazin,[56] who had so much wit, there is not a single letter, and I am sure that if he had written a lot of them, someone would have included them when printing his poems, as someone did those of Malherbe and Voiture."

"Since I have a friend who was his friend," said Cléante, "I am able to assure you that never did a man write more letters than he and that scarcely ever was there one who wrote better, whether to famous people, such as Balzac, Costar, and others, or to princes or mighty ministers and, above all, to the ladies. But he hardly ever kept his letters, so that at his death it was necessary to look for them in others' hands, not in his study. And when one of his female friends and two of his male friends undertook to collect his works after his death, the ladies to whom he had written were not obliged to release his letters. However, it is a great shame that they have been lost, because the serious and informative ones were very beautiful, and the playful ones very charming."

"At least," said Aminte, "do you agree with me that women have written less than men or, if they have responded, they have written badly, for I see very few letters from ladies in the very large number of volumes that you have given me; and since, generally speaking, all people are vain, they would have included answers from the ladies if they had answered well."

"One cannot doubt," objected Clindor, "that there have always been ladies who wrote admirably well, and one can see the incontestable proofs in Voiture himself. But the respect one owes to ladies does not permit one to print their letters without their consent, and they rarely give it from pure modesty."

"For my part," said Clariste, "I, who take an obvious pleasure in receiving letters from people whom I love, and who do not dislike replying to them, do not make a point of fussing over my notes. I write as I speak, I say what I think, and provided that I make myself understood, I am content. And I am sure that it is never necessary to have too much wit in ordinary letters. Someone has shown me," added Clariste, "a postscript from a love letter, where that idea is well explained. Here it is—it is a lady who speaks:

I forgot to ask your pardon for having wished for more wit when writing to you, for when one is not unhappy about oneself, but one is miserable, nothing is necessary except tenderness.

56. Jacques Sarrazin (1588–1660), French sculptor and painter, helped to found the *Académie royale* and favored a neoclassical style.

After Clariste had recited these four lines, Cléante exclaimed, "Ah, Madame, how much pleasure you have given me in praising the sentiment [in this letter], for it is certain that there is little need to have much wit in notes or letters of love. And that is the reason it makes it so difficult to find letters and notes of this nature that are perfect throughout: for there is little need at all for grand words; it is also not necessary to speak like the people; neither too much art nor too much negligence is necessary. There is little need of what one calls 'elegance,'[57] yet gallantry, politeness, and passion are needed. And it is finally so difficult to write well about love, because nothing more is [required, except love]."

"But for my part," said Bérise, "I do not understand at all why it should be any more difficult to write of one thing than another. For in the end I believe that in the case of letters one must simply say what one thinks and say it well. Thus when one has wit and judgment, one thinks concerning each matter more or less what it is appropriate to think and, as a result, one writes what it is appropriate to write. In effect, if I am writing for an important business, I will not write as if I had nothing more than a simple compliment to make; if I am sending some news, I will not play the elegant wit; if I am composing a friendly letter, I will not put on a high style; and if I wish to write love letters, I will consult only my heart. That is why I don't very well know why you assign such great difficulty to writing letters of this nature."

"In truth," said Aminte, "I hold there are many who write all sorts of letters very well, and there are a few persons who do so perfectly well."

"I'll go along with that," replied Cléante, "but I repeat that, out of all kinds of letters, those called love letters are the most difficult to compose. And also, concerning [love letters], there are fewer people who are able to judge well."

"Bérise speaks, however, as if she found all sorts of letters equally easy to compose," replied Aminte. "However, I believe, as does Cléante, that [writing love letters] requires more delicacy and judgment than most things."

"But in order to show you what I myself know," responded Bérise, "—and at least I know a little in general about how letters should be composed—is it not true that business letters should be precise, that [in them] common sense is more important than eloquence, that they [should] say all that is necessary and nothing else, that all superfluous words should be banished, leaving only those that are necessary, and that one should try principally to compose that

---

57. "Bel esprit," literally, "handsome spirit," but usually translated "wit" or sometimes "spirit" or "gallantry"; since Cléante says gallantry and passion *are* required, we have here translated it as "elegance."

which is orderly and clear? However," she added, "also required of business letters is a civility that distinguishes polite people from those who are not. Finally, it should be obvious that the person who is writing understands what she wishes to make others understand, for I know nothing more insupportable than to write a letter that needs explication, that muddles things instead of clarifies them."

"However," replied Aminte, "there are many people who believe they are understandable and aren't understandable at all."

"That is not true of Bérise," responded Cléante, "for I assure you that she understands quite well what she wants to say. That is why it would be a great pleasure to have her teach me how she thinks letters of consolation should be composed. For since occasions to write [such letters] present themselves often enough," he added, laughing, "I shall compose five or six following her advice, which I shall keep to use whenever I have to write one. Nothing is more contrary to my humor than such letters. Also, I have been tempted a hundred times, rather than to afflict myself with this sort of letter to the afflicted, to sooner choose to distract them than to sympathize with them. In effect, I know so little what one should say, or what one should not say, that I can never compose a letter of this nature without writing it more than once and without also making erasures after having put it down in clean copy. That is why the beautiful Bérise will do me a great favor by teaching me how to write [such letters]."

"In truth," replied Bérise, "you will not have such great trouble if you share my sentiments; for I can't stand these grand letters of consolation, which never have any effect and which do not console anyone. Nevertheless, you would think, after listening to the talk of some people, that their letters have a magical force against affliction and, after reading them, that you shouldn't feel any more regret for what was lost. Yet I wish people would be persuaded once and for all," she added, "that nothing but time is able to console such grief and it is not the business of eloquence to mess with this. And then, to tell you the truth, how is it possible to console people who are not at all afflicted? That is why I find that the best one can do on these occasions is to make letters of consolation very short, for to be reasonable requires simply that you demonstrate to the person you are writing that you share in his or her grief, without going into long complaints or grand eulogies and without employing all the morality and all the eloquence uselessly."

"It is true," said Cléante, "and you are right. For how can you console, for the death of their husbands, wives who have no need of consolation? And how can one console all sorts of people with whom it would be better to rejoice in order to suit the secret feelings of their hearts, since it is sometimes very convenient to be heirs of those concerning whose death one is supposed to console them? That is why, kind Bérise," added Cléante, "I make a vow never to write letters of consolation that are not short, to let all the morality and all the eloquence rest in peace on these occasions, no longer to compose lengthy exaggerations of the cruelty of death, as do some people, nor any more grand eulogies or long panegyrics and, in short, to conform completely to your instructions. I do not even ask you," he added, "how one should rejoice with those who have happened on some good fortune, for I know how to do that admirably, and I can offer you ten or twelve openings for that kind of letter without counting those said earlier, 'I take part . . . .' 'I am so interested in . . .' and other things too vulgar for witty people. But you would give me a rare pleasure if you would teach me how to compose properly letters of recommendation that would provide an introduction for the person you are writing about and, above all, teach me very precisely how it is possible to make clear to those you are writing to, if you wish them to do exactly what you say or if you don't care much at all about it. For when I am away from Paris I am overwhelmed with these sorts of things."

"For my part," said Bérise, "when I recommend for some business a person whom I do not much like, I write a letter short and dry; there is still courtesy, and the vocabulary of entreaty is included, but it is placed there without being supported by anything. On the other hand, when I wish to beg effectively, I first say that the favor I ask is reasonable; I say something good about the person for whom I am entreating; I testify to the friendship I have for her; I take upon myself the responsibility of protecting her; I even engage the person's pride in rendering her a service; and for greater certainty, I write her another note [saying] that I stick by everything that I have already written."

"For myself, in particular," said Clariste to Bérise, "I very much wish that you would explain to me how to write to those people with whom you must have a business relationship out of social obligation, but you do not esteem enough to give your friendship to nor to take pleasure in amusing them."

"First of all," replied Bérise, "I would write them as little as I could, for I cannot stand those people who write only in order to write, who voluntarily involve themselves, without any necessity, in receiving letters from people about whom they do not care at all and who love in general to receive and write letters indiscriminately. In second place, when constrained to write in the manner that you mean, I would not put in these kinds of letters either great wit or great friendship; for one assuredly makes a mistake when one writes a very beautiful and very obliging letter to a person of very mediocre worth. That is why it is necessary to have a kind of lukewarm civility on call that serves [well enough] for these people whom one does not value very much or like much at all, when some social reason requires us to write to them. And it is appropriate in these cases to compose letters, which we have called 'letters of compliment,' so that they contain nothing special, nothing good or bad—composed of some words and little content, so that they engage no one, neither those who write them nor those to whom they are written, and so that they have a style so general that they can fit nearly every kind of mediocre person without being especially appropriate to anyone."

"In truth," replied Aminte, "judgment is necessary in everything. For example, one might say that there is nothing easier to write than news. However, one often sees people who write even news very oddly."

"Those are the people," responded Cléante, "who very often write something without knowing anything, who believe all that anyone tells them, who write without plan and without charm, who entertain only themselves by writing those things no one else cares about at all, disagreeable things or things that no longer offer the pleasure of novelty. However, it is certain, too, that it is still not so necessary for a woman to be young to be beautiful, as it is necessary for news to be new to be interesting; and there is nothing more irritating than to receive a long narration of an old adventure."

"Yet it is true," resumed Aminte, "that there are certain grim events that one remembers and repeats from time to time and that circulate widely as if they had only just happened; these things are rather annoying for those who have extensive knowledge of them, when someone writes to them at length about these things, unless there are extenuating circumstances. But in my opinion, when composing these letters to recount the latest news, one should consider what type of news would please the person who is addressed. For I am sure that there are people who love nothing but this universal news with which rumor is usually concerned, and who only desire [to hear about] battles won or lost, sieges of cities, fires, floods, shipwrecks, uprisings of the people, and other similar grand events; there are also those who care little about the great happenings that one finds in the newspapers, who prefer what one calls the news of the 'cabinet,'[58] which is not told except in whispers and which is not well known except to worldly, well-informed

58. News of the "cabinet" would be the gossip or secrets one could only tell one's most intimate friends, since they were the ones in French aristocratic society who were admitted to the cabinet; this kind of room was an architectural innovation in the Renaissance, used as a study or for praying, bookkeeping, reading, for withdrawing after an argument with your spouse (according to Anne Clifford's diary), but also for private discussion or reading with a cleric or intimate visits with one or two close friends.

people, who have exquisite judgment and delicate taste. That is why it is always necessary to know the humor and the interests of the people to whom one writes when one engages to hand on some news to them. And there are also some things one should never hand on."

"That is right, Madame," replied Cléante. "But what I principally would like Bérise to tell us, since she seems to be already engaged in it, is in what letters it is permissible to display all one's wit and in what fashion it is best to display it."

"You know better than I, without doubt," she replied. "But in order to make you realize that I am capable of appreciating the beauty of your letters of gallantry, if you ever write some to me, I declare to you that these are the only ones that I know anything about and, with regard to those letters that I will call 'serious letters,' I would be lost."

"As far as these [serious] letters," responded Cléante, "it is without doubt permissible to avail oneself of a very elevated style; for example, if a person in high office were to write to another concerning some important matter or some scholarly people were to participate in an exchange of letters, they would employ, appropriately, history, moral philosophy, politics, the poets, and nearly all the power of eloquence."

"About such stuff," said Bérise, "I know nothing. But letters of gallantry, I understand them admirably. It is proper in these that wit should have all one's attention, that imagination should have freedom to play, and that judgment should not appear so severe that one may not mingle some agreeable foolishness among matters more serious. One is able to mock [everything] ingeniously [in these letters]; praise and flattery agreeably find their place in them; in them one speaks sometimes of friendship, as if one were speaking of love; in them one searches for novelty; in them one is able also to speak innocent lies; one makes up news when one knows none; one passes from one subject to another without constraint; and these sorts of letters are properly called a conversation between absent persons. You have to be sure to put in a certain type of wit that has a quality of restraint, that tastes of books and the study, and that is far removed from gallantry, which one might call the soul of this kind of letter. It is requisite in these letters that the style be easy, natural, and noble—all at once. Yet it is not necessary to refrain from employing a certain art that makes it possible to include almost anything in letters of this nature, following that popular proverb, transformed into the highest matter through a skillful wit, provided that a worldly air reigns throughout. But on these occasions one should refrain from using that grand eloquence that is particularly appropriate for orations, and one should employ another [eloquence] that at times conveys a more charming effect with less noise, principally among ladies; for, in a word, the art of speaking well about trifles is not known to all sorts of people."

"I assure you," responded Clariste, "and I can also assure you again, that it is unsuitable for all sorts of people to know such a thing."

"But amiable Bérise," said Cléante, "do us the favor in its entirety, and tell us very precisely how you would wish love letters to be composed."

"Since I have never written any and never received any," she replied, "I do not know very well what it is I should say. However, since today I feel myself in a mood to talk, I shall not refuse you. But first I shall tell you that in my opinion there are many more [kinds of] elegant love letters than one would think."

"I believe that as much as you do," replied Cléante, "but one should not be astonished if letters of gallantry are seen everywhere, while love letters only rarely, because one writes the first kind for the view of the whole world, while one writes the second kind only to hide them. Those who receive an elegant letter of friendship make a point of showing it, while those who receive an elegant love letter are embarrassed to publish it; thus one should not find it strange that one sees so few good ones of this last kind. Indeed, to speak truthfully, since there are a great many people who possess infinite wit, but far fewer who enjoy infinite love, one should also not be astonished that there are fewer fine letters of this kind than of all other sorts; since it is always true that in order to write exactly as necessary about these matters, one must love passionately and be capable of a certain delicacy of heart and spirit, which makes this passion agreeable both in conversation and in letters—and all this is infrequently found."

"But did someone not say a little while ago," responded Aminte, "that it was not necessary to employ much wit for these occasions?"

"I admit it," answered Bérise, "but do you not think that sometimes you need a great deal [of wit] in order not to show it? Thus one might also say that, while love letters do not need that burning wit that must sparkle in letters of gallantry, yet they require something else in place of that; the heat of passion takes the place of this fire of wit that I'm talking about. That is why I find that the true nature of love letters must be tender and impassioned, and that there is something gallant, something spiritual, and at the same time something playful in these sorts of letters, yet always joined to passion and respect. Expressions in these letters must be more tender and more touching, and one must always say those things that touch the heart, mixed with those that entertain the mind. If I am not wrong, you should likewise include a little anxiety, because happy letters get you nowhere in love. It is not that one cannot have joy; but, after all, it must never be a peaceful joy, and even when you do not have a reason for complaint, you should do it anyway."

"You speak about it so admirably!" responded Cléante. "For if you had done nothing else your whole life than experience love and write about it, you could not have spoken better about it."

"If I have not experienced it," she replied, smiling, "I have friends who have done it for me and who have taught me what to say about it. But finally, a love letter should have more sentiment than wit; the style should be natural, deferential, and impassioned; and I also maintain that there is nothing that contributes more to make a letter of this kind less touching than to make it too beautifully written. Also, it is for that reason that there are so few people who can judge love letters well. For in order to be a fair judge, one must put oneself in the place of those who love; one must know that it is their hearts that speak; one must understand a hundred little things that those who are writing know well and that others don't understand at all; finally, it is necessary to know how to make a very delicate distinction between the gallantry of a letter of friendship and the gallantry of a letter of love. As for the rest," she added, "I heard from a very courteous gentleman that ordinarily women write better love letters than do men, and I think he was right. For when a lover has resolved to write quite openly about his passion, it is no longer art if he just says, 'I die of love.' But with a woman, who cannot ever admit so precisely what she feels and must keep it more a secret, this love that she only shows a glimpse of delights more than that put on display without subtlety."

"But from what I have seen," said Aminte, "the love letters of a lover and his beloved should be different."

"Do not doubt it," responded Bérise, "for love and respect must prevail in the letters of a lover, while virtue, modesty, and fear must mingle with tenderness in the letters of the beloved, so far as I understand it. For I do not bother with talk about young scatterbrains who are more forward than men, who speak more than they are spoken to, and who make themselves despised by those whom they want to adore them. Nor do I speak about those women who are past youth except in spirit, and to whom an ingrained imprudence has given a ridiculous boldness."

"But my amiable Bérise," responded Cléante, "since you know so much, tell me also whether it is permissible to write long love letters. For I have a friend full of wit who says that love letters must be short."

"Speaking of all sorts of notes in general," answered Bérise, "I think that it is good not to be excessively long. But it would be strange if one thought it wrong that two people who love each other infinitely, who scarcely can speak freely, and who have a thousand little vexations to convey to each other are not able to write that which they are not able to say easily and that love, which is an exaggerated passion, which causes all things to grow, did not have the right at times to force them to write long letters. For how can one encompass great passion in few words? How can one put enormous jealousy in a little note, and express all the feelings of a tender heart in only three or four words? For those who write notes of gallantry," she added, "it is easy to make them brief, even when there is a great deal of wit. Because they have their judgment totally at liberty, they may choose what they say and reject those thoughts that do not please them. But a poor lover whose reason is muddled may choose nothing; he says everything that comes into his fancy and shouldn't be selective. For in the case of love, one never knows what to say and one never thinks that one has said enough. Thus I maintain that it is not forbidden to compose long letters from time to time, as long as they are characterized throughout by the love that begets them. And, to speak sincerely, nothing merits more praise than an exquisite love letter; for finally, despite what I've said earlier, I believe that when one writes such a letter, one's mind is so engrossed and so distracted that it is much more difficult to write well than on any other occasion. As I have said, it is not that the heart should not be involved but that sometimes the heart is so distressed that it does not very well know what it feels."

"But, pardon me," Cléante interrupted, "who are these friends who taught you so well how to talk of love?"

"She was a confidante in a passion so gallant and so virtuous," replied Aminte, "that if you knew all that she knows, you would not be surprised to find yourself speaking as she speaks. But after all," continued Aminte, "if one is able to commend a beautiful love letter in itself, one must never praise those ladies who make it known that they receive them or reply to them; for however innocent the passion that caused them to be written, those who view these sorts of letters are never convinced [that it is innocent]. And then, to speak sincerely, there is already a great deal of indiscretion among men in general, so that no matter how virtuous the fondness that one has for them, one must never confess it, and much less through letters or through kind words. That is why, despite all your anthologies of letters and all these charming precepts of Bérise, I remain unmoved from my first opinion that I do not like to write."

"That results, no doubt," responded Bérise, "from the fact that you do not care enough about your friends, for letters are the only consolation for absence. And even when one is in the same place, the use of notes is a convenience without equal: notes relieve you of having to talk to all the people you have employed; you are thereby informed of a thousand little things you would not otherwise know, because they would have forgotten them by the time you saw them. In a word, whoever would keep me from receiving notes from my friends and replying to them would deprive me of a great pleasure."

Aminte answered that she would let her follow her own inclination and that she would beg to be allowed likewise to follow hers.

The rest of the conversation was very playful and very agreeable; and since Bérise and Cléante found themselves in a humor to entertain themselves upon their return, they overwhelmed Aminte with all sorts of different letters written during the next eight days. Some told her about marriages, and so she wrote to congratulate them. Others told her of people who had died, and so she grieved with their kinsmen. At last she received a bunch of letters on all sorts of subjects, and without letting herself be fooled, to them she did not respond except by a profound silence. All this did not fail to entertain her, but also entertained others as a result, for on her return she made up a thousand charming reasons to justify it, or to excuse it, which made them all realize that she only had to write what she thought in order to write perfectly.

SERIES EDITORS'
BIBLIOGRAPHY

Note: Items appearing in the volume editors' bibliography are not repeated here.

PRIMARY SOURCES

Alberti, Leon Battista. *The Family in Renaissance Florence.* Translated by Renée Neu Watkins. Columbia, S.C.: University of South Carolina Press, 1969.

Arenal, Electa, and Stacey Schlau, eds. *Untold Sisters: Hispanic Nuns in Their Own Works.* Translated by Amanda Powell. Albuquerque, N.M.: University of New Mexico Press, 1989.

Astell, Mary. *The First English Feminist: Reflections on Marriage and Other Writings.* Edited and with an introduction by Bridget Hill. New York: St. Martin's Press, 1986.

Atherton, Margaret, ed. *Women Philosophers of the Early Modern Period.* Indianapolis, Ind.: Hackett Publishing Co., 1994.

Aughterson, Kate, ed. *Renaissance Woman: Constructions of Femininity in England: A Source Book.* London and New York: Routledge, 1995.

Barbaro, Francesco. *On Wifely Duties.* Translated by Benjamin Kohl. In Kohl and R. G. Witt, eds. *The Earthly Republic.* Philadelphia: University of Pennsylvania Press, 1978, 179–228. Translation of the Preface and Book 2.

Behn, Aphra. *The Works of Aphra Behn.* 7 vols. Edited by Janet Todd. Columbus, Ohio: Ohio State University Press, 1992–96.

Boccaccio, Giovanni. *Famous Women.* Edited and translated by Virginia Brown. The I Tatti Renaissance Library. Cambridge, Mass.: Harvard University Press, 2001.

———. *Corbaccio or the Labyrinth of Love.* 2d rev. ed. Translated by Anthony K. Cassell. Binghamton, N.Y.: Medieval and Renaissance Texts and Studies, 1993.

Brown, Sylvia. *Women's Writing in Stuart England: The Mother's Legacies of Dorothy Leigh, Elizabeth Joscelin and Elizabeth Richardson.* Thrupp, Stroud, Gloceter: Sutton, 1999.

Bruni, Leonardo. "On the Study of Literature (1405) to Lady Battista Malatesta of Moltefeltro." In *The Humanism of Leonardo Bruni: Selected Texts.* Translated and introduced by Gordon Griffiths, James Hankins, and David Thompson, 240–51. Binghamton, N.Y.: Medieval and Renaissance Texts and Studies, 1987.

Castiglione, Baldassare. *The Book of the Courtier.* Translated by George Bull. New York: Penguin, 1967.

Cerasano, S. P., and Marion Wynne-Davies, eds. *Readings in Renaissance Women's Drama: Criticism, History, and Performance 1594–1998.* London and New York: Routledge, 1998.

Christine de Pizan. *The Book of the City of Ladies.* Translated by Earl Jeffrey Richards. Foreward by Marina Warner. New York: Persea Books, 1982.

———. *The Treasure of the City of Ladies.* Translated by Sarah Lawson. New York: Viking Penguin, 1985. Also translated and with an introduction by Charity Cannon Willard. Edited and with an introduction by Madeleine P. Cosman. New York: Persea Books, 1989.

Clarke, Danielle, ed. *Isabella Whitney, Mary Sidney and Aemilia Lanyer: Renaissance Women Poets.* New York: Penguin Books, 2000.

Crawford, Patricia, and Laura Gowing, eds. *Women's Worlds in Seventeenth-Century England: A Source Book.* London and New York: Routledge, 2000.

Daybell, James, ed. *Early Modern Women's Letter Writing, 1450–1700.* Houndmills, UK, and New York: Palgrave, 2001.

Elizabeth I: Collected Works. Edited by Leah S. Marcus, Janel Mueller, and Mary Beth Rose. Chicago: University of Chicago Press, 2000.

Elyot, Thomas. *Defence of Good Women: The Feminist Controversy of the Renaissance.* Facsimile Reproductions. Edited by Diane Bornstein. New York: Delmar, 1980.

Erasmus, Desiderius. *Erasmus on Women.* Edited by Erika Rummel. Toronto: University of Toronto Press, 1996.

Female and Male Voices in Early Modern England: An Anthology of Renaissance Writing. Edited by Betty S. Travitsky and Anne Lake Prescott. New York: Columbia University Press, 2000.

Ferguson, Moira, ed. *First Feminists: British Women Writers 1578–1799.* Bloomington, Ind.: Indiana University Press, 1985.

Galilei, Maria Celeste. *Sister Maria Celeste's Letters to Her father, Galileo.* Edited and translated by Rinaldina Russell. Lincoln, Neb., New York: Writers Club Press of Universe, 2000.

Gethner, Perry, ed. *The Lunatic Lover and Other Plays by French Women of the 17th and 18th Centuries.* Portsmouth, N.H.: Heinemann, 1994.

Glückel of Hameln. *The Memoirs of Glückel of Hameln.* Translated by Marvin Lowenthal. New introduction by Robert Rosen. New York: Schocken Books, 1977.

Henderson, Katherine Usher, and Barbara F. McManus, eds. *Half Humankind: Contexts and Texts of the Controversy about Women in England, 1540–1640.* Urbana, Ill.: University of Illinois Press, 1985.

Humanist Educational Treatises. Edited and translated by Craig W. Kallendorf. The I Tatti Renaissance Library. Cambridge, Mass.: Harvard University Press, 2002.

Joscelin, Elizabeth. *The Mothers Legacy to Her Unborn Childe.* Edited by Jean leDrew Metcalfe. Toronto: University of Toronto Press, 2000.

Kaminsky, Amy Katz, ed. *Water Lilies, Flores del agua: An Anthology of Spanish Women Writers from the Fifteenth through the Nineteenth Century.* Minneapolis, Minn.: University of Minnesota Press, 1996.

Kempe, Margery. *The Book of Margery Kempe.* Translated and edited by Lynn Staley. A Norton Critical Edition. New York: W.W. Norton, 2001.

King, Margaret L., and Albert Rabil, Jr., eds. *Her Immaculate Hand: Selected Works by and about the Women Humanists of Quattrocento Italy.* Binghamton, N.Y.: Medieval and Renaissance Texts and Studies, 1983. 2d rev. ed, 1991.

Klein, Joan Larsen, ed. *Daughters, Wives, and Widows: Writings by Men about Women and Marriage in England, 1500–1640.* Urbana, Ill.: University of Illinois Press, 1992.

Knox, John. *The Political Writings of John Knox: The First Blast of the Trumpet against the Monstrous Regiment of Women and Other Selected Works.* Edited by Marvin A. Breslow. Washington: Folger Shakespeare Library, 1985.

Kors, Alan C., and Edward Peters, eds. *Witchcraft in Europe, 400–1700: A Documentary History.* Philadelphia: University of Pennsylvania Press, 2000.

Krämer, Heinrich, and Jacob Sprenger. *Malleus Maleficarum* (ca. 1487). Translated by Montague Summers. London: Pushkin Press, 1928. Reprint, New York: Dover, 1971.

Larsen, Anne R., and Colette H. Winn, eds. *Writings by Pre-Revolutionary French Women: From Marie de France to Elizabeth Vigée-Le Brun.* New York and London: Garland Publishing Co., 2000.

de Lorris, William, and Jean de Meun. *The Romance of the Rose.* Translated by Charles Dahlbert. Princeton: Princeton University Press, 1971. Reprint, University Press of New England, 1983.

Marguerite d'Angoulême, Queen of Navarre. *The Heptameron.* Translated by P. A. Chilton. New York: Viking Penguin, 1984.

Mary of Agreda. *The Divine Life of the Most Holy Virgin.* Abridgment of *The Mystical City of God.* Abridged by Fr. Bonaventure Amedeo de Caesarea, M.C. Translated from French by Abbé Joseph A. Boullan. Rockford, Ill.: Tan Books, 1997.

Myers, Kathleen A., and Amanda Powell, eds. *A Wild Country out in the Garden: The Spiritual Journals of a Colonial Mexican Nun.* Bloomington, Ind.: Indiana University Press, 1999.

Teresa of Avila, Saint. *The Life of Saint Teresa of Avila by Herself.* Translated by J. M. Cohen. New York: Viking Penguin, 1957.

Weyer, Johann (1515–88). *Witches, Devils, and Doctors in the Renaissance: Johann Weyer, De praestigiis daemonum.* Edited by George Mora with Benjamin G. Kohl, Erik Midelfort, and Helen Bacon. Translated by John Shea. Binghamton, N.Y.: Medieval and Renaissance Texts and Studies, 1991.

Wilson, Katharina M., ed. *Medieval Women Writers.* Athens, Ga.: University of Georgia Press, 1984.

———, ed. *Women Writers of the Renaissance and Reformation.* Athens, Ga.: University of Georgia Press, 1987.

Wilson, Katharina M., and Frank J. Warnke, eds. *Women Writers of the Seventeenth Century.* Athens, Ga.: University of Georgia Press, 1989.

Wollstonecraft, Mary. *A Vindication of the Rights of Men and a Vindication of the Rights of Women.* Edited by Sylvana Tomaselli. Cambridge: Cambridge University Press, 1995.

———. *The Vindications of the Rights of Men, The Rights of Women.* Edited by D. L. Macdonald & Kathleen Scherf. Peterborough, Ontario, Canada: Broadview Press, 1997.

Women Critics 1660–1820: An Anthology. Edited by the Folger Collective on Early Women Critics. Bloomington, Ind.: Indiana University Press, 1995.

Women Writers in English, 1350–1850. 15 volumes published through 1999 (projected 30-volume series suspended). Oxford, Oxford University Press.

Wroth, Lady Mary. *The Countess of Montgomery's Urania.* 2 parts. Edited by Josephine A. Roberts. Tempe, Ariz.: Medieval and Renaissance Texts and Studies, 1995, 1999.

———. *Lady Mary Wroth's "Love's Victory": The Penshurst Manuscript.* Edited by Michael G. Brennan. London: The Roxburghe Club, 1988.

———. *The Poems of Lady Mary Wroth.* Edited by Josephine A. Roberts. Baton Rouge, La.: Louisiana State University Press, 1983.

de Zayas Maria. *The Disenchantments of Love.* Translated by H. Patsy Boyer. Albany, N.Y.: State University of New York Press, 1997.

———. *The Enchantments of Love: Amorous and Exemplary Novels.* Translated by H. Patsy Boyer. Berkeley, Calif.: University of California Press, 1990.

SECONDARY SOURCES

Ahlgren, Gillian. *Teresa of Avila and the Politics of Sanctity.* Ithaca, N.Y.: Cornell University Press, 1996.

Akkerman, Tjitske, and Siep Sturman, eds. *Feminist Thought in European History, 1400–2000.* London and New York: Routledge, 1997.

Allen, Sister Prudence, R.S.M. *The Concept of Woman: The Aristotelian Revolution, 750 b.c.—a.d. 1250.* Grand Rapids, Mich.: William B. Eerdmans Publishing Company, 1997.

———. *The Concept of Woman: Volume II: The Early Humanist Reformation, 1250–1500.* Grand Rapids, Mich.: William B. Eerdmans Publishing Company, 2002.

Armon, Shifra. *Picking Wedlock: Women and the Courtship Novel in Spain.* New York: Rowman and Littlefield Publishers, Inc., 2002.

Ballaster, Ros. *Seductive Forms.* New York: Oxford University Press, 1992.

Barash, Carol. *English Women's Poetry, 1649–1714: Politics, Community, and Linguistic Authority.* New York and Oxford: Oxford University Press, 1996.

Battigelli, Anna. *Margaret Cavendish and the Exiles of the Mind.* Lexington, Ky.: University of Kentucky Press, 1998.

Beilin, Elaine V. *Redeeming Eve: Women Writers of the English Renaissance.* Princeton: Princeton University Press, 1987.

Benson, Pamela Joseph. *The Invention of Renaissance Woman: The Challenge of Female Independence in the Literature and Thought of Italy and England.* University Park, Penn.: Pennsylvania State University Press, 1992.

Benson, Pamela Joseph, and Victoria Kirkham, eds. *Strong Voices, Weak History? Medieval and Renaissance Women in Their Literary Canons: England, France, Italy.* Ann Arbor: University of Michigan Press, 2003.

Bilinkoff, Jodi. *The Avila of Saint Teresa: Religious Reform in a Sixteenth-Century City.* Ithaca, N.Y.: Cornell University Press, 1989.

Bissell, R. Ward. *Artemisia Gentileschi and the Authority of Art.* University Park, Penn.: Pennsylvania State University Press, 2000.

Blain, Virginia, Isobel Grundy, and Patricia Clements, eds. *The Feminist Companion to Literature in English: Women Writers from the Middle Ages to the Present.* New Haven, Conn.: Yale University Press, 1990.

Bloch, R. Howard. *Medieval Misogyny and the Invention of Western Romantic Love.* Chicago: University of Chicago Press, 1991.

Bornstein, Daniel, and Roberto Rusconi, eds. *Women and Religion in Medieval and Renaissance Italy.* Translated by Margery J. Schneider. Chicago: University of Chicago Press, 1996.

Brant, Clare, and Diane Purkiss, eds. *Women, Texts and Histories, 1575–1760.* London and New York: Routledge, 1992.

Briggs, Robin. *Witches and Neighbours: The Social and Cultural Context of European Witchcraft.* New York: HarperCollins, 1995. Reprint Viking Penguin, 1996.

Brink, Jean R., ed. *Female Scholars: A Tradition of Learned Women before 1800.* Montréal: Eden Press Women's Publications, 1980.

Brown, Judith C. *Immodest Acts: The Life of a Lesbian Nun in Renaissance Italy.* New York: Oxford University Press, 1986.

Brown, Judith C., and Robert C. Davis, eds. *Gender and Society in Renaissance Italy.* London: Addison Wesley Longman, 1998.

Bynum, Carolyn Walker. *Fragmentation and Redemption: Essays on Gender and the Human Body in Medieval Religion.* New York: Zone Books, 1992.

———. *Holy Feast and Holy Fast: The Religious Significance of Food to Medieval Women.* Berkeley: University of California Press, 1987.

Cervigni, Dino S., ed. *Women Mystic Writers. Annali d'Italianistica* 13 (1995) (entire issue).

Cervigni, Dino S., and Rebecca West, eds. *Women's Voices in Italian Literature. Annali d'Italianistica* 7 (1989) (entire issue).

Charlton, Kenneth. *Women, Religion and Education in Early Modern England.* London and New York: Routledge, 1999.

Chojnacka, Monica. *Working Women in Early Modern Venice.* Baltimore: Johns Hopkins University Press, 2001.

Chojnacki, Stanley. *Women and Men in Renaissance Venice: Twelve Essays on Patrician Society.* Baltimore: Johns Hopkins University Press, 2000.

Cholakian, Patricia Francis. *Rape and Writing in the Heptameron of Marguerite de Navarre.* Carbondale and Edwardsville, Ill.: Southern Illinois University Press, 1991.

———. *Women and the Politics of Self-Representation in Seventeenth-Century France.* Newark: University of Delaware Press, 2000.

Clogan, Paul Maruice, ed. *Medievali et Humanistica: Literacy and the Lay Reader.* Lanham, Md.: Rowman and Littlefield, 2000.

Conley, John J., S.J. *The Suspicion of Virtue: Women Philosophers in Neoclassical France.* Ithaca, N.Y.: Cornell University Press, 2002.

Crabb, Ann. *The Strozzi of Florence: Widowhood and Family Solidarity in the Renaissance.* Ann Arbor: University of Michigan Press, 2000.

Cruz, Anne J., and Mary Elizabeth Perry, eds. *Culture and Control in Counter-Reformation Spain.* Minneapolis: University of Minnesota Press, 1992.

Davis, Natalie Zemon. *Society and Culture in Early Modern France.* Stanford: Stanford University Press, 1975, especially chapters 3 and 5.

———. *Women on the Margins: Three Seventeenth-Century Lives.* Cambridge, Mass.: Harvard University Press, 1995.

DeJean, Joan. *Ancients against Moderns: Culture Wars and the Making of a Fin de Siècle.* Chicago: University of Chicago Press, 1997.

————. *Tender Geographies: Women and the Origins of the Novel in France.* New York: Columbia University Press, 1991.

————. *The Reinvention of Obscenity: Sex, Lies, and Tabloids in Early Modern France.* Chicago: University of Chicago Press, 2002.

Dictionary of Russian Women Writers. Edited by Marina Ledkovsky, Charlotte Rosenthal, and Mary Zirin. Westport, Conn.: Greenwood Press, 1994.

Dixon, Laurinda S. *Perilous Chastity: Women and Illness in Pre-Enlightenment Art and Medicine.* Ithaca, N.Y.: Cornell University Press, 1995.

Dolan, Frances E. *Whores of Babylon: Catholicism, Gender and Seventeenth-Century Print Culture.* Ithaca, N.Y.: Cornell University Press, 1999.

Donovan, Josephine. *Women and the Rise of the Novel, 1405–1726.* New York: St. Martin's Press, 1999.

De Erauso, Catalina. *Lieutenant Nun: Memoir of a Basque Transvestite in the New World.* Translated by Michele Ttepto and Gabriel Stepto; foreword by Marjorie Garber. Boston: Beacon Press, 1995.

Erdmann, Axel. *My Gracious Silence: Women in the Mirror of Sixteenth-Century Printing in Western Europe.* Luzern: Gilhofer and Rauschberg, 1999.

Erickson, Amy Louise. *Women and Property in Early Modern England.* London and New York: Routledge, 1993.

Ezell, Margaret J. M. *The Patriarch's Wife: Literary Evidence and the History of the Family.* Chapel Hill: University of North Carolina Press, 1987.

————. *Social Authorship and the Advent of Print.* Baltimore: Johns Hopkins University Press, 1999.

————. *Writing Women's Literary History.* Baltimore: Johns Hopkins University Press, 1993.

The Feminist Encyclopedia of German Literature. Edited by Friederike Eigler and Susanne Kord. Westport, Conn.: Greenwood Press, 1997.

Ferguson, Margaret W., Maureen Quilligan, and Nancy J. Vickers, eds. *Rewriting the Renaissance: The Discourses of Sexual Difference in Early Modern Europe.* Chicago: University of Chicago Press, 1987.

Ferraro, Joanne M. *Marriage Wars in Late Renaissance Venice.* Oxford: Oxford University Press, 2001.

Fletcher, Anthony. *Gender, Sex and Subordination in England 1500–1800.* New Haven: Yale University Press, 1995.

Frye, Susan and Karen Robertson, eds. *Maids and Mistresses, Cousins and Queens: Women's Alliances in Early Modern England.* Oxford: Oxford University Press, 1999.

Gallagher, Catherine. *Nobody's Story: The Vanishing Acts of Women Writers in the Marketplace, 1670–1820.* Berkeley: University of California Press, 1994.

Garrard, Mary D. *Artemisia Gentileschi: The Image of the Female Hero in Italian Baroque Art.* Princeton: Princeton University Press, 1989.

Gelbart, Nina Rattner. *The King's Midwife: A History and Mystery of Madame du Coudray.* Berkeley: University of California Press, 1998.

Glenn, Cheryl. *Rhetoric Retold: Regendering the Tradition from Antiquity through the Renaissance.* Carbondale and Edwardsville, Ill.: Southern Illinois University Press, 1997.

Goffen, Rona. *Titian's Women.* New Haven: Yale University Press, 1997.

Goldberg, Jonathan. *Desiring Women Writing: English Renaissance Examples.* Stanford: Stanford University Press, 1997.

Goldsmith, Elizabeth, ed. *Writing the Female Voice.* Boston: Northeastern University Press, 1989.

Goldsmith, Elizabeth, and Dena Goodman, eds. *Going Public: Women and Publishing in Early Modern France.* Ithaca, N.Y.: Cornell University Press, 1995.

Greer, Margaret Rich. *Maria de Zayas Tells Baroque Tales of Love and the Cruelty of Men.* University Park, Penn.: Pennsylvania State University Press, 2000.

Hackett, Helen. *Women and Romance Fiction in the English Renaissance.* Cambridge: Cambridge University Press, 2000.

Hall, Kim F. *Things of Darkness: Economies of Race and Gender in Early Modern England.* Ithaca, NY: Cornell University Press, 1995.

Hampton, Timothy. *Literature and the Nation in the Sixteenth Century: Inventing Renaissance France.* Ithaca, N.Y.: Cornell University Press, 2001.

Hardwick, Julie. *The Practice of Patriarchy: Gender and the Politics of Household Authority in Early Modern France.* University Park, Penn.: Pennsylvania State University Press, 1998.

Harvey, Elizabeth D. *Ventriloquized Voices: Feminist Theory and English Renaissance Texts.* London and New York: Routledge, 1992.

Haselkorn, Anne M., and Betty Travitsky, eds. *The Renaissance Englishwoman in Print: Counterbalancing the Canon.* Amherst, Mass.: University of Massachusetts Press, 1990.

Herlihy, David. "Did Women Have a Renaissance? A Reconsideration." *Medievalia et Humanistica,* NS 13 (1985): 1–22.

Hill, Bridget. *The Republican Virago: The Life and Times of Catharine Macaulay, Historian.* New York: Oxford University Press, 1992.

A History of Central European Women's Writing. Edited by Celia Hawkesworth. New York: Palgrave Press, 2001.

A History of Women in the West. Volume 1: From Ancient Goddesses to Christian Saints. Edited by Pauline Schmitt Pantel. Cambridge, Mass.: Harvard University Press, 1992.

A History of Women in the West. Volume 2: Silences of the Middle Ages. Edited by Christiane Klapisch-Zuber. Cambridge, Mass.: Harvard University Press, 1992.

A History of Women in the West. Volume 3: Renaissance and Enlightenment Paradoxes. Edited by Natalie Zemon Davis and Arlette Farge. Cambridge, Mass.: Harvard University Press, 1993.

A History of Women's Writing in Russia. Edited by Alele Marie Barker and Jehanne M. Gheith. Cambridge: Cambridge University Press, 2002.

Hobby, Elaine. *Virtue of Necessity: English Women's Writing 1646–1688.* London: Virago Press, 1988.

Horowitz, Maryanne Cline. "Aristotle and Women." *Journal of the History of Biology* 9 (1976): 183–213.

Howell, Martha. *The Marriage Exchange: Property, Social Place, and Gender in Cities of the Low Countries, 1300–1550.* Chicago: University of Chicago Press, 1998.

Hufton, Olwen H. *The Prospect before Her: A History of Women in Western Europe, 1: 1500–1800.* New York: HarperCollins, 1996.

Hunt, Lynn, ed. *The Invention of Pornography: Obscenity and the Origins of Modernity, 1500–1800.* New York: Zone Books, 1996.

Hutner, Heidi, ed. *Rereading Aphra Behn: History, Theory, and Criticism.* Charlottesville, Va.: University Press of Virginia, 1993.

Hutson, Lorna, ed. *Feminism and Renaissance Studies.* New York: Oxford University Press, 1999.

Jaffe, Irma B., with Gernando Colombardo. *Shining Eyes, Cruel Fortune: The Lives and Loves of Italian Renaissance Women Poets.* New York: Fordham University Press, 2002.

James, Susan E. *Kateryn Parr: The Making of a Queen.* Aldershot and Brookfield, UK: Ashgate Publishing Co., 1999.

Jankowski, Theodora A. *Women in Power in the Early Modern Drama.* Urbana, Ill.: University of Illinois Press, 1992.

Jansen, Katherine Ludwig. *The Making of the Magdalen: Preaching and Popular Devotion in the Later Middle Ages.* Princeton: Princeton University Press, 2000.

Jed, Stephanie H. *Chaste Thinking: The Rape of Lucretia and the Birth of Humanism.* Bloomington, Ind.: Indiana University Press, 1989.

Jordan, Constance. *Renaissance Feminism: Literary Texts and Political Models.* Ithaca, N.Y.: Cornell University Press, 1990.

Kagan, Richard L. *Lucrecia's Dreams: Politics and Prophecy in Sixteenth-Century Spain.* Berkeley: University of California Press, 1990.

Kehler, Dorothea, and Laurel Amtower, eds. *The Single Woman in Medieval and Early Modern England: Her Life and Representation.* Tempe, Ariz.: Medieval and Renaissance Texts and Studies, 2002.

Kelly, Joan. "Did Women Have a Renaissance?" In her *Women, History, and Theory.* Chicago: University of Chicago Press, 1984. Also in Renate Bridenthal, Claudia Koonz, and Susan M. Stuard, eds., *Becoming Visible: Women in European History.* 3d ed. Boston: Houghton Mifflin, 1998.

———. "Early Feminist Theory and the *Querelle des Femmes.*" In *Women, History, and Theory.*

Kelso, Ruth. *Doctrine for the Lady of the Renaissance.* Foreword by Katharine M. Rogers. Urbana, Ill.: University of Illinois Press, 1956, 1978.

King, Carole. *Renaissance Women Patrons: Wives and Widows in Italy, c. 1300–1550.* New York and Manchester: Manchester University Press (distributed in the U.S. by St. Martin's Press), 1998.

King, Margaret L. *Women of the Renaissance.* Foreword by Catharine R. Stimpson. Chicago: University of Chicago Press, 1991.

Krontiris, Tina. *Oppositional Voices: Women as Writers and Translators of Literature in the English Renaissance.* London and New York: Routledge, 1992.

Kuehn, Thomas. *Law, Family, and Women: Toward a Legal Anthropology of Renaissance Italy.* Chicago: University of Chicago Press, 1991.

Kunze, Bonnelyn Young. *Margaret Fell and the Rise of Quakerism.* Stanford: Stanford University Press, 1994.

Labalme, Patricia A., ed. *Beyond Their Sex: Learned Women of the European Past.* New York: New York University Press, 1980.

Laqueur, Thomas. *Making Sex: Body and Gender from the Greeks to Freud.* Cambridge, Mass.: Harvard University Press, 1990.

Larsen, Anne R., and Colette H. Winn, eds. *Renaissance Women Writers: French Texts/American Contexts.* Detroit: Wayne State University Press, 1994.

Lerner, Gerda. *The Creation of Patriarchy* and *Creation of Feminist Consciousness, 1000–1870.* 2 vols. New York: Oxford University Press, 1986, 1994.

Levin, Carole, and Jeanie Watson, eds. *Ambiguous Realities: Women in the Middle Ages and Renaissance.* Detroit: Wayne State University Press, 1987.

Levin, Carole, et al. *Extraordinary Women of the Medieval and Renaissance World: A Biographical Dictionary.* Westport, Conn.: Greenwood Press, 2000.

Lewis, Jayne Elizabeth. *Mary Queen of Scots: Romance and Nation.* London: Routledge, 1998.

Lindsey, Karen. *Divorced Beheaded Survived: A Feminist Reinterpretation of the Wives of Henry VIII.* Reading, Mass.: Addison-Wesley Publishing Co., 1995.

Lochrie, Karma. *Margery Kempe and Translations of the Flesh.* Philadelphia: University of Pennsylvania Press, 1992.

Love, Harold. *The Culture and Commerce of Texts: Scribal Publication in Seventeenth-Century England.* Amherst, Mass.: University of Massachusetts Press, 1993.

MacCarthy, Bridget G. *The Female Pen: Women Writers and Novelists 1621–1818.* Preface by Janet Todd. New York: New York University Press, 1994. Originally published by Cork University Press, 1946–47.

Maggi, Armando. *Uttering the Word: The Mystical Performances of Maria Maddalena de' Pazzi, a Renaissance Visionary.* Albany: State University of New York Press, 1998.

Marshall, Sherrin. *Women in Reformation and Counter-Reformation Europe: Public and Private Worlds.* Bloomington, Ind.: Indiana University Press, 1989.

Matter, E. Ann, and John Coakley, eds. *Creative Women in Medieval and Early Modern Italy.* Philadelphia: University of Pennsylvania Press, 1994. Sequel to the Monson collection, below.

McLeod, Glenda. *Virtue and Venom: Catalogs of Women from Antiquity to the Renaissance.* Ann Arbor: University of Michigan Press, 1991.

Medwick, Cathleen. *Teresa of Avila: The Progress of a Soul.* New York: Alfred A. Knopf, 2000.

Meek, Christine, ed. *Women in Renaissance and Early Modern Europe.* Dublin-Portland: Four Courts Press, 2000.

Mendelson, Sara, and Patricia Crawford. *Women in Early Modern England, 1550–1720.* Oxford: Clarendon Press, 1998.

Merrim, Stephanie. *Early Modern Women's Writing and Sor Juana Inés de la Cruz.* Nashville, Tenn.: Vanderbilt University Press, 1999.

Messbarger, Rebecca. *The Century of Women: The Representations of Women in Eighteenth-Century Italian Public Discourse.* Toronto: University of Toronto Press, 2002.

Miller, Nancy K. *The Heroine's Text: Readings in the French and English Novel, 1722–1782.* New York: Columbia University Press, 1980.

Miller, Naomi J. *Changing the Subject: Mary Wroth and Figurations of Gender in Early Modern England.* Lexington, Ky.: University Press of Kentucky, 1996.

Miller, Naomi J., and Gary Waller, eds. *Reading Mary Wroth: Representing Alternatives in Early Modern England.* Knoxville, Tenn.: University of Tennessee Press, 1991.

Monson, Craig A., ed. *The Crannied Wall: Women, Religion, and the Arts in Early Modern Europe.* Ann Arbor: University of Michigan Press, 1992.

Musacchio, Jacqueline Marie. *The Art and Ritual of Childbirth in Renaissance Italy.* New Haven: Yale University Press, 1999.

Newman, Barbara. *God and the Goddesses: Vision, Poetry, and Belief in the Middle Ages.* Philadelphia: University of Pennsylvania Press, 2003.

Newman, Karen. *Fashioning Femininity and English Renaissance Drama.* Chicago and London: University of Chicago Press, 1991.

Okin, Susan Moller. *Women in Western Political Thought.* Princeton: Princeton University Press, 1979.

Ozment, Steven. *The Bürgermeister's Daughter: Scandal in a Sixteenth-Century German Town.* New York: St. Martin's Press, 1995.

Pacheco, Anita, ed. *Early [English] Women Writers: 1600–1720.* New York and London: Longman, 1998.

Pagels, Elaine. *Adam, Eve, and the Serpent.* New York: Harper Collins, 1988.

Panizza, Letizia, ed. *Women in Italian Renaissance Culture and Society.* Oxford: European Humanities Research Centre, 2000.

Panizza, Letizia, and Sharon Wood, eds. *A History of Women's Writing in Italy.* Cambridge: Cambridge University Press, 2000.

Parker, Patricia. *Literary Fat Ladies: Rhetoric, Gender and Property.* London and New York: Methuen, 1987.

Pernoud, Regine, and Marie-Veronique Clin. *Joan of Arc: Her Story.* Revised and translated by Jeremy DuQuesnay Adams. New York: St. Martin's Press, 1998. French original, 1986.

Perry, Mary Elizabeth. *Crime and Society in Early Modern Seville.* Hanover, N.H.: University Press of New England, 1980.

———. *Gender and Disorder in Early Modern Seville.* Princeton: Princeton University Press, 1990.

Petroff, Elizabeth Alvilda, ed. *Medieval Women's Visionary Literature.* New York: Oxford University Press, 1986.

Perry, Ruth. *The Celebrated Mary Astell: An Early English Feminist.* Chicago: University of Chicago Press, 1986.

Rabil, Albert. *Laura Cereta: Quattrocento Humanist.* Binghamton, N.Y.: Medieval and Renaissance Texts and Studies, 1981.

Rapley, Elizabeth. *A Social History of the Cloister: Daily Life in the Teaching Monasteries of the Old Regime.* Montreal: McGill-Queen's University Press, 2001.

Raven, James, Helen Small, and Naomi Tadmor, eds. *The Practice and Representation of Reading in England.* Cambridge: Cambridge University Press, 1996.

Reardon, Colleen. *Holy Concord within Sacred Walls: Nuns and Music in Siena, 1575–1700.* Oxford: Oxford University Press, 2001.

Reiss, Sheryl E., and David G. Wilkins, ed. *Beyond Isabella: Secular Women Patrons of Art in Renaissance Italy.* Kirksville, Mo.: Turman State University Press, 2001.

Rheubottom, David. *Age, Marriage, and Politics in Fifteenth-Century Ragusa.* Oxford: Oxford University Press, 2000.

Richardson, Brian. *Printing, Writers and Readers in Renaissance Italy.* Cambridge: University Press, 1999.

Riddle, John M. *Contraception and Abortion from the Ancient World to the Renaissance.* Cambridge, Mass.: Harvard University Press, 1992.

———. *Eve's Herbs: A History of Contraception and Abortion in the West.* Cambridge, Mass.: Harvard University Press, 1997.

Rose, Mary Beth. *The Expense of Spirit: Love and Sexuality in English Renaissance Drama.* Ithaca, N.Y.: Cornell University Press, 1988.

————. *Gender and Heroism in Early Modern English Literature.* Chicago: University of Chicago Press, 2002.

————, ed. *Women in the Middle Ages and the Renaissance: Literary and Historical Perspectives.* Syracuse: Syracuse University Press, 1986.

Rosenthal, Margaret F. *The Honest Courtesan: Veronica Franco, Citizen and Writer in Sixteenth-Century Venice.* Foreword by Catharine R. Stimpson. Chicago: University of Chicago Press, 1992.

Sackville-West, Vita. *Daughter of France: The Life of La Grande Mademoiselle.* Garden City, N.Y.: Doubleday, 1959.

Sánchez, Magdalena S. *The Empress, the Queen, and the Nun: Women and Power at the Court of Philip III of Spain.* Baltimore: Johns Hopkins University Press, 1998.

Schiebinger, Londa. *The Mind Has No Sex?: Women in the Origins of Modern Science.* Cambridge, Mass.: Harvard University Press, 1991.

————. *Nature's Body: Gender in the Making of Modern Science.* Boston: Beacon Press, 1993.

Schutte, Anne Jacobson, Thomas Kuehn, and Silvana Seidel Menchi, eds. *Time, Space, and Women's Lives in Early Modern Europe.* Kirksville, Mo.: Truman State University Press, 2001.

Shannon, Laurie. *Sovereign Amity: Figures of Friendship in Shakespearean Contexts.* Chicago: University of Chicago Press, 2002.

Shemek, Deanna. *Ladies Errant: Wayward Women and Social Order in Early Modern Italy.* Durham, N.C.: Duke University Press, 1998.

Smith, Hilda L. *Reason's Disciples: Seventeenth-Century English Feminists.* Urbana, Ill.: University of Illinois Press, 1982.

————, ed. *Women Writers and the Early Modern British Political Tradition.* Cambridge: Cambridge University Press, 1998.

Sobel, Dava. *Galileo's Daughter: A Historical Memoir of Science, Faith, and Love.* New York: Penguin Books, 2000.

Sommerville, Margaret R. *Sex and Subjection: Attitudes to Women in Early-Modern Society.* London: Arnold, 1995.

Soufas, Teresa Scott. *Dramas of Distinction: A Study of Plays by Golden Age Women.* Lexington, Ky.: The University Press of Kentucky, 1997.

Spencer, Jane. *The Rise of the Woman Novelist: From Aphra Behn to Jane Austen.* Oxford: Basil Blackwell, 1986.

Spender, Dale. *Mothers of the Novel: 100 Good Women Writers before Jane Austen.* London and New York: Routledge, 1986.

Sperling, Jutta Gisela. *Convents and the Body Politic in Late Renaissance Venice.* Foreword by Catharine R. Stimpson. Chicago: University of Chicago Press, 1999.

Steinbrügge, Lieselotte. *The Moral Sex: Woman's Nature in the French Enlightenment.* Translated by Pamela E. Selwyn. New York: Oxford University Press, 1995.

Stephens, Sonya, ed. *A History of Women's Writing in France.* Cambridge: Cambridge University Press, 2000.

Stocker, Margarita. *Judith, Sexual Warrior: Women and Power in Western Culture.* New Haven: Yale University Press, 1998.

Stretton, Timothy. *Women Waging Law in Elizabethan England.* Cambridge: Cambridge University Press, 1998.

Stuard, Susan M. "The Dominion of Gender: Women's Fortunes in the High Middle Ages." In Renate Bridenthal, Claudia Koonz, and Susan M. Stuard, eds. *Becoming Visible: Women in European History*. 3d ed.. Boston: Houghton Mifflin, 1998.

Summit, Jennifer. *Lost Property: The Woman Writer and English Literary History, 1380–1589*. Chicago: University of Chicago Press, 2000.

Surtz, Ronald E. *The Guitar of God: Gender, Power, and Authority in the Visionary World of Mother Juana de la Cruz (1481–1534)*. Philadelphia: University of Pennsylvania Press, 1991.

———. *Writing Women in Late Medieval and Early Modern Spain: The Mothers of Saint Teresa of Avila*. Philadelphia: University of Pennsylvania Press, 1995.

Teague, Frances. *Bathsua Makin, Woman of Learning*. Lewisburg, Penn.: Bucknell University Press, 1999.

Todd, Janet. *The Secret Life of Aphra Behn*. London, New York, and Sydney: Pandora, 2000.

———. *The Sign of Angelica: Women, Writing and Fiction, 1660–1800*. New York: Columbia University Press, 1989.

Valenze, Deborah. *The First Industrial Woman*. New York: Oxford University Press, 1995.

Van Dijk, Susan, Lia van Gemert,and Sheila Ottway, eds. *Writing the History of Women's Writing: Toward an International Approach*. Proceedings of the Colloquium, Amsterdam, 9–11 September. Amsterdam: Royal Netherlands Academy of Arts and Sciences, 2001.

Vickery, Amanda. *The Gentleman's Daughter: Women's Lives in Georgian England*. New Haven: Yale University Press, 1998.

Vollendorf, Lisa, ed. *Recovering Spain's Feminist Tradition*. New York: Modern Language Association, 2001.

Waithe, Mary Ellen, ed. *A History of Women Philosophers*. 3 vols. Dordrecht: Martinus Nijhoff, 1987.

Wall, Wendy. *The Imprint of Gender: Authorship and Publication in the English Renaissance*. Ithaca, N.Y.: Cornell University Press, 1993.

Walsh, William T. *St. Teresa of Avila: A Biography*. Rockford, Ill.: TAN Books and Publications, 1987.

Warner, Marina. *Alone of All Her Sex: The Myth and Cult of the Virgin Mary*. New York: Knopf, 1976.

Warnicke, Retha M. *The Marrying of Anne of Cleves: Royal Protocol in Tudor England*. Cambridge: Cambridge University Press, 2000.

Watt, Diane. *Secretaries of God: Women Prophets in Late Medieval and Early Modern England*. Cambridge, UK: D. S. Brewer, 1997.

Weber, Alison. *Teresa of Avila and the Rhetoric of Femininity*. Princeton: Princeton University Press, 1990.

Welles, Marcia L. *Persephone's Girdle: Narratives of Rape in Seventeenth-Century Spanish Literature*. Nashville: Vanderbilt University Press, 2000.

Whitehead, Barbara J., ed. *Women's Education in Early Modern Europe: A History, 1500–1800*. New York and London: Garland Publishing Co., 1999.

Wiesner, Merry E. *Women and Gender in Early Modern Europe*. Cambridge: Cambridge University Press, 1993.

———. *Working Women in Renaissance Germany.* New Brunswick, N.J.: Rutgers University Press, 1986.

Willard, Charity Cannon. *Christine de Pizan: Her Life and Works.* New York: Persea Books, 1984.

Wilson, Katharina, ed. *An Encyclopedia of Continental Women Writers.* New York: Garland, 1991.

Winn, Colette, and Donna Kuizenga, eds. *Women Writers in Pre-Revolutionary France.* New York: Garland Publishing, 1997.

Woods, Susanne. *Lanyer: A Renaissance Woman Poet.* New York: Oxford University Press, 1999.

Woods, Susanne, and Margaret P. Hannay, eds. *Teaching Tudor and Stuart Women Writers.* New York: Modern Language Association, 2000.

INDEX

Abrams, David, 106 n. 9
absolutism, 9
Académie Française, 4, 7
academies, 12
Acciaiuoli, Andrea, xxv
Adam, xv–xvi, xxiii
aesthetics, 15, 28
affectation, 109
Africa, 67, 72, 133 n. 34, 137
Agrippa II, 86 n. 46
Agrippa, Henricus Cornelius, xxiii–xxv
Alberti, Leon Battista, xxiii
Alexander the Great, 121
Alexandria, 132, 137
Altman, Janet Gurkin, 19 n. 47
Amasis, 132
Amazons, xxvii–xxviii
Anacharsis, 127
Ancyra, 79
Andreadis, Harriette, ix, 6 n.18, 34
androgyny, xxvii
Anne of Austria (queen and regent of
    France), 5, 30
Anne of Brittany, (queen of France),
    xxv
Anne of Denmark (princess), xxv
Antioch, 79
Antiochus IV of Syria, 56 n. 4
Antipater, 66
Antony, Mark, 22, 60–62, 65, 77 n. 28,
    86

anxiety, 44–46
Aphthonius, 10, 20
Apollo, 91–92
Aquinas, Saint Thomas, xiv, xvi
Arabia, 85, 133
Arabic, language, 1, 12, 132, 137
Aragona, Tullia d', 11
Ariosto, Ludovico, xxviii
Aristobulus, 59, 63, 66
aristocracy, 9, 14–15, 18, 30
Aristotle, xii–xiii, 10–11, 28, 109 n. 11
Armenia, 80, 85
Aronson, Nicole, 3–8, 21 n. 51, 32, 34
    n. 66
Aronson, Stuart R., 3 n. 4
ars dictaminis, 19. See also letter-writing
Artemisia, xxvii
Asia, 80, 133 n. 34, 137
Asia Minor, 75 n. 24
Astell, Mary, xxv, xxvii, xxix
Augustine, Saint, xvi, 25
Augustus Caesar (Caius Julius Caesar
    Octavius Augustus; emperor of
    Rome), 60 n. 9, 77, 82–83
Aurelian, Lucius Domitius, 23, 75–76,
    78–85

Baader, Renate, 15 n. 42
Babylonia, 77 n. 31
Backer, Dorothy, 15 n. 42
Bacon, Francis, Sir, 25

Balzac, Jean Louis Guez de, 15, 139–42
Barbaro, Francesco, xxiii, xxviii
Barbin, Claude, 138
Barbour, Paula, 12 n. 38
Barsaphane, 59
Barzun, Jacques, 7 n. 19
Bassnett, Susan, 11 n. 31
Bean, Robert D., 106 n. 9
Beasley, Faith E., 5 n. 11, 15 n. 42
Beauchamp, Virginia Walcott, ix, 9 n. 28
beauty, 88–89, 92, 94
Bembo, Pietro (cardinal), 140
Bentivoglio, Guido (cardinal), 140
Berenice, 86
Bergamo, Filippo da, xxi–xxii
Biancardi, Elisa, 3–4, 8
Bible, xii, xv, xxi, 45–46
Bithynia, 79
Boccaccio, Giovanni, xvii–xviii, xxi, xxv
Bodin, Jean, xxiv
Boileau-Desprèaux, Nicolas, 138 n. 49
Bommakanty, Shivani, 106 n. 9
Bosporus, 79
Brantôme, Pierre de, xxii
Brown, Jeff, 106 n. 9
Bruni, Leonardo, xxviii
Brutus, Marcus Iunius, 83
Burke, Mary E., 11 n. 30
Burke, Peter, 16 n. 44

Camara, Juan Rodríguez de la. *See* Rodríguez de la Camara, Juan
Cantelma, Margherita of Mantua, xxv
Capella, Galeazzo Flavio. *See* Capra, Galeazzo Flavio
Capra, Galeazzo Flavio, xxiii
Caro, Annibale, 140
Carrhae, 78
Cartesianism, 15 n. 42
Carthage, 67 n. 18, 69–70, 72
Cary, Elizabeth (Lady Falkland), 22
Cassell, Anthony K., xviii
Cassius, Gaius Longinus, 83 n. 44
Castiglione, Baldassare, xxii, 14, 16, 25–26

catalogs of famous women, xxi–xxiii, xxv–xxvi, xxviii, 1, 17, 20
Catherine de' Medici (queen and regent of France), xxvii, 14
Catherine of Aragon, xxv, 11
Cato, Marcus Porcius, 83
Catullus, Caius Valerius, 33
Cavendish, Margaret, duchess of Newcastle. *See* Newcastle, Margaret Cavendish, duchess of
Celts, 80
Cereta, Laura, xxv, 11–12
Chalcedon, 79
Chapelain, Jean, 15, 140
Charles V (king of France), xxv
Charles VIII (king of France), xxv
chastity, xxi, xxiii–xxix, 9, 58, 60–62, 66, 79
childbirth, xviii
children, 97
Christine de Pizan, xxii, xxix; *Book of the City of Ladies*, xvii, xx–xxi, xxv, xxvii; *The Treasure of the City of Ladies*, xxv
Cicero, Marcus Tullius, 10, 17–19, 22, 25–26, 140 n. 53
Claude Catherine de Clermont-Dampierre (maréchal de Retz), 14
Claudius, Marcus Aurelius II (emperor of Rome), 85
Cleopatra VII (queen of Egypt), 60–61, 77, 82–83, 86 n. 46
Clifford, Anne. *See* Dorset, Anne (Clifford), countess of
Col, Gontier, xxii
collaboration, 4, 20
commonplaces, 25
Condé, Louis II de Bourbon, prince de, 5
Coogan, Robert, ix
Corneille, Pierre, 15, 140 n. 53
Cosimo I (duke of Florence), 11
cosmetics, xxviii
constancy, 58, 73, 75–76, 81–84
convent, xix, 35
conversation, 2–3, 6–7, 9, 13–18, 25–29, 32, 35–37, 51–53, 96–117, 147
Costar, Pierre, 139–41

courage, 76–85, 89
Courbé, Augustin, 138
courtesy, 100, 104–5
courtly love, xvii
courtship, 36, 47
Crane, Mary Thomas, 11 n. 30
Ctesiphon, 78, 85
Cumae, 113
Cyrus the Great, 133. *See also* Scudéry,
 Madeleine de, *Artamène; ou, Le grand
 Cyrus*

Daedalus, 53 n. 8
Dalmatia, 80
decorum, 104
DeJean, Joan, 4 n. 9, 20, 33–34, 37 n.
 71
Delaney, Catherine, 106 n. 9
Denis, Delphine, 1, 25, 37, 96 n. 1, 117
 n. 20, 127 n. 23, 139 n. 52
Descartes, Catherine, 6, 33
dialect, 28, 129 n. 27
dialectic, 25, 28
diaries, xxv
divorce, xv
Doherty, Lillian, ix, 117 n. 20
Doña María (queen of Castile), xxv
Donawerth, Jane, 13 n. 40
Dorset, Anne (Clifford), countess of,
 146 n. 58
dowry, xv, xviii
dream allegory, xvii
Duchêne, Roger, 2 n. 2
Dunhill, Anne, 12 n. 36

education, for women, xiii, xix, xxi–
 xxiii, xxviii–xxix, 2–3, 8–12, 24–25,
 86–95
Egypt, 60–61, 75 n. 24, 77, 79, 85,
 132–37
Eleanora of Aragon, xxv
Elizabeth I (queen of England), xxvii,
 11
Elyot, Sir Thomas, xxvii
embroidery, xviii
Emesa, 79
empiricism, 22, 25
England, 34

English Civil War, 12
epigram, 95
Equicola, Maria, xxiii, xxv
Erasmus, Desiderius, xxiii, 10–11, 109
 n. 11
Ercole I d'Este (duke of Ferrara), xxv
Erinna, 1, 8, 23–25, 33, 35, 86–95
ésprit, 18, 27
ethopoeia, 20–21
Euphrates, 135
Eve, xv–xvi, xxi, xxiii

Faderman, Lillian, 34
fashion, in clothing, 97, 100
Fedele, Cassandra, xxv, 11
Ferguson, Margaret, 22 n. 53
Field, Catherine, ix
figurative language, 10, 17
Flanders, xix
Fonte, Moderata, xxvii
Fortune, 58–59, 68, 73–79, 82–84, 119,
 135
Fouquet, Nicolas, 7
France, 1, 21, 119
Freedman, Tama, 106 n. 9
friendship, 124, 130, 147–49, 151;
 female, 2, 19, 33–37, 44–55. *See also*
 homoeroticism
Fronde, 2 n. 2, 4–5, 9, 15, 30

Galatia, 79
Galen, xii
Galindo, Beatrix, 11
Gallienus, Publius Licinius Egnatius
 (emperor of Rome), 78–79, 81, 85
Gerson, Jean, xxii
Gibson, Joan, 9–10
Glenn, Cheryl, 13 n. 39
glory, 91, 94, 96
Goggio, Bartolommeo, xxiii, xxv
Goldsmith, Elizabeth, ix, 1, 7 n. 21, 15
 n. 43, 32
Gondi, Albert de, 14
Goodman, Dena, 15
gossip, 27, 98, 103
Goths, 85
Gournay, Marie de, xxix

Goutimesnil, Madeleine de Martel de, 3
Grafton, Anthony, 9 n. 28
grammar, 9 n. 29
Grande, Nathalie, 3, 5–6
Greece, 16, 21, 86, 132
Greek language, xx, 3, 11–13, 112, 133
Guazzo, Stefano, xxiv
Guevaro, Antonio, 140
Guillaume de Lorris, xvii, xv

Hageman, Elizabeth H., 9 n. 28
Hallett, Judith, ix, 33 n. 63
Handel, Lauren, 106 n. 9
Hannay, Margaret, 10 n. 29
Harth, Erica, 15 n. 43, 21, 32 n. 60
Hasdrubal, 67 n. 18, 69, 72
Hassan, Chris, 106 n. 9
Henry IV (king of France), 140 n. 53
Henry VIII (king of England), xxv
Heraclianus (Roman general), 79
Hercules, 132
Herod the Great, 22, 56–67
Herod (king of Chalcis), 86 n. 46
Herodotus, 132–33
Hesiod, 33
Hester, Thaddeus, 106 n. 9
heterosexuality, 34
Hinds, Leonard, 20 n. 48
Hircanus, 58–59, 63, 66
Homer, 33
homoeroticism, 2, 6, 16–17, 19, 33–37, 44–50
honnête gens, 15, 18, 30, 96, 99–101, 111, 116, 129, 138
Horace, 27, 52 n. 6, 128 n. 26, 140 n. 53
Hôtel de Rambouillet, 3, 14
Howell, Wilbur Samuel, 11 n. 30
Hubbell, H. M. 26 n. 57
Hull, Suzanne W., 9 n. 28
humanism, xx, xxiii–xxv, xxviii–xxix, 2, 8–13, 16–20, 24–25, 31, 36
humors, four, xiii
hysteria, xiii, 35

Icarus, 53
imagination, 29, 89–90, 93–94, 112

imitation, 28, 53–54
impersonation, 129
incest, xxviii
Innes, James, 94 n. 60
Irwin, Joyce L., 12 n. 37
Isocrates, 26 n. 57
Italy, xix–xx, 21, 36

Japan, 20
Jardine, Lisa, 9 n. 28
Jean de Meun, xvii, xxii, xxv
Jean de Montreuil, xxii
Jensen, Katherine A., 15 n. 43
Jerome, Saint, xvi
Jesus, xvi
Joan of Arc, 140 n. 53
John the Baptist, 56 n. 2
Joseph Ben Gurion, 56 n. 3
Josephus, 56 n. 3
Juan II (king of Castile), xxv
Juana Inez de la Cruz, Sor, 95 n. 62
Judea, 58, 65
judgment, 29, 47, 89–90, 104, 112–14, 125, 129, 143, 146–47, 150
Julius Caesar (emperor of Rome), 60 n. 9, 65 n. 15, 77 n. 28, 121
Jupiter, 70 n. 21
Justinian (emperor of Rome), xiv

Kelly, Ann Cline, 16 n. 44
Kerkylas of Andros, 33
Keyes, Clinton Walker, 26 n. 57
King, Margaret L., ix, xi–xxxi, 9
kingship, ideal, 133–39
Kleis of Mytilene, 33
Knox, John, xxvii
Krajewska, Barbara, 8 n. 23
Krämer, Heinrich, xxiv

lactation, xviii
Laelius, 68
La Fayette, Marie Madeleine Pioche de La Vergne, comtesse de, 15
language: French, 28; purity of, 112; vulgar, 29, 114–15, 125
Lanser, Susan, ix, 6 n. 18, 34–35
Laodicea, 61, 65
La Rochefoucauld, François, duc de, 15

Latin language, xvi–xvii, xix–xx, xxix,
  3, 10–13, 20, 23, 33–34, 36, 133
Lazard, Madeleine, 11 n. 34, 14 n. 41
Le Franc, Martin, xxii
Le Moyne, Pierre, xxii
Lenkey, Stephanie, ix, 96 n. 1, 139 n.
  52
Lepidus, Marcus Aemilius, 60 n. 9, 77
  n. 28
lesbianism, 34–35. *See also* friendship;
  homoeroticism
letter-writing, xxv, 1, 6, 11, 13, 18–20,
  25, 30–37, 44–55, 139–51
Levin, Carole, 13
liberty, 68, 70, 72–75, 78, 80, 84
Logan, Shirley, ix
logic, 10
Longueville, Anne Geneviève de
  Bourbon-Condé, duchesse de, 5, 15
Lougee, Carolyn, 15
Louis XIII, 140 n. 53
Louis XIV (king of France), 2 n. 2, 5, 7,
  9, 30, 138–39
love, xvii, 47–48, 59, 61–62, 72, 98,
  147. *See also* love letters
love letters, 32, 36, 141, 143, 148–50
Luna, Alvaro de, xxv
Lunsford, Andrea A., 13 n. 39
lust, xxvi

Maccabees, 56
Maccabeus, Judas, 56 n. 4
Mack, Peter, 13 n. 39
Maclean, Ian, 2 n. 2, 5 n. 11, 9 n. 28,
  15 n. 42, 18 n. 45
Maguire, James, 106 n. 9
Maintenon, Françoise d'Aubigné,
  marquise de, 25
Maître, Myriam, 2 n. 2, 4 n. 9
Makin, Bathsua, 12
Malherbe, François de, 15, 139–42
manuscript culture, xx
Marcus, Leah, 11 n. 30
Margaret (duchess of Austria, regent of
  the Netherlands), xxv
Marguerite de Navarre (queen), 14
Mariam (queen), 22, 37, 56–67
Marinella, Lucrezia, 12

marriage, xv–xix, xxiii, 2 n. 2, 4 n. 8,
  22–24, 33–35, 58–59, 69, 73
Martinvast, Marie-Madeleine de
  Montcal de, 6
martyrs, xxi
Mary (mother of Jesus), xvii
Mary Stuart (queen of Scotland), 11
Masinissa, 23, 67–75
Mathéolus, xvii, xx
maxims, 131
Mazarin, Jules, 5, 30, 138 n. 46
McDougall, Dorothy, 5–6
McGuire, Greg, 106 n. 9
Mecapor, 80
medallion, 57, 68, 76, 78, 87
Medici, Giuliano de', xxii
medicine, 45
melancholy, xxiv, 63
memory, 47, 50, 58, 89–90, 93–94,
  114, 129
men, as head of household, xiv, xviii,
  xxvi
Mercury, 91
Merry, Bruce, 11 n. 33
Mesopotamia, 78, 80
meter, 86, 95
Mikesell, Margaret, 9 n. 28
Minerva, 91
Miseno, 80
misogyny, xi–xiii, xx, xxiii, 1–2
Mithridates VI (king of Pontus), 83
modesty, 62, 149
Molière, Jean Baptiste Poquelin, 2 n. 2
Molitur, Ulrich, xxiv
Montaigne, Michel Eyquem de, 140
Montesquieu, Charles Louis de
  Secondat, baron de la Brède et de,
  127 n. 23
Montpensier, Anne Marie Louise
  d'Orléans, duchesse de, 15
Moors, 80
moral philosophy, 45–46, 55
Morata, Olympia, xxv
Muses, 14, 86, 91–92
mutability, 88

nature, 24, 88–91, 93, 112, 125, 128
needlework, 3

Nenichka, Denise, 106 n. 9
Newcastle, Margaret Cavendish,
    duchess of, 13, 22
Newman, Karen, 96 n. 1
news, 102, 143, 146
Nichols, Shelley, 106 n. 9
Niderst, Alain, 7 n. 20
Nile, 120
Nisibis, 78
Nogarola, Isotta, xxv, xxviii, 9 n. 28
Norbrook, David, 13 n. 39
Norlin, George, 26 n. 57
Numidia, 67, 72, 74
nuns, xxiv–xxv

oaths, 28
obedience, required of women, xxi,
    xxiii, 9, 22, 58
O'Brien, Katelyn, 106 n. 9
Octavius Caesar. *See* Augustus Caesar
Odenatus, 77–79, 85
Olympus, Mount, 45
Onorio, Diana, 106 n. 9
opera, 139
oratory, 2, 10–11, 16–17, 20–25, 56–95
original sin, xv–xvi, xxvi
Ovid (Publius Ovidius Naso), 33–34,
    86 n. 47, 140 n. 53

Padron, Juan Rodríguez del. *See*
    Rodríguez de la Camara, Juan
Palestine, 80
Pallavicino, Gasparo, xxii
Palmyra, 75 n. 24, 77, 80
panegyric, 145
Panicker, Suja, 106 n. 9
Panizza, Letizia, 12 n. 36
Pannonia, 80
Paone, Kimberlee, 106 n. 9
Parnassus, 92
paterfamilias, xiv
patience, 61, 84
patronage, xxv, 19, 21
Paul, xvi
Pellisson, Paul, 6–7, 34
periodic sentence, 10, 17, 22
Perry, Jamila, 106 n. 9

Persia, 77–81, 85, 124, 133 n. 37
Phaon, 6, 34
Pheroras, 66
Phoenicia, 80
Pillet, Stephane, ix
Plato, xiii, 11, 25, 34 n. 66, 92 n. 57,
    133 n. 36, 138
Platonism, 36
pleonasm, 17
Pliny the Younger (Caius Plinius
    Caecilius Secundus), 140 n. 53
Plutarch, 138
Policy, Amy, 106 n. 9
politics, 102. *See also* Scudéry,
    Madeleine de, politics
Pompey (Cneius Pompeius Magnus),
    77 n. 28
Porter, Robin, 106 n. 9
Portia, daughter of Cato, 83
précieuses, xxvii, 2, 16, 21
pregnancy, xviii
Protestantism, xix
proverbs, 29, 126, 129
Ptolemy (ruling family of ancient
    Egypt), 77
Pythagoras, 106

querelle des femmes. See women, pamphlet
    controversy about
Quintilian, 10, 18, 28

Rabil, Albert, ix, xi–xxxi, 9
Rabinowitz, Nancy Sorkin, 33 n. 62
Rackham, H., 26 n. 57
Rambouillet, Catherine de Vivonne,
    marquise de, 4, 14
Ramée, Pierre de la. *See* Peter Ramus
Ramus, Peter, 11
Rayor, Diane, 33 n. 62
Rebhorn, Wayne, 12–13
Rémy, Nicolas, xxiv
Renaissance, xi, 10, 14, 16, 19–22,
    24–25, 33–36
reproduction, xxii, xxvi
reputation, 60, 65–67, 82
rhetoric, xx, 9–14, 16, 19–22, 24–28,
    34,
Rhetorica ad Herennium, 10

rhetorical argument, 20–25, 28, 32
Rhodes, 65
Ribera, Pietro Paolo de, xxii
Richards, Earl Jeffrey, xx n. 4
Richelieu, Armand Jean du Plessis, duc de (cardinal), 15
Richlin, Amy, 33 n. 62
Rivard, Christopher, 106 n. 9
Robin, Diana, 11–12
Roches, Catherine des, 11
Roches, Madeleine des, 11
Rodríguez de la Camara, Juan, xxii
Rodríguez del Padron, Juan. *See* Rodríguez de la Camara, Juan
Roman Catholicism, xii, xxvi, xix, 55 n. 10
Roman imperialism, critique of, 68–71
Roman law, xiv
Rome, xx, 21, 23, 60–61, 67–83, 86, 107, 137
Romulus, 107
Rose, Mary Beth, 11 n. 30
Russell, Rinaldina, 11 n. 33

Sainte-Beuve, Charles Augustin, 3 n. 5, 8
saints, xix
Salome, 56 n. 2, 62–66
salon, xxvii, 1–3, 6, 12–16, 21, 23–28, 35–36
Samedis, the Scudéry salon, 6, 15
Sands, Tamara, 106 n. 9
Sapor, king of Persia, 78, 85
sapphics, 86,
sapphistry. *See* friendship; homoeroticism; lesbianism
Sappho, 1, 3, 6, 8, 19, 23–25, 32–35, 37, 86–95
Saracens, 80, 85
Sarrazin, Jacques, 142
satire, xvii, 28, 34, 128, 130
Schurman, Anna Maria van, xxix, 12
Scipio Africanus Minor, 23, 67–70, 72–74
Scudéry, Georges (brother of Madeleine), 1, 3–7, 14–15, 20, 37; *Le Prince Déguisé*, 3

Scudéry, Georges (father of Madeleine), 3
Scudéry, Madeleine de: *Artamène; ou, Le grand Cyrus (Artamene; or, Cyrus the Grand)*, 3, 5–6, 8, 96 n. 1, 117 n. 20, 127 n. 23; *Célinte, nouvelle première (Celinte, the First Novel)*, 7; *Clélie, histoire romaine (Clelie, a Roman History*, 7–8, 33, 106 n. 9; *Conversations morales (Moral Conversations)*, 7; *Conversations nouvelles sur divers sujets (New Conversations on Diverse Subjects)*, x, 1, 6–7, 30–32, 139–51; *Conversations sur divers sujets (Conversations on Diverse Subjects)*, xxxii, 1, 4 n. 9, 7, 14, 18, 25–30, 32, 96–139; *Discours de la gloire (Discourse about Glory)*, 7; *Entretiens de morale (Conversations about Morality)*, 7; as feminist, 8; *La Promenade de Versailles (A Walk Through Versailles)*, 7; *Les femmes illustres; ou, Les harangues héroiques (Famous Women; or, Heroic Speeches)*, x, 1–2, 4, 17, 20–25, 33, 35, 38, 56–95; *Ibrahim; ou, L'illustre Bassa (Ibrahim; or, The Famous Bassa)*, 4; *Lettres amoureuses de divers autheurs de ce temps (Amorous Letters by Various Contemporary Authors)*, 1–2, 4, 16–20, 35–38, 44–55; *Mathilde d'Aguilar*, 7; *Nouvelles conversations de morale (New Moral Conversations)*, 7; and politics, 5–7, 30; published anonymously, 3–4; style, 2
Semiramis, 138
Seneca, Lucius Annaeus, the younger, 138, 140 n. 53
Sesostris, 133
Sévigné, Marie de Rabutin-Chantal, marquise de, 15
sewing, xviii
sexuality, xvii, 33
Sicily, 112
silence, required of women, xxi, xxiii–xxiv, xxviii, 9, 59, 64, 107
Skamandronymos, 33
Skinner, Marilyn B., 33 n. 62
slavery, 68, 70, 72–74, 82, 84

Snyder, Jane McIntosh, 33 n. 62, 89 n. 52
Socrates, 138
Solon, 127
sophistry, 10, 21–24, 26, 28, 44–46, 75
Sophonisba, 22–23, 37, 67–75
Spain, 118–19
Spence, Ferrand, 105 n. 9, 137 n. 45
Spenser, Edmund, xxviii
spinning, xviii
Sprenger, Jacob, xxiv
Stanton, Domna, 18
Stark, John, 13 n. 40
stoicism, 23, 58 n. 7, 73–74, 79, 81, 84
style, 16–20, 22, 24, 28, 31, 52–54, 146–47
suffrage, 24
suicide, 67–86
Sullivan, Patricia A., 13 n. 39
Sutherland, Christine Mason, 13 n. 40
Sutton, E. W., 26 n. 57
Syphax, 67, 69–70, 72, 74
Syracuse, 101, 112
Syria, 77 n. 31, 80
Syrte, 67

Tarentum, 113
Tertullian, xvi
Theanea, 79–80
Tigris, 135
Timmermans, Linda, 8
Titus Flavius Vespasianus (emperor of Rome), 86
Tivoli, Gardens of, 85, 138
Traub, Valerie, 6 n. 18, 34
travel narrative, 29–30, 120–22
tribade, 34
Triumph, 23, 67–68, 71–78, 81–85, 95

Ulley, Dawn, 106 n. 9
Ulpian, xv
uterus, xiii

Valerian (Publius Licinius Valerianus; emperor of Rome), 78

Venesoen, Constant, 8
Venus, 81, 119
Versailles, 7
virginity, xxvi
Vives, Juan Luis, xxiii, xxv, xxviii, 9 n. 28, 11
Voiture, Vincent, 15, 139–42
Vosevich, Kathi, 11 n. 30

Wahl, Elizabeth, 6 n. 18
Walker, Clinton, 26 n. 57
warfare, art of, 78–81, 85
Weil, Maggie, 106 n. 9
Weller, Barry, 22 n. 53
Wentz, Victoria, 106 n. 9
Wertheimer, Molly, ix, 13
West Indies, 119
Weyer, Johann, xxiv
Whigham, Frank, 16 n. 44
widows, xxvii
wit, 10, 18, 27–32, 37, 51, 89–90, 99, 103–5, 111–14, 117, 132, 135, 142–43, 147–49
witchcraft, xxiii–xxiv, xxviii
Wolfe, Phillip J., 1, 25, 37, 105 n. 9
women: accused of sexual misconduct, xxviii; and community, xxi, xxvii, xxix, 34; equal to men, xi, xxii–xxiii, xxix, 14, 16, 24; excluded from political power, xxvii; inferior to men, xii–xiii, xxi–xxii, 9, 24; medical theories of, xii; pamphlet controversy about, xx–xxii, xxv, 12, 20, 24–25; property rights of, xv, 24; superiority of, xxii–xxiii; as vehicles for transmission of property, xxvi; virtues of, xxi–xxii, xxvi, 51
Woodbridge, Linda, 24
wordplay, 10, 18
Wormeley, Katherine P., 3 n. 5

Xenophon, 133, 138

Zabdas, 79
Zenobia (queen), 22–23, 37, 75–86